Europe in Upheaval

EUROPE IN UPHEAVAL: THE REVOLUTIONS OF 1848

RAND McNALLY EUROPEAN HISTORY SERIES

GEORGE FASEL

Reed College

RAND McNALLY & COMPANY · Chicago

THE RAND MCNALLY EUROPEAN HISTORY SERIES
George L. Mosse, advisory editor

GEORGE FASEL, Europe in Upheaval: The Revolutions of 1848
BRISON D. GOOCH, The Reign of Napoleon III
HANS J. HILLERBRAND, Men and Ideas in the Sixteenth Century
BARBARA JELAVICH, The Habsburg Empire in European Affairs,
1814–1918
HARRY J. MAGOULIAS, Byzantine Christianity: Emperor, Church and
the West
JOHN B. WOLF, Toward a European Balance of Power, 1620–1715

To Louise and George W. Fasel, Sr.,
my mother and father

Editor's Preface

It used to be thought that the sole object of history was to discover and set forth the facts. When the *English Historical Review* was founded it recommended such a procedure, for through it one "can usually escape the risk of giving offense." While much of this tradition has remained active in the teaching and writing of history, it has led, in turn, to a sharp reaction against such timidity and narrowness. History became a branch of philosophy or of the social sciences, and scholarship was in danger of being displaced by the search for general laws that might govern the development of all mankind. There is a hunger for history abroad in the land, but many of those who want to know about the past are rightly dissatisfied with arid narrations of fact (and turn to the historical novel instead), while others are bewildered by abstruse generalizations that seem to ignore the particular for the universal.

The books in the Rand M?Nally European History Series do not place themselves in either of these traditions. Instead, they recognize both the importance of accurate and detailed scholarship and the obligation to place such scholarship within a meaningful historical setting. They do not shun general ideas and assumptions; they test them in the crucible of research. This combination is always exciting, because it penetrates historical development; and this development, in each of its stages, illuminates a new dimension of mankind. A prominent historian once wrote, "What man is, only history tells."

Here "what man is" is told by scholars who have researched and reflected upon a significant period of history. They have taken this opportunity to present their conclusions in a manner that will attract and stimulate those who long for a lively account of the past. All of the authors in this series are specialists presenting their original insights, making it possible for all those interested in history to partake of their work.

George L. Mosse, *advisory editor*
Rand M?Nally European History Series

Preface

Twenty years ago, at the time of the centenary of the revolutions of 1848, there occurred a great outpouring of historical literature devoted to the revolutions—much of it broadly general and synthetic in character, summarizing what we had learned of the revolutions in the hundred years since their outbreak. But the centenary seems also to have revived scholarly interest in 1848; in the past two decades not only historians but sociologists, demographers, economists, and political scientists as well have produced a remarkable number of detailed monographs on the period. There is still a great deal we do not know, yet much of this recent scholarship forces us to revise a number of notions about 1848 that we held in 1948. For some years, however, there has been no attempt to synthesize this work, no general account concentrating on the revolutions which tries to update the question. Such is the purpose of this book.

There are some peculiarities in my approach which require explanation. First of all, I have not tried to write a history of Europe in 1848; rather, my focus is on the revolutions themselves. While I have dealt at length with the areas in which revolution struck (France, the German Confederation, the Hapsburg Empire, the Italian peninsula), I have almost systematically ignored those touched only by minor disturbances or not at all (Belgium, the Netherlands, the Iberian peninsula, Russia, and Great Britain). Second, I have conceived of this book not as a detailed narrative, but rather as an essay. Narrative accounts, whose authors had more space in which to work, are available elsewhere. While I have maintained a roughly chronological organization throughout and have tried to provide a factual skeleton so that the newcomer will not be utterly bewildered, I have nonetheless emphasized interpretation at the expense of narrative. Only in Chapter 2, The Outbreak of Revolution, have I strayed from this intention, since it seemed important to provide a reasonably detailed account of just how the revolutions materialized.

This work itself is primarily a synthesis, and thus my principal intellectual debts are to the men and women who have created such a rich and fascinating scholarly literature on the subject of the revolutions. In addition, John Rothney of the University of Missouri took time off from an already overburdened schedule to lend some badly needed advice and extremely helpful criticism for which I am deeply grateful. Donald Baker of Michigan State University also contributed some pertinent suggestions. An anonymous reader commissioned by Rand McNally and Company made me rethink large blocs of the book with his caustic and telling critique. These persons may perhaps be able to see their own influence on the pages that follow; I suspect that they will frequently see my own stubbornness, too. Alexander Cohen was of invaluable assistance with the index. My wife understood sooner and better than I that a little book can cause big problems; only her ability to bear with them made it possible for me to do so.

Paris   George Fasel
July 1969

Contents

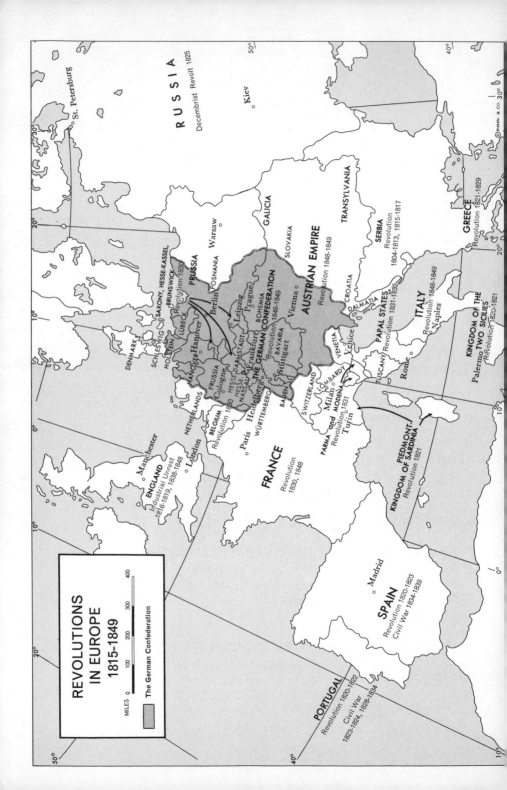

REVOLUTIONS
IN EUROPE
1815-1849

MILES 0 100 200 300 400

The German Confederation

RUSSIA

St. Petersburg

Decembrist Revolt 1825

Kiev

Warsaw

POSNANIA

PRUSSIA

BRUNSWICK

SAXONY, HESSE-KASSEL

Revolution 1830

Berlin

Leipzig

Prague

BOHEMIA

GALICIA

SLOVAKIA

TRANSYLVANIA

AUSTRIAN EMPIRE

Revolution 1848-1849

Vienna

Revolution 1848-1849

THE GERMAN CONFEDERATION

Frankfurt

HESSE-DARMSTADT

NASSAU

Heidelberg

BAVARIA

Stuttgart

WÜRTEMBERG

BADEN

PRUSSIA

Cologne

Revolution 1830

HANOVER

HANOVER

LÜBECK

HOLSTEIN

SCHLESWIG

DENMARK

NETHERLANDS

BELGIUM

Revolution 1830

Paris

FRANCE

Revolution
1830, 1848

SWITZERLAND

LOMBARDY

Milan

VENETIA

Venice

PARMA and MODENA

Revolution 1831

Turin

KINGDOM OF SARDINIA

Revolution 1821

PIEDMONT

TUSCANY

PAPAL STATES

Revolution 1831-1832

Rome

ITALY

Revolution 1848-1849

Naples

KINGDOM OF THE
TWO SICILIES

Revolution 1820-1821

Palermo

CROATIA

DALMATIA

SERBIA

Revolution
1804-1813, 1815-1817

GREECE

Revolution 1821-1829

SPAIN

Revolution 1820-1823
Civil War 1834-1839

Madrid

PORTUGAL

Revolution 1820-1822

Civil War
1823-1824, 1828-1834

ENGLAND

Industrial Unrest
1816, 1819, 1838-1848

Manchester

London

©RMN. & CO

50°

40°

30°

20°

10°

0°

10°

20°

30°

40°

50°

Chapter 1

Europe in the 1840s

Historians generally agree that in the nineteenth century western and central Europe underwent a profound transformation from a rural-agrarian society to an urban-industrial one. For the present purposes, however, the important questions are: how far had the process gone by 1848? in what sorts of societies did the revolutions strike? On this point, there is far less accord.

Obscuring sound judgment on this issue is an old and respected historiographical tradition which places at the end of the eighteenth century, and spreading in either direction for fifteen or twenty years, the great watershed between modern times and whatever one wishes to call what went before. This tradition argues that, at the turn of the eighteenth century into the nineteenth, two irresistible forces began to reshape the western world—the political and social changes proceeding from the great French Revolution, and the economic and social changes entailed by the industrial revolution.

One of the difficulties with this way of structuring modern European history is that it tempts us to take the notion of watershed too literally, so that we separate events on its two sides more than is justified. Actually, those dual revolutionary forces took a great deal of time to remake European society. Someone who revisited the continent in the 1840s, not having seen Europe since the 1780s, would have found a great deal that was familiar, a great deal to suggest that the old regime was tenaciously clinging to life, watershed or no watershed.

"Modern industry," wrote Karl Marx and Friedrich Engels, "has converted the little workshop of the patriarchal master into the great factory of the industrial capitalist." It is hard to believe that this line from *The Communist Manifesto* was written in January 1848. A Prussian census of 1846 showed that only 4 per cent of the total male population over age fourteen worked in factories. In mid-century Paris, the continent's largest city, only 7,000 *patrons* employed more than ten workers each (as opposed to 32,000 *patrons* who worked alone or with but one employee). France was, with Belgium, the most industrially advanced country on the continent in 1848, and yet possessed fewer than 5,000 steam-powered machines.

In the 1840s, as in the 1780s, most manufacturing remained the province of small producers—independent artisans operating in the tradition of the old craft guilds (which in many places still existed). The basic unit of industrial production was the small shop, owned by an independent craftsman who might employ two or three skilled or semi-skilled laborers, though frequently such shops were one-man operations. In these circumstances, the division of labor was simply non-existent, and notions of cheap, efficient mass production were generally alien. The small artisan had no sense of a vast market that he might corner by slashing costs. Rather, he thought in terms of a relatively small, secure market with prices protected by controls—sometimes legal, sometimes informal—upon production.

In any case, industrial production, whether in large factories or small shops, played a relatively minor role in the European economy of the 1840s. Most of the continental countries were still basically agricultural. In France, fully three-fourths of the population lived in the countryside and took its livelihood from the soil; elsewhere, the rural population formed an even larger percentage of the whole. Only a few cases may be found—those of Belgium, France, the Rhenish states of Prussia, and perhaps Saxony—where economies were approaching what W. W. Rostow has called industrial "take-off."

Moreover, to speak of the European economy is to conceal the unevenness of industrial progress and economic development on the continent. The most advanced single region was in northwestern Europe. The Belgians were the continent's earliest and most energetic railway builders, and also nurtured a lively textile industry.

More than a third of all France's power looms were concentrated in Alsace and Lorraine.

In the neighboring German Rhineland, there were similar improvements in the mechanization of textile production, though the convenience of water transportation tended to impede railway development. Elsewhere in the German states, industrialization tended to spring up near the larger cities—Berlin, Leipzig, Dresden—though none had yet approached the status of a Manchester or a Leeds. Here again, as in central and southern France, factories were scarce, and manufacturing centered in artisan shops. And the farther east one proceeded, the more Europe's fundamentally agrarian character asserted itself. In south-central and southern Europe, there was little to challenge the economic preponderance of agriculture, little to threaten the small craftsman in the manufacture of goods. There was some industrial activity around Vienna, and in a few other Austrian towns; northern Italian cities were experiencing a decided commercial renaissance. But in other vast areas—Hungary and southern Italy, for instance—industrialization remained completely remote; there, cities served as markets for agricultural products and as centers for services and administration.

If, in looking at the Europe of the 1840s, one seeks to identify the forces that would ultimately transform the continent, then of course one emphasizes the little pockets of factory industry, the embryonic railway networks, the early metallurgical experiments. But if the goal is rather to describe the still-prevailing structure of European economy and society, the Europe which experienced the revolutions of 1848 rather than the one which ultimately emerged from the revolutions, then the emphasis must lie on the persistence of traditionalism, on the continuities of eighteenth-century practices. Given the latter objective, a sketch of European economy and society in the 1840s ought properly to begin with the countryside.

The European peasantry manifested the greatest internal differences of any social group of the time. It included property-owners and day-laborers, tenant farmers and sharecroppers, prosperous little winegrowers in France and miserable serfs in East Prussia or Hungary. It ranged from cash-crop producers to subsistence farmers trying to scratch a living from their little strip of land, and everywhere numbered many families who avoided starvation only by taking in occasional piecework—usually by spinning cloth.

In this last respect, the peasants point up the danger of overemphasizing the separation between city and countryside. Peasants who were heavily dependent upon piecework could be just as susceptible as urban artisans to the threat of factory competition, to market fluctuations, and to pressures exerted by wholesalers and middlemen. And many such peasants there were, especially in places where agriculture was neither highly capitalized nor still predominantly manorial. Peasant smallholders in central and southern France, for example, or central and southwestern Germany, were heavily dependent upon the demand for their manufacturing skills. Piecework might be the responsibility of the woman of the family, while the man worked the soil; then the man might well seek employment in a nearby town during the winter agricultural off-season. Whatever the arrangement, such non-agricultural employment often buffered the marginal peasant from utter extinction.

Many peasants, especially in central, eastern, and southern Europe, were simply the victims of outright exploitation. In these regions, most peasants remained in a legal bondage scarcely distinguishable from serfdom, tilling the huge aristocratically owned estates that dominated the countryside. Even where this formal bondage had been lifted, as in Prussia, the peasant was hardly better off. He could purchase his own land only by plunging himself deeply into debt, and as a free agent he could not even avail himself of the few benefits afforded serfs by paternalistic lords.

An even more general problem was the pressure of the population on the land. The European population was still growing rapidly in a demographic surge that had begun around the middle of the eighteenth century. In the first half of the nineteenth century alone, the four major areas hit by revolution in 1848 grew at the remarkable rate of roughly 35 per cent:

STATE	POPULATION: 1800 (in millions)	POPULATION: 1850 (in millions)
France	28.2	35.8
German Confederation	23	35.1
Hapsburg Empire	28	36
States of the Italian Peninsula	18	25
	97.2	131.9

Yet productive capacities were barely able to keep pace with this growth rate. Modern agrarian technology was only beginning to make its debut on the continent, where the ancient system of crop rotation which let land lie fallow was still widely practiced. The enrichment of the soil by various root crops which could also be used for animal fodder was in a relatively experimental stage. More commonly, outmoded methods persisted behind high tariff walls designed to keep domestic agricultural prices at a level profitable for cash-crop producers.

This conjunction of rapid population growth with sluggish agricultural progress led to a number of consequences. First, like most everything else in this period, it spelled hard times for peasant smallholders, who were producing at a virtually constant rate but forced to support a larger family. There was little sense in such peasants converting to one-crop market production unless they owned or rented a large enough plot of land. Yet the rising population was increasing pressure on the land, increasing the density of the rural population, and making enlargements of one's holdings —or even procurement of a strip of land at all—that much more difficult. Moreover, the technological backwardness of continental agriculture meant that it could hardly employ some of the methods common in England for clearing unarable land and bringing waste areas under cultivation. Finally, the failure of agriculture to match growing consumer demands with increased production, when combined with tariffs, resulted in a steady rise in the price of most foodstuffs.

Two qualifying observations ought to be made on the issue of population pressure in the countryside. A familiar hypothesis suggests that, where peasant proprietorship had become increasingly common, as in France, the peasantry tended to be politically conservative, anxious to preserve the small gains it had made. Conversely, it could be expected that where land-hunger and exploitation were worst, one would find a more radical peasantry. In fact, the hypothesis does not hold up. True, the worst rural disorders of 1848 occurred in the German states, many of them not characterized by a high degree of peasant proprietorship. But there was also widespread turbulence in the French countryside, while little was heard from the serfs on the huge Hungarian latifundia. Though a new hypothesis will have to wait for more detailed studies of the European countryside during this period, it seems clear that it is an oversimplification to equate rural dissatisfaction with land-hunger alone.

Also, the pressure of rural overpopulation could be somewhat relieved by migration (except for some areas in eastern Europe where feudal remnants restricted the peasant's freedom of movement). As already hinted, migratory movements were not something new; movement from countryside to town according to the season was a traditional feature of many regions. Nor was all rural migration directed at factory towns, since relatively few of them existed then. Migrants might move from one rural region to another, or from the countryside into the small towns—there to learn some artisanal trade—not to mention the possibility of migration out of the country. Yet it is still true that the most novel feature of rural migration in mid-nineteenth-century Europe was the increasing number of migrants who went to the large cities, attracted by employment opportunities or higher wages or an easier life or whatever. Such migrations did more than create Europe's great metropoli. They also led to the underpopulation of a number of rural areas, and agricultural progress was then inhibited by serious labor shortages. In such places, not only were workers in short supply when a landowner wished, say, to drain a marsh on his property, but the very shortage forced agricultural wages up to the point where financing improvements became impossible.

Besides these general problems, there were a variety of other rural difficulties and peasant complaints not so readily classifiable; only a few of the more common may be mentioned here. In many places, special privileges for the nobility rankled deeply: tax exemptions, hunting rights denied the peasantry, controls over grazing and forest land. There were objections to the intrusion of the central government: the French census-takers of 1841, whose inquiry seemed certain to lead to the raising of taxes, met with widespread and sometimes violent rural resistance. When bad harvests brought scarcities in certain staple foods, peasants protested vigorously against shipping locally-produced grain or potatoes to the voracious nearby cities. Finally, rural discontent was not always peasant discontent; rural and small town artisans also contributed to the protest. Boatmen on canals and rivers resisted the introduction of steampower and railways, for example, and village craftsmen were as incensed as tenant farmers by grain requisitions.

In short, the dissatisfactions of rural Europe at mid-century were

neither exclusively agricultural nor were they voiced exclusively
by peasants. They were sometimes directed against the inroads made
by outside influences into hitherto relatively isolated areas, but often
they were also related to desires for reform in those areas. They
depended very much on local conditions, and varied radically from
place to place. Variations aside, it is still important to remember
that deep dissatisfactions existed. It is too easy to be hypnotized
by the social problems of cities, by the fact that the revolutions of
1848 erupted for the better part in the large urban centers, and to
relegate rural Europe to a politically unimportant status, passive
and apathetic, sunk in miserable silence. As a matter of fact, the
rural disorders of 1848 were the culmination of a generation of food
and tax riots, poaching incidents and other forest disorders, attacks
upon railroad tracks and trestles, and a variety of other forms of
protest. They were only a violent intensification of the regular
rhythms of rural life.

For all the complexity of rural society, one factor remained relatively constant: the continued predominance of the noble landlord.
Only in France had the nobility suffered substantially from the
Great Revolution's assaults upon aristocratic privilege and property. Elsewhere, the aristocracies of Europe emerged from the
revolutionary and Napoleonic episode with remarkable vitality and
influence. For all the persistent dissatisfaction with continued noble
privileges, outside of France, there had been no serious threat to
the nobles' elite position in the countryside. By the 1840s, some of
the mystique of noble birth was doubtless wearing off. But large
landed estates remained a formidable power base, and aristocrats
felt increasingly free to supplement income derived therefrom with
various commercial ventures. In most countries, high bureaucratic
positions remained the exclusive preserve of the grandees; in those
states experimenting with parliamentary government, the aristocrats
unfailingly took a prominent place in the legislatures. But most
aristocrats' power and prestige were still rooted in the local soil—in
their tremendous economic power in the countryside, their influence
over peasants, and their exercise of various local administrative
responsibilities.

European cities were growing in the first half of the century,
and they were swelled largely by rural and small-town migrants.
But still the proportion of rural and urban population in the continental countries remained relatively constant, due to the general

population growth. The countryside was having great difficulties supporting its population, but the cities could not always promise more. There were some opportunities for work in the city, usually connected with building construction. When the French government decided, in 1840, to erect new fortifications around Paris, it drew on migrant peasant labor. But such jobs were usually temporary, and few cities had the large factories with which to absorb an excess labor force permanently. Thus, Europe on the eve of the revolutions was still characterized by a heavy imbalance tilted toward the rural population, by the predominance of agriculture and landed wealth, and by ruling elites drawn from the landed nobility's ranks. It was an imbalance that only shifted after—and, to some extent, because of—the revolutions of 1848.

Perhaps it is unfair to read *The Communist Manifesto* as a descriptive treatise, since Marx and Engels were probably most concerned with identifying the incipient forces of change that they could see early in 1848. Indeed, one of their most famous sentences can only be read as anticipation. "Society as a whole," they wrote, "is more and.more splitting up into two great hostile camps, into two great classes directly facing one another: Bourgeoisie and Proletariat." By bourgeoisie, of course, they meant primarily industrial entrepreneurs, and more generally those who owned the means of production; by proletariat, primarily factory laborers, and more generally the propertyless poor. They announced, in other words, the social divisions of the urban-industrial age, on the threshold of which continental Europe stood but had not yet entered as they wrote. Forty years later, Engels himself admitted that it was only *after* 1848 that widespread industrialization "produced clarity in class relations" and "created a genuine bourgeoisie and a genuine largescale proletariat."

In the Europe of the 1840s, there hardly existed a class which could be described, in the *Manifesto's* words, as "masses of laborers, crowded into the factory ... privates in the industrial army." Where they did exist, their lot was not always utterly miserable; in Berlin, for example, factory workers were comparatively well paid, and they treated the outbreak of revolution in 1848 with marked suspicion. Other social critics of the time tended to use the word "proletariat" more loosely, applying it to the "working classes" in general, the urban poor—most of whom, once more, had never been inside a factory. The difficulty with this use of "proletariat" is that it suggests a certain social homogeneity where none existed. The European working classes, ranging from skilled artisan to unskilled menial laborer, were a remarkably complex and variegated group. Most skilled artisans indignantly rejected the appellation of proletarian. Often, their work demanded a special competence and training beyond that needed to operate a large machine in a factory. Moreover, many trades could point to long and honorable traditions of quality craftsmanship. Many artisans were literate, and they drew added pride from their relative independence. Working in small shops, they were not submerged in the anonymity of a gigantic mill; there could be a more personal relationship with employer, with product, and even with consumer. The skilled artisans were clearly the elite of the working-class community, but they were by no means homogeneous themselves, especially when it came to politics. Some trades might be particularly hard-hit by economic crises, or (less often) undercut by cheaper factory production, and thus more receptive to radical appeals. Others—the printing trades, for example, or in many places the tailors might simply have nurtured a tradition of left-wing protest. Others still might have avoided serious privations by one means or another, and would thus have tended to go little beyond moderate reformism.

In addition to this sort of vertical differentiation, there was rather frequent horizontal differentiation, usually between master craftsman-employer and journeyman-employee. Often such divisions were more than a matter of disputes over wages and working conditions, common as these were. The master aspired to, and often attained, a social status superior to that of his employees; as a modest property owner, he was at pains to keep the distinction between master and journeyman distinct. Artisan tradition usually demanded that his relations with his workers be more paternal in spirit than the cold detachment of the large factory owner. Nonetheless, masters attempted to keep their own ranks exclusive, and often the masters of a town would join together to do so—much to the frustration of ambitious journeymen. Social relationships between the two groups were informally restricted, and intermarriages infrequent. On the other hand, master-journeyman cooperation was not unknown. The outlawing of guilds in France in 1791 had helped (at least partially) to obliterate the formal distinctions. In trades that produced not directly for the market but rather at the demand of a wholesaler, the employer and employees alike might find themselves at the economic mercy of a particularly tough middleman, so that their interests clearly coalesced.

The artisan craftsman, however, constituted only one segment of the urban working classes. The cities of Europe included also a large number of semi-skilled laborers—from carriers to chimney-sweeps, from coal-heavers to dock-workers. Their tasks had little to do with production, and were often more menial and more physically strenuous than those of the skilled craftsmen.

It is difficult to locate much in the way of class cohesiveness in these urban masses. It is true that contemporary observers had a disturbing tendency to lump the urban poor together—the skilled craftsman, the semi-skilled or unskilled laborer, the factory worker, even the consistently unemployed who frequently turned to beggary or crime. The crisis of 1848 belied this sort of generalization, for the urban workers of Europe showed their astonishing heterogeneity, indeed their fragmentation and inner division, with a broad range of responses to revolutionary developments. Certainly the historian's difficulty in making intelligent internal categorizations of the working classes stems largely from ignorance; relatively little detailed research on working-class life and communities has been undertaken, so that it is difficult to say much about their structure, the extent to which a class or classes existed, the extent to which there was consciousness of them. But also, complexity was built into the structure; it took the advent of modern industrialism to diminish occupational diversity and create that "clarity in class relations" of which Engels wrote.

The unevenness of social conditions in mid-century Europe is well illustrated by a brief glance at different working-class grievances. In the German states, concern centered on the guild system—sometimes its reinstatement, sometimes its modification. The first half of the nineteenth century had seen increasing governmental reluctance to enforce guild regulations; in 1845, for instance, the Prussian government issued its *Gewerbeordnung* (or industrial decree) which effectively abolished the last remaining guild regulations. At the same time, the creation of a customs union, the Zollverein, embracing nearly all the German Confederation, subjected the artisan to new, remote competitors. In response to just such pressures, master craftsmen in particular sought the reestablishment and strengthening of the guilds, and they turned for help to the very powers who were dismantling them—the state authorities. The masters' idea of social reform was to get the state to resume the role of protector of the guilds and thus replace competition in a free market with the more secure, if less dynamic, system of regulated production and prices.

These demands had some appeal to journeymen, for the guild system also attempted to protect them against a flooding of the labor market and a debasement of wages by placing restrictions upon the number of persons that could be employed in a given craft at a given time and by sanctioning the institution of apprenticeship. But here the master-journeyman conflict also appeared. Journeymen generally approved of the guild system, but they wanted it with modifications that would loosen up its internal structure, provide more upward social mobility, and give them some leverage —such as the right to organize and strike—for the improvement of conditions. Prior to 1848, however, the journeymen did tend to follow the masters' lead, centering their demands for reform on the guild system and directing their appeals to the state.

In France, working-class demands had a different tone altogether. There, a formal guild structure seemed less relevant, and French artisans and workers sought their guarantees in other forms. If there was a single demand which had close to universal appeal, it was encapsulated in the slogans "the organization of labor" and "the right to work." These phrases, associated with the social theorist Louis Blanc but soon acquiring a much more general meaning than he gave to them, asked simply for permanent employment or its equivalent. In other words, French workers— probably plagued more by unemployment than by any other problem—expected to have jobs from which they could earn a living. If such jobs were not available, they still expected to be provided with an income. The demand had in common with German guild reformism a pronounced statism. It was directed at the state, which was supposed to create employment or, at the very least, sustain life. And it implicitly denounced the notion of a free labor market in which some persons might go jobless while others worked for rock bottom wages.

French workers were more overtly political than their German counterparts. It is true that the Germans' demands had political content, but the artisanate was not clearly aligned with any political movement or persuasion. In France, it was the existence of a revolutionary tradition in the cities, dating to the *sans culotte* forebearers of the nineteenth-century workers, which determined that working-class politics would be more openly (if not exclusively) republican and revolutionary. It was no accident that, on the morrow of the 1848 revolution, there suddenly appeared in all the major cities political clubs of a decidedly left-wing coloration and numbering large working-class memberships. In a sense, the French working classes in the larger cities were already organized before 1848. That is, they shared common political experiences—the uprisings of the 1830s in Paris and Lyon, for example—which bound them together as much as the formal structures of underground secret societies. The social complexity of the urban poor perhaps forestalls any reference to a uniform "class consciousness," and there were enough internal political differences among them to make one wary of sweeping generalization. But there was still widespread consciousness of certain common circumstances and common goals. Perhaps the working classes of Paris were not yet in fact a class, but they were developing remarkable solidarity. In Germany, it took the experience of 1848 itself to lay the foundations for that solidarity.

If it is difficult to generalize about European workers of the 1840s, it is equally difficult even to define Europe's middle classes of the same period. Embracing as they did so many persons from humble shopkeepers to wealthy financiers, the middle classes hardly justified *The Communist Manifesto*'s oversimplifying label, "the bourgeoisie."

Lacking a widespread development of large factory industry, we cannot expect to find a European bourgeoisie dominated by "captains of industry." There were an increasing number of important industrial entrepreneurs on the continent, but far more characteristic representatives of the business classes were those men involved in finance and commerce. The great middle-class fortunes of the mid-nineteenth century, as of the late eighteenth century, were made less in industry than in banking and trade.

Still, it would be a mistake to think of the middle classes of the 1840s simply as the owners of the means of production, identifying them completely with the business classes. Many bourgeois, and especially the most politically visible and articulate, were not involved in business but in the professions—law, medicine, teaching, and journalism. Government service of one sort or another also remained a popular middle-class vocation, though in most countries it was still difficult to rise to the top of the bureaucracy without a noble title. Similarly remote from production were the petty retailers, the small shopkeepers and tradesmen of city and town whom Marx expected the modern industrial system to reduce to proletarian status.

In view of the diversity of the middle classes, it is hard to see how some historians find, in the Europe of this period, the development of something characterized as "bourgeois society." It is true that the middle classes of the 1840s enjoyed a somewhat enhanced prestige over their counterparts of a century earlier. The French revolution began the erosion of aristocratic privilege, though its work was far from being completed a half-century later; equally as important was the Napoleonic creed of the "career open to talents." Positions of power and status hitherto denied commoners began to open up; it was far less common to imagine that working for a living was demeaning. But it is one thing to note a steady growth of bourgeois self-confidence and pride. It is quite another to suppose that the middle classes set the tone and style of European society, that middle-class values—insofar as common values can be ascribed to the broad range of persons thus referred to—epitomized European social values. In many places, the middle classes remained relatively small and relatively impotent. Again, in the absence of large-scale factory industry, there could be no large entrepreneurial class to dominate the economy and to force political recognition. Where parliamentary government did not exist, the middle classes were virtually excluded from the political arena; where it did, property qualifications might restrict politics to the very wealthiest (which very often meant primarily landowners).

Even in France, where the so-called bourgeois monarchy of Louis Philippe had abolished hereditary aristocracy in 1831, it would be difficult to detect anything like middle-class dominance, if by middle-class one means businessmen, professionals, and non-noble bureaucrats. It can be put forward with some confidence that 1830 represented nothing like a profound social revolution. Recent work has shown that there was little change in the nature of the ruling elite to accompany the flight of Charles X, that power remained firmly in the hands of the large landowners—some of them titled, some not. Now if such persons did not bear a title, contemporaries naturally referred to them as bourgeois; and many times such persons had begun their careers in finance or commerce or law or state service. But their decisions to invest much or all of their wealth in land testify to the continuing prestige of land as the most respectable (if not always the most profitable) form of wealth. And their political behavior—as electors and deputies under the Orléans monarchy—testifies to the relative solidarity of landholding interests, both noble and non-noble.

The French case seems decisive, and it reflects once more the tenacity of eighteenth-century values, even among the allegedly rising bourgeoisie. Businessmen and professionals manifested the same urge as their eighteenth-century predecessors, if somewhat less frantically, to remove themselves from bourgeois occupations for more genteel forms of income. Again, there is evidence of some growing bourgeois pride in their traditional pursuits. But as an historian of the early nineteenth-century Parisian bourgeoisie has written, "almost all the wealthy Parisians gave a preponderant place to rural properties among their real estate investments." Such persons may have somehow remained middle-class, but not in the sense that we customarily attach to that word.

It is time to return to the question that opened this chapter and try to characterize the societies in which the revolutions erupted. As sharply as these societies differed one from another in certain respects, they still displayed some important common features. By nearly every meaningful measure, these were rural and agricultural societies. The barely incipient large-scale industries of the continent had just begun to exert the changes forecast by social critics like Marx. Only in Germany and France were some hints of the future available. Nearly everywhere else, the forms and the rhythms of economic life were as they had been a century or two before. As of 1848, Europe still awaited the industrial revolution. Similarly, in terms of social structure, the late eighteenth-century watershed looks less imposing. Everywhere on the continent, a traditionalistic social structure persisted, and even where some of the most typical old regime features had been destroyed—legal aristocratic privilege, formal serfdom—still the occupations and sources of income for the majority of the populations were strongly reminiscent of the eighteenth century.

The notion of Europe in 1848 as still basically preindustrial may be difficult to accept, especially since it minimizes the importance of the dual revolutions which were supposed to have transformed

the western world. Perhaps a more graphic demonstration of the
stage of continental development would be a brief sketch of a
nation passing out of the preindustrial period. There was only one
such nation in the world in the mid-nineteenth century: Great
Britain.

One of the most striking features of British social history during
this period is the astonishing growth of the population. The population of the entire British Isles grew, between 1800 and 1850, from
16 million persons to 27.5 million—a growth rate over the half-
century of 71 per cent, just double that of the principal continental
countries. England itself, as the recipient of huge migratory waves
from elsewhere in the Isles, grew during the same period at something just over 90 per cent. Ever more staggering are the raw
numbers on urban growth. In 1800, only London of all English cities
could count more than 100,000 residents. By 1850, there were
twenty-eight cities over 100,000, which collectively comprised one-
fifth of the entire British population. France, by contrast, had only
five cities over 100,000, and only one-fourth of the French population lived in towns with 2,000 or more persons. It is difficult to
say just when a nation has become urbanized without resorting to
completely arbitrary categories—when more than half its population
resides in towns of at least 2,000 persons (the French official
definition)? of 5,000 persons? or of 10,000? Nonetheless, it seems
safe to say that, by mid-century, Britain was no longer a predominantly rural society.

If Britain was well on the way to transformation into an urbanized society, this does not mean that its rural population or its
agriculture had ceased to be of importance. On the contrary, British
agriculture was probably the most advanced and, proportionately,
the most productive in the world, and still half the population
remained in the countryside. The great advances in agriculture
stemmed primarily from a number of technical innovations dating
from the late seventeenth and eighteenth centuries which had allowed
the British to make maximum use of their agricultural resources.
Landlords long accustomed to living solely on their rents began to
convert their domains into capitalistic enterprises. In order to
practice some of the new techniques of cultivation more efficiently,
they began to consolidate their holdings into large, unified blocks—
which often meant squeezing out the owners of tiny strips which
interfered with this consolidation, or the landlord reasserting his

residual rights over common land which had become crucial to small farmers and village folk as a place for gathering firewood, grazing animals, and so forth. In other words, large-scale agricultural progress was frequently accomplished at the expense of the marginal peasants. At the same time, the need for agricultural labor was declining, since many large farmers were turning to more profitable, and labor-saving, activities such as animal breeding. In these circumstances, large segments of the British peasantry had little choice but to leave the land, and ultimately provide the huge urban labor force that makes heavy industrialization possible. By the late 1840s, nearly a century after these developments had begun, migration from countryside to city had become a steady flow, now further stimulated by the attraction of allegedly higher wages in factories.

If these sorts of social forces were urbanizing Britain, steam power was just as dramatically industrializing it. The steam engine had not been introduced universally into British industrial production; rather, the first experiments, followed by large-scale applications, came in coal mining and in cloth spinning. During the first half of the nineteenth century, British coal production tripled and accounted for more than half the total world product. Steam-powered spinning, and later weaving, quickly revolutionized the textile industry, making possible increased production at cheaper cost. Soon after, steam power combined with other technological refinements to turn the British metallurgical industry into another world leader: between 1815 and 1848, production of iron and steel leaped by 800 per cent. Finally, of course, the British were quick to recognize the potential of steam power for transportation. They were pioneers in the development of steam-powered water vessels, and even more vigorous in the building of railroads. By 1850, Britain was crosshatched with 6,600 miles of railroad track; at the same time, the German Confederation could count less than 3,500 miles, France only about 1,800 miles.

The pressures forcing people off the land and the growth of large-scale factory industry combined to produce the first industrial proletariat of modern times. This propertyless factory worker suffered miseries which may not—though it is difficult to measure such things—have been any worse than those which afflicted the continental urban poor. Yet he did have to suffer the extremely rigid discipline of the factory, a sharp difference from the relative freedom of the artisan shop. He often ran greater health risks, due to various sorts of unsanitary conditions in the factories, and the frequency of heavy machinery led to a high rate of industrial casualties. The typical factory hand had no real skill, no trade, no occupational identity; he was trained to do a very simple task and nothing more, so that the prospect for any advancement (as from journeyman to master) was remote.

Britain, then, was beginning to develop a proletariat that would fit Marx's description, and the appearance of this new social layer is, in retrospect, significant and conspicuous. Yet it should not obscure the fact that, in the 1840s, the more traditional sorts of working-class groups—skilled artisans and the numerous semi-skilled or unskilled non-factory laborers—were even more numerous. The continued existence of these groups, and particularly the artisans who were manufacturing goods in competition with the large factories, is a useful check on any tendency to exaggerate the extent of Britain's industrial development in the mid-nineteenth century. For, again, industrialization was far from complete in the British economy, and in numerous areas where steam-powered machines had not yet revolutionized the modes of production, the small craftsmen continued to rule.

One of the more familiar perspectives for viewing British history during the early nineteenth century is that of conflict between the landlord classes and the new industrial middle classes. Of course, middle-class wealth and power were nothing new in Britain, especially with some of the enormous fortunes made from colonial trade in the eighteenth century. The urban-commercial bourgeoisie had always had a modest representation in the House of Commons, and the ruling nobility and landed gentry were generally quicker than their continental counterparts to co-opt prominent bourgeois into the elite. This, however, became less easy to do as the entrepreneurial class began to expand rapidly, and at the same time demonstrated considerable dissatisfaction with the political arrangements which relegated it to a distinctly minor role. The business interests were able to find champions among the Whig aristocrats in Parliament who were anxious to end a long period of Tory rule. The result was the Great Reform Bill of 1832, which reordered parliamentary representation and the franchise to the benefit of the non-landed elements—and, significantly, was forced through over the objections of the House of Lords.

The bill may have been a landmark in British constitutional history, but what was its effect upon the relations between the landed elite and the new industrial interests? Probably it did ease some of the worst tensions, but it is hard to see that it unseated the landed element in favor of the business classes or even put them on an even social footing. The aristocracy and the gentry continued to dominate politics and government; of particular importance, they retained the influence to manipulate economic policy in their own interests. The industrialists, at the same time, suffered a number of legislative restraints upon their operations, such as laws restricting child and female labor. For all the productivity of British agriculture, it still could not feed the booming population, and Britain was dependent upon imports of food. Landed elements, fearful that frequently cheaper foreign imports—and especially wheat—would drive them out of their own market, were able to get a tariff on many of these items which boosted their prices to the British level. Industrial interests, on the other hand, had no need of tariff protection; indeed, they were convinced that if they could get foreign duties lowered, their own mass-produced products could compete successfully in any market. Besides, the British food tariffs—symbolized by the tariff on wheat (in British usage, "corn," and thus known as the Corn Laws)—kept the cost of living artificially high, forcing factory owners to pay higher wages than were actually necessary for the workers' subsistence.

The so-called free-trade interests, predominantly urban and middle-class, began their organized assault upon the Corn Laws in the late 1830s; by 1846, Parliament began to repeal most of these laws, inaugurating a new era in British economic history. But the social implications were important too, for the new industrial interests and the middle classes had extracted a concession of enormous importance from a social and political system which was still run by landed, often aristocratic, groups. It was another indication that the balance was shifting in Britain—far more so than in any continental country.

This brief sketch has tried to indicate, in the broadest terms, how European society and economy in the 1840s were ordered; it remains to be seen how Europe was governed, and to specify more concretely what the political and ideological forces for change were.

In the most general terms, European governments of the 1840s could be divided into those which had and those which had not made some concession to the liberalizing forces of the French Revolution. Such concessions usually took the form of constitutionalism and some version of parliamentary government. Belgium and France were the two most prominent constitutional monarchies, both the product of revolutions. The Belgians had combined their battle for liberal reforms with a war for national independence from Dutch rule in 1830. The French had been granted a constitution by the restored Bourbon monarchy in 1814; the revolution of July 1830 which permanently evicted the Bourbons also led to a new, somewhat more liberal constitution. In addition, there were constitutions in a handful of the smaller German states of the west and southwest. The French and Belgian constitutions had been written and approved by elected parliaments (elected, it is true, by a suffrage confined to the wealthier property owners). Most of the German constitutions, with their provisions for parliaments, had been handed down by the reigning monarchs with little pretence of consultation. Still, these constitutions all followed a general pattern: the parliament had some nominal power, greater in France and Belgium than in the German states, but still with only vague control over the royally appointed ministries. The executive retained considerable jurisdiction, including repressive powers over press, speech, assembly, and so forth, in spite of the constitution's general affirmation of fundamental civil liberties. The legislatures were bicameral, with aristocratic assemblies offsetting the lower houses which were themselves generally selected by a franchise with high property qualifications.

Such institutional arrangements hardly sound like the fullfillment of the revolutionary ideal. They were designed, however, not to please the Robespierres of nineteenth-century Europe, but the Mirabeaus. Moreover, they were signal advances over the governments of non-constitutional states—Prussia, Saxony, Hanover, Bavaria, the Hapsburg Empire, and the several Italian principalities. There, the eighteenth-century mode of government still prevailed: nominal autocracy, large bureaucracy, and the absence of any public politics whatsoever. The real power of the monarch in these states depended in no small part upon the personality and capacities of the man in question. The Hapsburg Emperor Francis I had maintained much of the decision-making authority in his own hands. His death in 1835 delivered the throne to his mentally incompetent successor, Ferdinand. But the new Emperor could not begin to control the huge Hapsburg governmental machine, so that real power soon resided in the ministries and even in various personalities at court.

Constitutionalism, even conservative constitutionalism, represented a compromise on the part of authoritarian elements, usually a reluctant concession to the forces of moderate reformism made in order to fend off the more awful prospect of revolution. It was just such a compromise that the non-constitutional states refused to make. Prince Metternich, Chancellor of the Hapsburg Empire, wrote in January 1848, "The [impending] conflict will tear the mask from the face of *reform* to show in all its horror the specter of radicalism, which is still trying to veil itself behind a form that it has never had and behind claims that will never be more than phrases for it to exploit as a trap for fools." All the assumptions of the old regime are in this brief statement—the sense of an impending Armageddon between revolution and the status quo, the unwillingness to discriminate among the several forces demanding change, the identification of compromise with sheer foolishness.

The principal voice for reform in the 1840s came from the liberals—a word which has perennially raised problems of definition as thorny as those associated with the social groupings already discussed. In fact, it ought not to be too difficult to work out an acceptable notion of liberalism which is generally applicable for most of the continental countries.[1]

Liberal demands were fundamentally political demands; they dealt with constitutions, parliaments, and civil liberties. These concerns betrayed the legalistic tendencies of liberalism, its desire to have autocratic government converted into a government of laws enshrined in a constitution and see certain freedoms guaranteed by law. The goals of constitutionalism and parliamentarism had by no means been fulfilled by the already existing constitutions. Liberals in the German constitutional states were still dissatisfied with the absence of ministerial responsibility to the parliament, with the weak parliamentary powers over the state budget, and with the loopholes in civil liberties. The more moderate French liberals were

---

[1] The word's contemporary usage derived from a group of Spanish reformists of the early nineteenth century, the *Liberales,* whose proposed constitution of 1812 was something of a model for later liberal constitutions.

satisfied with the July Monarchy, but others complained that Louis Philippe still wielded too much power and that the franchise was too restricted for sound representative government. Not that the liberals in any country promoted universal suffrage; a further common characteristic of liberal doctrine was its open opposition to democracy. " '*Vox populi, vox Dei,*' " wrote Odilon Barrot, leader of the largest French liberal party, "which gives to a majority the infallibility of God is the most dangerous and the most despotic absurdity that has ever emerged from a human brain. If you want to ruin a state, give it universal suffrage. . . ." Liberals sought rather a franchise extended not merely to the very wealthy, but to well-to-do and educated persons in general.

Liberalism is probably best known as the ideology of the middle classes. In part, this identification is correct; clearly, the concerns of liberalism were the concerns neither of an aristocratic elite nor of poverty-stricken masses. The liberals sought broader middle-class representation and participation in government, and while they were not blind to the social problems that afflicted the poor, neither were they much enamoured of social welfare schemes which increased government's responsibilities and might have implications concerning the existing distribution of property and the social structure. To some extent, this attitude may have arisen from a class selfishness which commentators hostile to liberalism have seen as its very core. It must also be recalled that the governments liberals were trying to reform were characterized by broad jurisdictions and responsibilities, by a scope of authority which liberals found far too great. Thus, liberal opposition to state welfare schemes was an outgrowth of the same attitude which opposed state censorship, police powers, and so forth.

Historians, perhaps thinking too much of developments in England, have also tried to cast liberalism as the ideology of the industrial entrepreneurs, men for whom liberty meant the freedom to compete, to remove government restrictions upon their operations, to keep wages and overhead low. Economic conditions on the continent, however, meant that this version of liberalism was far less prevalent there prior to 1848. While there were liberals who could define themselves in terms of economic laissez-faire, the issues were more often political. This frequently political flavor of continental liberalism may help to explain the fact that its personnel was by no means exclusively middle-class. There were prominent aristocratic liberals in every state, and indeed their prestige and wealth often propelled them to leadership of the movements.

Liberals were most immediately concerned with constitutional guarantees of civil liberties—freedom of speech, of the press, of assembly. Since, in the 1840s, no continental nation had anything approaching a free press and since freedom of assembly was sharply restricted in all states, it is easy to see how these could be very live issues. They were in fact the issues, though not exactly the causes, which prompted the revolutions of 1848.

Liberalism constituted the most important force for reform, for orderly, legal, political change; but liberals to a man abhorred revolution. They tended strongly to identify the idea of revolution with the memory of the first French republic. As Benedetto Croce put it, "terror of the Terror became one of the fundamental social convictions" of the early nineteenth century. Although many liberals harked back to the principles of 1789 and restated the principles of the Declaration of the Rights of Man and Citizen, they also feared that revolution only opened wide the doors to extremists—to democrats and Jacobins, or to the even more frightful socialist revolutionaries who were cropping up during the 1830s and '40s.

The first half of the nineteenth century saw the spectrum of left-wing ideologies broaden so that it ran from political democrats all the way to the first modern communists, including between them a bewildering variety of shadings and nuances. The "left" in Europe no more constituted a homogeneous bloc than did the "bourgeoisie" or the "peasantry."

If one disregards Metternich's advice and distinguishes liberalism from radicalism, it is convenient to make that distinction at the point between ardently reformist liberals and the more moderate democrats. Divided first of all on the issue of universal suffrage, they further disagreed on the very form of government: liberals were almost uniformly monarchist, and democrats almost uniformly republican. It is true that most liberals relegated royalty to a limited constitutional role, with relatively few significant powers and perhaps only a suspensive veto over the decisions of a representative government. Yet monarchy also provided their system with a certain theoretical stability by giving the constitutional mechanism an element independent of day-to-day political struggles, something like an impartial executive endowed with special perspective as well as dynastic prestige. Even for liberals unimpressed with these arguments, monarchy was still better than a republic, widely identified with democracy and the unleashing of the unruly masses. The democrats, for their part, saw in royalty the preeminent symbol of the old regime, of privilege and prerogative, a living denial of the democratic principle of "popular sovereignty." Clearly, these were important differences; but beyond them, it could at times be difficult to distinguish the more moderate democrats from the advanced liberals. Both admitted the existence of serious social ills, both were reluctant to upset the social status quo to cure them, both were appalled by the socialist revolutionaries and preferred the route of gradual, piecemeal social tinkering. The prospect of social revolution was likely to drive moderate democrats to the right, just as it did liberals.

Next came men to whom we can refer as the radical republicans. Closer to the Jacobin tradition, they were also political democrats, but more strident in tone than the moderates and less reluctant to talk of social reform. Moderate republicans courted a broad popular audience, but the nature of their appeal was such as to attract primarily a middle-class following. The radicals turned more openly toward disgruntled petty bourgeois and the urban poor, dwelling on the idea of "the people," in whom all sovereignty and political virtue resided. Less squeamish about revolutionary rhetoric than the moderates, the radicals were still not notable for their revolutionary efforts until independent events brought about the upheavals of 1848. Thereafter, radicals like Arnold Ruge in Germany or Alexandre-Auguste Ledru-Rollin in France had a brief (and miserably unsuccessful) fling at it themselves.

The radicals have been well described as "integralists"—men who wanted an integral application of democratic doctrines, and not the patchy, gradual approach of the moderates. But, again, it would be mistaken to cast them as social revolutionaries. Their adulation of "the people" was more political than social. In France, the radicals' social program arose from a sort of sentimental Jacobin egalitarianism which thought that the state ought to intervene to protect the little man. The handful of Viennese radicals, who surfaced only after the revolution, advocated a small dole to the poor and boggled when workers talked of increasing it. German democrats like Ruge and Robert Blum were expansive in their expressions of sympathy for the poor, and vague in their programs for change. Most agreed that political liberation had to precede social amelioration.

It would be convenient if one could continue this survey of the European left in the familiar terms of an array of neatly distinguishable groups, each more radical than the last, stretching ever outward across the political horizon. Unfortunately, the subject fails to fit the scheme. For example, the socialists ought to go next, to the left of the radicals, and, indeed, some of them belong there, by virtue of their more far-reaching social reform programs. One of these is Louis Blanc, probably the most famous French socialist of the period and author of the popular little treatise, *L'Organisation du travail*. Blanc shared most of the radical democrats' political sympathies, and even worked as an editor on Ledru-Rollin's newspaper, *La Réforme*. But Blanc also explicitly called himself a socialist, an appellation justified by his version of state socialism in which the central government—once it became an expression of the popular will—would reorganize production and distribution on a more egalitarian basis. Property was not to disappear; it would rather, like labor, be organized in the form of cooperatives owned by workers themselves but initially subsidized by state funds. "It is not a question of taking wealth away," wrote Blanc in 1847, "it is a question of fertilizing it so that it becomes universal."

The difficulty is that far from all socialists during the 1840s will also fit into this slot. A few socialist thinkers were also political royalists; a great many more were simply apolitical, utterly indifferent to the form of the government, and highly suspicious of the radicals' slogan that political change had to precede social change. Still, in 1848, most socialists supported the revolutions, and found themselves thrown together with the radicals, many of whom began to call *themselves* socialists, as if to defy any effort at neat categorization.

The word 'socialist' referred to men with such widely divergent ideas that the usefulness of the word may be called into doubt. Far from being a coherent body of doctrine or political movement, socialism embraced virtually anyone demanding fundamental reforms of the social system. As a political movement, socialism amounted to very little indeed prior to 1848: a handful of militant secret societies scattered across the continent, probably with sympathetic support from some segments of the working classes. As an intellectual movement, however, socialism had profound importance. Taken together, and ignoring momentarily the internal contradictions, the total body of socialist writings offered a thoroughgoing critique of contemporary society and proposed a variety of remedies, from moderate change to total renovation, which badly rattled the property-owning elite. It is difficult to understand some of the atmosphere of panic that permeated 1848 without grasping the genuine fear that the socialists had for years been inspiring in middle- and upper-class society.

Historians have customarily traced nineteenth-century socialism to some of the more radical phases of the French Revolution. Such connections may well exist. But there is another sense in which the kind of change that socialism sought was just the sort that the Revolution overlooked. The Revolution had abolished legal privilege; it had not guaranteed social equality. Its ethos of freedom could, when translated into economic terms, mean a kind of laissez-faire in which the strong were free to exploit the weak. Indeed, the Revolution never seriously addressed itself to the problem of an economic and social system which exposed great masses of people to poverty and misery while favoring the wealth and comfort of a few.

If socialism had a prophet, he was to be found not in the French Revolution, but in the person of a déclassé French aristocrat whose most fruitful work was done in the first quarter of the nineteenth century, the Comte de Saint-Simon. Saint-Simon was a brilliant, if somewhat unsystematic, thinker who never succeeded in putting his essential ideas into a single, comprehensive work. But his writings are rich with insights and suggestions, later developed and popularized by the circle of bright young men who had gathered around him in Paris during the 1820s. Saint-Simon was fascinated by the productive capacities of modern society, how much they could achieve if properly organized and how sadly their potential was wasted. Wasted, first, by a foolish social system: in a famous essay, Saint-Simon asked which would do more harm to France, the loss of its fifty leading physicians, fifty leading scientists, fifty leading businessmen, bankers, industrialists, and so on through a long list of "productive" professions, or instead the loss of all the members of the royal family, all the ministers of state, the bureaucracy, the clergy, the magistracy, the ten thousand richest nobles. But there was further waste engendered by a senselessly inefficient system of competition in which the productive powers worked against one another instead of cooperating for the good of all. Saint-Simon envisioned the union of all the productive forces of society into a single class, obliterating social distinctions, working cooperatively under unified direction. It would be difficult to find a concept that more thoroughly saturated the socialism of the 1830s and '40s than this principle of association, posed as an alternative to competition.

Saint-Simon supplied the ensuing generation of socialists with the rudiments for a critique of contemporary society, some principles for reform, and a vocabulary of which much would persist in socialist writings no matter how the doctrines changed. But where later socialism frequently turned in libertarian directions, Saint-Simon's thought had a broad authoritarian streak. The goal of organic social unity and the maximization of productive powers required management, direction, and control. Like most people of his tendency, Saint-Simon imagined that his system would give the only true freedom; liberals and democrats were not so sure. Some modern commentators have wanted to see Saint-Simon less as a socialist than as the prophet of modern technocracy, of the society run by industrial and scientific managers, one in which all persons may share in economic progress but everything is subordinated to the smooth functioning of the machine. However that may be, it is interesting to note that a remarkable number of Saint-Simon's young disciples of the late 1820s turned up thirty years later as prominent financiers and industrial leaders in Napoleon III's Second Empire.

Saint-Simon's ideas tried to go beyond the social advances of the French Revolution. His contemporary, Charles Fourier, bitterly rejected all that was associated with the Revolution. Fourier did not begin to publish his work until 1808; but he lived through the Revolution, which brought him financial ruin and near death at the radicals' hands, and he conceived his later work as an intellectual refutation of the "civilization," as he called it, that the Revolution produced.

Fourier is often recalled as a delightful little eccentric whose social prophecies included a world in which the sea would turn to lemonade. Beneath the eccentricities, however, lay a serious and thoughtful social critic whose work contained some of the most telling critiques of modern capitalism. For the present purposes, however, it is more profitable to consider Fourier's principal contribution to the early socialism of his century, the idea of creating an ideal society. Fourier helped revive this ancient pastime of political and social philosophy, and infused it with a passion for detail hardly precedented in the utopian tradition. He rested his plans for ideal human communities—phalansteries, in his arcane jargon—

on a complete social and economic system and an analysis of human psychology; he left nothing to chance, not the size of the rooms people would live in, nor the clothes they would wear, nor anything of possible significance. Again, at the center of Fourier's system, as of Saint-Simon's, was the notion of association, of the cooperative efforts of a society working for a common benefit rather than individuals working against one another. Probably Fourier's handful of disciples cared little for the details of his phalansteries' organization; but the idea of constructing ideal communities—both in thought and in practice—was central to early nineteenth-century socialism. The most spectacular attempts were carried out in America, thought to be detached from the decadence of European civilization, a fresh and pure place where a new start was possible. Fourierists, both French and American, helped found some experimental communities in the new world, as did some of the followers of the Frenchman Étienne Cabet, and disciples of the Englishman Robert Owen. This strain in socialist thought is interesting not merely for its colorful history; it indicates also the extent to which alienation from existing society had progressed, how serious socialists could be in their will to create a new social system.

The generation of socialists, almost all French, who inherited and reshaped the work of Saint-Simon and Fourier, are most commonly known as Utopians. The label was first pasted on them by Marx and Engels, who were trying to underscore the superiority of their own "scientific" socialism. In fact, Marx read widely and profitably in the French socialists. Many of the elements of his own theory— regarding the concentration of industry and the development of monopoly, refinements of the labor theory of value and the notion of surplus value, the development and polarization of class consciousness, the "withering away" of the state in the ideal society—were first glimpsed by the Utopians. It is true that the Utopians' work was often speculative, and they did have some weird schemes for social reorganization. Yet their critiques of society—and surely criticism was their most valuable contribution—were founded on careful empirical observation, and long before anything like large-scale industrialization had emerged on the continent they saw most of the directions it would take.

The socialist position on private property was one important issue on which the movement could get no agreement. Actually, very few theorists supported the total abolition of private property. But, as critics, they frequently attributed social ills to the abuse of private property or to its inequitable distribution, and it was these attacks which drew attention. Similarly, socialists were badly split on what ought to be the role of the state in the socialist society. Blanc, many of the Saint-Simonians, and a few other sectarians argued for an extremely strong central authority which, in the name of the people, would have jurisdiction over broad sections of economic and social life. In many quarters, therefore, socialism picked up the reputation of a dictatorial persuasion. In fact, many socialists were decentralizers, anti-statists, or just plain anarchists who felt, with Proudhon, "The government of man by man (under whatever name it be disguised) is oppression."

On no point were the socialists in greater disarray than on how they should proceed to the realization of their ideas. Since they were treated as little better than criminals by the authorities, clearly they could not work through established political channels. Indeed, everywhere in Europe, the least hint of socialist organization was savagely assaulted by authority and driven underground. Some socialists cast their works in the form of exhortations to the ruling elite, begging them to lead reforms themselves; others besieged the influential men of their society with copies of their works, hoping for some well-placed converts. An impatient handful disdained the tactic of persuasion and organized covertly for revolution. Of these, none was more famous than Louis Auguste Blanqui, who fought on his first barricade in July 1830 in Paris and spent thirty of his last forty-three years in jail for assorted revolutionary activities. For Blanqui, overthrow of the old order assumed priority over theorizing about the nature of the new one. His socialism was simple, even crude, violent. For example, in the course of a little essay entitled "The Man Who Makes the Soup Should Get to Eat It," Blanqui wrote: "Axiom: the nation is impoverished by the loss of a worker; it is enriched by the loss of an idler. The death of a rich man is a benefaction."

For Saint-Simon, the workers had been but one of the productive elements which was done less than justice by the prevalent state of affairs. In the second generation of socialist thinkers, the emphasis shifted drastically, and soon the urban working classes became the whole focus of the movement. Indeed, the notion of association fit nicely with the dispositions of artisans who sought something like a return to the stable, controlled world of the guild. If anything, the socialist involvement with the problem of the urban poor went too far. It is true that in the cities were to be found the most visible social ills, the most clear-cut warnings of what unchecked competition and exploitation could do. But to ignore the countryside, and its abundant poverty and discontent, was not only an intellectual oversight; it was a political mistake of the highest order. In the crisis of 1848, the socialists found that they had no way to mobilize the peasant masses. Moreover, their own reputation in rural areas consisted primarily in their theoretical attacks upon the ownership of private property, which to a peasant was likely to mean the little plot of land from which he drew his subsistence.

The extent of support for socialism among the urban poor is still hard to specify for some areas. Of course, in such cities as Naples, Venice, Milan, even Vienna, the question presents no difficulties, since there were hardly any socialists around to be supported. But in cities such as Berlin and Paris, socialist spokesmen were more numerous. Still, even in Berlin, the socialist movement was relatively small, and did not really get underway until the late summer of 1848. Even then, socialists like Stephan Born found it hard to attract much of a following. French socialists, building on a longer tradition of working-class protest, were more fortunate. There were a large number of socialist clubs and newspapers in Paris and the other major cities after the February 1848 revolution. Still, moderate republicans dominated Paris during the general election of April 1848, and the great left-wing rising of June probably arose more from social conditions than from ideological commitments.

Once more, the socialists of Europe inspired alarms out of all proportion to their strength—to some extent, perhaps, because of the virulence of their rhetoric. Even the comparatively calm ones, like Blanc, were liable to be confused with Blanqui, and tarred with the brush of violent revolutionary intent. The very fact that the socialists could raise such a stir throughout the 1840s reflects a substantial commitment to the social status quo as well as a deep reservoir of social fear.

Thus far, this examination of the groups advocating change in the Europe of the 1840s has concentrated on movements for domestic reform and renovation, on persons and ideologies intent on altering the institutions of a given country. It is time to turn to another great force, this one proposing international change, advocating the destruction of existing states and the creation of new ones.

In later decades, it was common to find liberalism and nationalism pitted against one another, a situation somewhat anticipated by 1848. By and large, in the first half of the nineteenth century, nationalists employed the vocabulary of liberalism and defined their goals too in terms of freedom. In the broadest sense, nationalism sought to replace dynasty, church, and province with the nation as the main object of loyalty. In a somewhat narrower sense, nationalism sought to attain for culturally homogeneous areas and peoples some degree of independence and unity.

"Culture" was doubtless the key concept in early nineteenth century nationalism; the degree of a people's cultural awareness and advancement was closely related to the form their nationalist demands took. In Germany, the great cultural efflorescence of the eighteenth century made political fragmentation even more obviously "unnatural." The handful of politically aware Germans took for granted that they ought to be united, and viewed the problem as a political one of achieving this goal. Much the same was true of the Italians, who shared a long cultural heritage, and whose nationalists agreed on the rightness of unification while disagreeing on the form it ought to take. But among the Slavic peoples of the Hapsburg Empire, drastically different political, cultural, and religious backgrounds made it difficult to forge a common Slavic nationalism. Slavic intellectuals had a hard time developing any sense of cultural identity, since most of them were educated in schools where German was the official language and Roman Catholicism the dominant faith. Thus, it followed that Slavic nationalism initially took a different tone than the German or the Italian, demanding first of all the parity of Slavic tongues and culture with German and concerning itself less with political independence.

Even where nationalism rested upon solid cultural foundations, as in most of the German states, it was still by no means a popular movement, one that engaged the energies and enthusiasm of the masses. While the peasants and the urban poor might rally momentarily to the nationalist cause, it was still a remote concern compared to their social and economic grievances. The unification movement was largely a middle-class concern, and one usually central to the liberal program. German liberals saw unification as a means to greater prosperity, as a way of cancelling out the power of the petty princes who resisted political reform, and also as an end in itself. Political unity seemed the inevitable fulfillment of German cultural superiority, the natural goal of a people who, in the eyes of the liberals, both desired and were destined to be free. For liberals simply could not separate the notion of freedom from that of national unity. One of the leading liberal spokesmen of the 1840s, Heinrich von Gagern, reflected this mentality in his opening address to the Frankfurt National Assembly of 1848. "We have the greatest task to perform," he said. "We must create a constitution for Germany, for the whole empire. The call and the capacity for such work are inherent in the sovereignty of the people."

Right-wing nationalism, emphasizing the primacy of the state and the subordination of all other considerations to its power, was indeed present in the 1840s, but it was not yet dominant. The liberal variety, with its emphasis upon freedom rather than authority, still maintained the initiative, and the liberals saw unification as the necessary correlate of constitutional and parliamentary government. The German Confederation, or Bund, established in the diplomatic aftermath of the Napoleonic wars, was in all respects the antithesis of liberal aspirations. To begin with, it hardly offered unity at all; there was no central government, and the Diet was composed of representatives chosen by the member governments. The two principal central European powers, Prussia and the Hapsburg Empire, used the weak structure of the Bund to keep their advantage over the smaller states and also to keep liberal reformism in hand. They worked through the Bund to repress liberal and nationalist movements—which were generally one and the same—and to try to prevent the spread of constitutionalism from the handful of lesser states which had nominally adopted it. From the Austrian point of view in particular, the Confederation had enormous advantages; it preserved Hapsburg predominance in central Europe, which would certainly have been challenged by a united Germany, and served as an effective mechanism for control of the idea of nationality—one which was anathema to the very existence of the Empire. Like the liberals themselves, the supporters of the status quo saw a close linkage between liberalism and nationalism.

Just as in the German states, Italian nationalism was fundamentally a program of the educated elites; and, like the Germans, such

Italians had a well-developed consciousness of their cultural unity. Italy did not have the powerful economic forces simultaneously creating and demonstrating the desirability of political unity which were operating in Germany; but the nationalist movement was no less vocal for that. With the peninsula politically fragmented and its several parts under the control of conservative monarchs, the same connections between unification and liberalism were present; the Italians' awareness of them was manifest in several schemes for unity that competed for popularity.

The most famous Italian nationalist was surely the colorful Giuseppe Mazzini, a republican who spent most of his years both before and after 1848 in political exile. Mazzini personified the generous, expansive idealism and the romantic nationalism of his age. He envisioned, in innumerable pamphlets, books, and speeches, a Europe of free and independent peoples, united in republican democracies, and coexisting fraternally. To this end, he formed a little underground organization named Young Italy which quickly spawned counterparts in other fragmented areas of the continent. Mazzini's writings bristle with all the confident visions that the nineteenth century could frequently generate: humanity, association, progress— the terms appear on nearly every page. Given the later somewhat sordid history of nationalism, it may seem odd to find this early nationalist ideologue writing that he believes in "the *unity* of the human race, and in the moral *equality* of all the children of God," or that:

> We believe that to make politics an *art*, and sever them from morality, as the royal statesmen and diplomatists desire, is a sin before God and destructive to the peoples. The *end* of politics is the application of the moral law to the civil constitution of a nation in its double activity, domestic and foreign.

Mazzini's call for a unified Italian republic met resistance from conservatives and liberals alike. The old regime—in the grotesquely reactionary Kingdom of Naples and Sicily ruled by the Bourbon King Ferdinand, in the Papal states, in Tuscany—could only hope to perpetuate itself by holding off unification; too weak to do so alone, these monarchs depended heavily upon Hapsburg aid. But liberals also opposed Mazzini, for the same reason they opposed democrats everywhere. Even though Mazzini explicitly rejected socialism, Italian liberals—drawn mostly from the aristocracy and the commercial classes—equated republicanism with mob rule.

Liberal unificationism chose rather to depend upon established authority to create a new Italy. One large faction—the so-called Neo-Guelphs—turned to the Papacy, which commanded the prestige and moral force to achieve unification, though it lacked the will and even the desire. Moderate liberals hoped to convince the Papacy that its leadership would ensure the achievement of unification on sound political principles. But the Papacy showed little interest in nationalism until 1846 and the election of Cardinal Mastai-Ferretti as Pius IX. The new Pope was an unwavering conservative. Yet in his first months in office he carried out some administrative reforms which had coincidentally been part of the liberal program. At the same time, his anxiety for popularity led him to make some remarks which wishful liberals interpreted as favorable to their cause. Hopes for Pius IX, further buoyed up by the new Pope's surprise amnesty for political prisoners, ran high in the liberal camp, which made their disappointment in 1848 all the more painful. Another group of liberals pinned their hopes upon the Kingdom of Piedmont-Sardinia, where the ruling House of Savoy had shown some sympathy for nationalist causes since the early 1820s. The Piedmontese dynasty, however, was not exactly unificationist. Rather, it saw itself at the head of a movement which would expand its hegemony over northern Italy rather than merge itself into united Italy. It is doubtful if the ambitions of Charles Albert, King after 1831, even extended beyond Lombardy and Venetia.

Whichever direction an Italian nationalist took—Mazzinian, Papal, Piedmontese—he was bound to come to the same conclusion: the unavoidability of a war of liberation against Austria. It was not a conclusion which any of them particularly relished. Hapsburg military might, centered in the forces of Marshal Radetzky which controlled Lombardy-Venetia from their base in Milan, was demonstrably greater than that of any Italian state. Moreover, the military resources of all the Italian states could only be pooled *after* Hapsburg influence had been destroyed. The most likely candidate for military leadership, however, was Piedmont, whose geographic location and political interests put it in the best position to battle Austria. Long before the revolutions of 1848, Italian liberal nationalists began to think of Charles Albert as the leader of national unification.

The German nationalist writer Friedrich Jahn once observed that "a people is first made into a nation by its mother-tongue." Certainly it was the realization that they spoke a unique language that was central to the Slavs' cultural awakening. The Austrian rulers of the Hapsburg Empire had fortified their political domination with systematic cultural domination; German was the language of the schools, the bureaucracy, the law courts. Slavs who aspired to any position of even relative status within the Empire were forced to master German and put aside their own language. But toward the end of the eighteenth century, there developed an increasing interest among Slavic (but also among German) intellectuals in the Slavic languages, and this soon broadened into busy study of Slavic popular literature and folkways. Historians began to reconstruct the Slavic past; the Czech scholar Francis Palácky labored over a gigantic history of Bohemia, giving the intelligentsia some basis for pride and a sense of identity. Just as Jakob and Wilhelm Grimm were trying to delineate the essence of a German national character through its folktales, scholars unearthed Slavic counterparts in the form of songs, stories, popular poetry, and customs. Educated Slavs were beginning to discover that their political inferiority within the Empire had no basis in cultural history.

And yet the political implications of Slavic nationalism were by no means clear. There were no existing Slavic dynasties around which independence movements could group, and the idea of republicanism was disturbing to the Slav liberals. None of the major Slavic groupings in the Empire—Czech, Slovak, Ruthene, Pole, Croatian, Slovene, Serb—had the economic wherewithal for viable independence; all were accustomed to depending upon the Hapsburg Empire for their economic life. As independent states, the several Slav peoples would have been weak and virtually defenseless. They would in particular have been prey to the Magyars of Hungary, who shared their subject status within the Empire, but who were notorious for their repression of Slavic minorities within Hungary. To the extent that Slav nationalists gave serious thought to political considerations, they rarely went further than demanding recognition of their cultural identity—the right to use their languages in their schools and in their local government—and some vague requests for provincial self-government.

Magyar liberal nationalists, like the Slavs, were eager to see some

loosening up of the rigid centralization and systematic Germani-
zation of the Empire. Magyar cultural nationalism centered upon
efforts to preserve and purify the mother tongue; much of this work
went on at the Hungarian Academy, founded in 1825, which also
sponsored the new works of Magyar literature. At about the same
time, there were stirrings in the Hungarian Diet, which began to
press for establishment of Magyar as the official language; in 1833,
Magyar was first used in Diet debates, and by 1844 it had become
the recognized language for the administration and for education
as well. These were significant victories for the time, won perhaps
because they had the support of Hungary's little knot of great
landed magnates. On political matters, the magnates were less
unified. Many of them were doing well enough under the Hapsburg regime and had no complaints; their idea of reform was to
increase agricultural productivity. But there was a vocal minority
of roughly western-style liberals among the magnates, and an even
noisier group of lesser landholding gentry who talked of complete
separation from the Empire. In the 1840s, one of the gentry's spokesmen, Lajos Kossuth, founded Hungary's first newspaper and demanded publication of the Diet's debates. The Magyar ruling
classes were becoming increasingly sensitized to political questions,
increasingly exposed to talk of constitutionalism and reforms. When
Metternich dared tamper with some minor vestiges of Hungarian
autonomy in 1847, he was answered with an unprecedented storm
of protest from the Diet.

The issue of nationalism appeared time and again during the
revolutions, and for that reason 1848 has appeared in the pages
of some historians as "the springtime of the peoples." It is true
that the revolutions unleashed the first full-scale nationalist wars in
central and southern Europe; it is true that 1848 laid the foundations for the great period of unification and international restruc-
turing in the 1860s. But again, this early nationalism was not a
"peoples' nationalism," a popular force which captured the imagination and mobilized the dedication of the masses as it was later to
do. Only in France, characteristically a decade or two more politically sophisticated than its continental neighbors, was nationalism
a live issue for the urban poor, and even there it was still overshadowed by social concerns. It would take both the political
experience of 1848 and the advance of industrialization—knitting

nations more closely together, facilitating communications and transportation—before national consciousness and nationalist politics spread beyond the educated and already politicized elite.

Historians have exerted a great deal of energy in debate over the outbreak of the revolutions of 1848, some arguing that revolution was widely expected during the middle '40s, others insisting that it was a sort of astonishing accident which caught everyone off guard. It is possible, of course, to cite evidence for both sides—sometimes the same evidence. "I believe that at this moment we are sleeping on a volcano," Alexis de Tocqueville told the French Chamber of Deputies at the end of January 1848, though he later admitted that "the event justified me more promptly and more completely than I foresaw."

The fact is that while prophets of doom abounded in Europe of the 1840s—as they do in most times and places—very few persons (with the possible exception of a handful of diehard revolutionary conspirators) had given much serious thought to revolution. The revolutions were not the product of calculation. They arose from a peculiar conjunction of circumstances, and were to that extent accidental; indeed, they could probably have been avoided altogether by efforts which ought not to have been beyond human capacity. On the other hand, the conditions which produced those circumstances were anything but accidental; they grew naturally (if not quite inevitably) from the structure of European society and politics.

In economies so heavily overbalanced toward the agrarian sector, it should be no surprise that economic crises would begin in that sector. In 1845, European countries experienced a series of crop failures which set off widespread economic and social reverberations. The failures struck almost exclusively staple foods, the ones that formed the principal element in the diet of the masses. They began in 1845 with a potato disease which decimated the crop in Ireland, the Netherlands, and large sections of northern and eastern Germany. In 1846, there were the first serious wheat crises, brought on by unusual heat and drought, which cut badly into the harvest in France and Germany. The next year saw an even worse harvest.

The precise impact of the agricultural crises varied, of course, from country to country, but there were enough common features to permit the following somewhat abstract model. Crop failures naturally drove up the prices of the staple commodities hit. Small cash-crop producers could hardly take advantage of this situation, since they had so much less to sell, and were careful to hold on to reserves for themselves; subsistence farmers now found themselves hard put to exist. In order to compensate for the soaring prices they were now forced to pay for bread or potatoes, they naturally cut back on their other purchases. In effect, the crisis sharply curtailed consumer purchasing power, something to which manufacturing had to adjust quickly. Facing the prospect of serious overproduction, manufacturers large and small had to lay off employees, or at the very least whittle wages down to the bone. In other words, at the very moment when food prices were rising, urban workers frequently found themselves out of a job.

This dimension of the crisis can hardly appear strange; it is strikingly similar to the sort of crisis that struck France in the late 1780s, and again in the late 1820s—both occasions which ultimately resulted in revolution. Moreover, popular response to the crisis had a familiar ring, generally in the form of the food riot. The food riot was one of the most common (though curiously little-studied) forms of popular protest, one that stretched back in European history for more than two centuries and generally reached a crescendo in times of dire scarcity. Usually, it consisted of mob assaults upon owners or sellers of food—grain-dealers, for example, or even bakeries. The mob would insist upon a price reduction and sale at a reasonable or "just" price; outright theft or "popular requisition" was relatively rare, and crowds more frequently drew upon some rough-and-ready notion of a fair price. In any case, a crowd was generally ready to resort to violence if necessary, and food riots often required calling in the local police or troops. The food riot was so common in early nineteenth century Europe that it is often overlooked, taken for a phenomenon that is equivalent to aimless protest or common crime. But in fact, as has recently been shown, food riots were rarely without political significance. Rioters often directed their complaints not merely at food dealers, but at local authorities as well. The riots reflected real dissatisfaction with a "system," however dimly conceived, which gave rise to scarcity by (for instance) supplying large towns before rural areas. And they could sometimes grow to significant proportions, as with the so-called potato revolution of Berlin in the spring of 1847, which required vigorous action by regular army troops to disperse the rioters.

The subsistence crisis of the 1840s was a characteristic spasm of the European economy, only larger and more intense than many similar ones of the preceding generation. Its high food prices, unemployment, declining prices for manufacturing, and consequent popular protest were all relatively familiar features. But there were also new features to the economic crisis, ones which heralded the sorts of economic crises that would typify the new industrial age of the coming generations.

The 1850s and '60s were surely the great age of continental railroad building, but the appeal of railways was already growing rapidly in the 1840s. In 1842, the French Chamber of Deputies passed a law to stimulate railroad growth by agreeing to provide land for private builders. At the same time the Prussian Junker aristocracy was pressing the government to stimulate railway building, particularly into the eastern provinces, in order to speed the grain produced on their estates to agricultural markets. While building was comparatively slow compared to future decades, the financial foundations for growth were laid in the 1840s. There were heavy investments in French and German railroads during these years, which resulted in the drastic reduction of available supplies of liquid capital. This situation was complicated by the agricultural crisis of 1845–47; governments employed their credit supply to buy foreign grain, and, given the large amounts of assets frozen in railroad investment and speculation, the credit supply shrank dangerously. Thus there were few available funds on hand for aid to small businesses in the middle '40s; financial overextension forced some bankruptcies, and a number of banks—particularly in the German states—closed up. A serious crisis of confidence struck the business community, and Europe experienced in miniature the sort of financial panic that would mark its later economic depressions, as in the 1870s.

It is easy enough to sketch out the main lines of the economic crisis of the 1840s; it is quite another matter to establish firmly its relationship to the political crisis that followed. For example, by the winter of 1847–48, and before revolution had broken out any place, the economic crisis began to subside. Food prices began to drop, and here and there were faint signals that manufacturing might revive and create once more the badly-needed jobs. The revolutions struck in the midst of what might, given time to develop, have become an economic upswing. If one is seeking to emphasize the economic determinants in the outbreak of revolution, this fact can be disturbing, though it might be argued that, while there were some signs of improvement in February and March of 1848, misery and privation were still widespread and severe; recovery was very far from complete. Even so, it has to be admitted that economic crises were nothing new. Within the living memory of those who experienced the one of the 1840s, there had been many such crises. Why should this particular one have led to revolution for masses of people for whom economic crisis was something like a way of life? And, of course, there are even more general questions here, regarding the relationship of revolution to misery, questions which ask whether extreme hunger, in and of itself, may ever be said to have launched a revolution.

Yet it is just as difficult to sever the crisis from the revolutions. Rioting peasants in southwest Germany, working-class violence in the Viennese suburbs, artisan insurrection in Paris all testify to the existence of profound economic discontent. The economic crisis provided a goad, it sharpened tensions, it helped create an atmosphere in which the revolutions could take place. But the difference between, say, the Berlin potato revolution of 1847 and the Berlin revolution of 1848 was that in the latter crisis people used a political vocabulary for the expression of their discontent, so that social and economic grievances took on an even greater political significance than they had before. In a sense, 1848 saw the politicization of traditional popular violence.

Many European liberals of 1846 and 1847 felt their cause was beginning to make important international advances. In 1846, the British liberals of the Anti-Corn Law League finally achieved their goal when Parliament began to reduce tariffs; shortly thereafter, the League's most prominent spokesman, Richard Cobden, made a tour of Europe, meeting with continental counterparts and urging them to organize for legal, constitutional agitation. The election of Pius IX in 1846 raised liberal-nationalist hopes in Italy. In 1847, succumbing to liberal appeals, Friedrich Wilhelm IV of Prussia summoned the United Diet, presumably to hear various programs for reform. Belgium introduced a greater degree of ministerial responsibility into its parliamentary system, and the liberals further consolidated their control. A brief civil war in Switzerland ended in the victory of the liberals and the defeat of conservative regions backed by Metternich. In France, opposition elements mounted a campaign for electoral reform, and a coalition running from moderates of the center to moderate republicans submitted a reform bill to the Chamber. And everywhere, liberals were alive to the activities of their counterparts in other countries.

Had these various reformist efforts borne any fruit, it is possible that the revolutions of 1848 would never have occurred. But the Prussian United Diet only provided liberals there with more frustration, and produced no worthwhile reforms. In France, the conservative majority easily defeated the proposal for electoral reform. The victory of François Guizot's government badly demoralized the minority coalition, which thereupon organized a nationwide campaign of political banquets at which various reformist leaders spoke in favor of reform. The banquets were in fact a traditional and rather tame form of political agitation, and their purpose was to rebuild confidence and maintain solidarity among the defeated reformist ranks. Only Pius IX seemed to offer much hope, though even he would soon prove to be a weak reed on which to rest liberal hopes. And throughout it all, the Hapsburg government maintained its stance of total refusal to compromise with the left.

This climate of political frustration was as crucial to 1848 as the economic crisis. In many places, the miserable peasants and urban poor already held the government responsible for the economic situation; refusal of the authorities to concede political reforms only fortified the widespread hostility to the political status quo. It is true that these antagonisms varied from one stratum of society to the next, from region to region, from country to country. But while the economic crisis heightened the level of popular violence, the patent failure of reformist politics made the situation all the more dangerous. It tended to channel the various discontents, focus them upon the governments in power, and give the vague slogans of reform some momentary specificity among the masses. It was the failure, rather than the victory, of reformism that helped politicize popular discontent, and the upheavals of 1848 thus began as something like revolutions of frustration.

Chapter 2

The Outbreak of Revolution

The February Revolution in Paris

Louis Philippe, King of the French, owed his crown to a revolution in the streets of Paris during July 1830. The revolution had begun as a violent protest against the repressive rule of the last Bourbon King, Charles X; it ended with moderates and liberals maneuvering the Duc d'Orléans onto the throne before the republicans could attempt anything untoward. Some of the personalities prominent in the revolutionary days recalled an eruption which had occurred forty years earlier: the Marquis de la Fayette was there, and old Talleyrand too, both of whom endorsed Louis Philippe. The new King himself, who was fifty-seven years old, was no stranger to revolution: his father, the previous Duc, known more popularly during the 1790s as Philippe Égalité, had voted for the execution of Louis XVI, only to fall victim himself to the blade a few months later. Louis Philippe served in the republican army before going into exile in 1793. He had none of his father's political impetuousness, and yet by 1830 he saw that some of the claims of liberalism could not be denied. He was chosen King by the parliament (or, at least, by the liberal rump in the Chamber of Deputies which acted as the parliament at the end of the revolution). He began his reign by taking an oath to the revised version of the Constitutional Charter of 1814.

On nearly all counts, there was reason for optimism with the inauguration of the July Monarchy. The Charter had been modified on several points respecting civil freedoms, and the new constitutional arrangements satisfied the liberals. Though hard-core legitimists—that is, supporters of the 'legitimate' Bourbon dynasty—refused to recognize the new monarch, Louis Philippe was able to rally most conservatives and moderates, after a period of uncertainty. Any fears that the regime's revolutionary origins would shape its nature were allayed when the government vigorously put down republican risings in Lyon and Paris during 1831 and 1832. In addition to building a political consensus which excluded only the far right and the far left, the monarchy lowered the property qualifications on the vote, thereby winning the support of important layers of the middle classes hitherto disenfranchised. When a surge of economic prosperity further stabilized the regime in the mid-1830s, it seemed that France had at last found the formula for orderly liberal government, what its more enthusiastic supporters called government of the golden mean. What, then, went wrong?

To begin with, the scope of the consensus was illusory. The July Monarchy is also well-known as the "bourgeois monarchy"; if it had in fact had the profound and sustained support of the bourgeoisie, it would not have met its end as it did. The regime's principal support came from a small set of elites, what the French would call *grands notables,* men of great wealth, prestige, and influence. But the July Monarchy never won the deep commitment of any social class, any important institution, any large region. In nearly eighteen years of existence it was unable to strike deep roots and its passing in 1848 was curiously unregretted by a people still monarchist in the majority. Moreover, while the regime had begun by making major adaptations to liberal constitutionalism, it thereafter made a career of inflexibility. Partly because of royal resistance, partly because of the recalcitrance of conservatives in parliament and government, liberal reform proposals were turned down time and again. After François Guizot came to dominate the ministry in 1840, this antireformist posture stiffened noticeably, perhaps because Guizot commanded a large and safe majority in the Chambers.

The July Monarchy was as intent as any European government of the time upon repressing radical protest; a law of September

1835 even made use of the word 'republican' illegal. But the regime never learned the trick of co-opting dissent. The electorate created by the new franchise law of 1831 numbered 160,000 persons, a substantial increase over the Restoration; moreover, since the franchise was linked to payment of direct taxes, prosperity would naturally enlarge the electorate. When critics complained that the political class, the *pays légal,* was too narrow, Guizot liked to remind them that these "natural" processes had expanded the electorate by 50 per cent, to around 240,000, by 1846. This argument had little effect on the several hundred thousand men of education and often substantial means who were denied the vote.[1] The opposition groups in the Chamber seized upon this growing dissatisfaction and began to concentrate largely on the issue of electoral reform.

In July 1847, the opposition staged a large political banquet in Paris. This was the first of more than fifty such banquets held throughout the country during the next six months, for the purpose of stirring up sentiment for electoral reform. They were inspired and coordinated by a central committee consisting of moderate republicans associated with the Paris newspaper *Le National,* liberal monarchists of Odilon Barrot's so-called Dynastic Left group, and a few of Adolphe Thiers' more moderate centrist followers. Thiers himself refused to participate in the banquets, uncertain of their political impact. In retrospect, Thiers' caution seems excessive. The banquets were, by and large, harmless affairs, at the farthest remove from revolutionary agitation, and marked primarily by bad food and bad speeches vaguely advocating a larger electorate. The clientele was, for the most part, kept respectably middle-class by the price of admission (although there were a few radical and socialist banquets organized by factions unassociated with the central committee). Probably, the banquet campaign gained few converts to suffrage reform; rather, its principal effect was to bolster the sagging morale of those already committed to the cause. For the election of 1846 had in fact increased Guizot's parliamentary majority, and already in the spring of 1847, the Chamber of Deputies had voted down proposals for an extension of the franchise to an additional 200,000 voters. Guizot could thus afford to treat the banquets as little more than a tasteless annoyance; if anything, they merely called

---

[1] One interesting case was that of Victor Cousin, a professor at the Sorbonne, created a Peer of France, and for a time even a cabinet minister. He still did not meet the requirements for the vote.

attention to the opposition's weakness. This official indifference can only have discouraged the banqueters further by underscoring the political irrelevance of their efforts. It was only when the government foolishly decided to make an issue of the banquets that they became significant.

In December, Louis Philippe delivered his annual Address from the Throne to the legislature, in the course of which he made reference to those who were fomenting "blind and hostile passions." The opposition was stung, for it had gone to great pains to keep the banquets well within the bounds of respectable political protest. It now appears that the King was alluding to a socialist banquet held in Limoges early in December and not to the parliamentary opposition's campaign at all. But the deputies of the center and left took the remark as evidence of royal enmity toward free speech and assembly; they tried to block the Chamber's usually routine acceptance of the Address, and debate dragged on into the new year.

Meanwhile, in early January, a group of reform-minded members of the Paris National Guard—a citizen, and largely middle-class, militia—decided to organize yet another banquet to be held in the capital. They attempted, unsuccessfully, to interest leaders of the parliamentary opposition in co-sponsoring the affair. The deputies were preoccupied with the debate on the royal address, and in any case had little reason to engage in yet another futile banquet. Lacking any political celebrities, the banquet would hardly have been worthy of note. Once again, however, government intervention alone manufactured a major incident; the authorities refused to issue the permit necessary for the banquet to be held in a public building.

Perhaps the government overestimated opposition strength; or perhaps it was unwilling to risk the excitement that a banquet might provoke among the Parisian population. In any event, the refusal to sanction the banquet dovetailed neatly with the opposition's complaints in the Chamber. The issue of free speech and assembly broke out of the confining arena of parliamentary debate and squarely confronted the entire population of Paris. The opposition, previously so indifferent to the idea of another banquet, now assumed responsibility for its organization. The affair was rescheduled for a new date, Sunday, February 20, on a private site in the Champs-Élysées, free from the need for official authorization.

It was not very long, however, before the opposition leaders, and particularly the monarchist contingent led by Barrot, began to find their position uncomfortable. Some considerable care had been exercised to keep this banquet, like its predecessors, unimpeachably moderate. But the dangers that the authorities had probably imagined when they initially prohibited the banquet now began to trouble the reformers. Would a large antigovernmental banquet, they wondered, run the risk of reviving the revolutionary traditions of the Parisian working classes? Barrot doubtless began to regret that the opposition had become committed to the banquet, that the whole business had inflated into a matter of principle, and he welcomed the opportunity provided by the government for a graceful withdrawal.

On February 18, Barrot negotiated with government spokesmen a compromise arrangement designed both to assuage official discontent with the very idea of a banquet and still save face for the opposition. The banquet was postponed to February 22—a Tuesday, when there were likely to be smaller crowds than on a Sunday—at which time the participants would gather at the Church of the Madeleine and march from there to the banquet site. They would then submit peaceably to prearranged police intervention and, after a formal toast to the freedom of assembly, would disperse. On the 19th, some two hundred opposition deputies and journalists met and voted overwhelmingly to accept the compromise. Among the politicians, at least, the desire to preserve order had superseded hostility to Guizot.

Such anxieties were ill-founded. From the beginning, the radical left treated the banquet as a contemptible charade, an irrelevant squabble within the ranks of the comfortable bourgeoisie. True, there was serious dissatisfaction among the Paris poor, and there were persons to whom the idea of revolution appealed—members of the underground secret societies and a few radical student groups. But no one foresaw revolution resulting from the Paris banquet, and no one seriously attempted to ensure that it would.

On the morning of February 21, *Le National* published the marching orders for the next day's gathering at the Madeleine and trek to the Champs-Élysées, along with a formal acceptance of the invitation to attend the banquet, signed by one hundred and ten opposition deputies. Harmless as this might sound, it gave—when splashed across the front page of *Le National* in bold-face type—a menacing (and not altogether accurate) impression of opposition unity and determination in the face of government hostility. Beneath the imposing lists of names were the details of the preliminary procession, in which not only deputies, various reformist sympathizers, and students would participate, but also "the National Guard." This latter referred merely to those individual Guardsmen who had volunteered to take part in the parade, in uniform but of course unarmed. It could easily, however, give the impression that the opposition was inciting the Guard to defy the government. This was a challenge Guizot could not ignore.

If the provocative tone of *Le National* was at all intentional, it probably aimed at nothing more than to provoke Guizot into a flagrant violation of the right of assembly, and thus bring down the ministry either by legal measures or perhaps even by the decision of an intimidated King. Guizot did indeed respond, around midday on the 21st, by flatly prohibiting the banquet. Most of the opposition deputies decided to back down once again. Assembled at Barrot's on the afternoon of the 21st, they voted to dispense with the demonstration entirely. When the pro-reform units of the National Guard learned of their decision, they concluded that demonstration without the deputies was futile. Late that evening, the Minister of the Interior countermanded his earlier order alerting the troops.

The banquet crisis was over. Very shortly, the revolution would begin.

Unquestionably, the whole banquet affair had helped create tensions in Paris. The confrontation between government and opposition had served once more to underscore Guizot's unswerving resistance to reform, and to give added reason—though such was hardly needed—for his immense unpopularity. It may well have stirred up some of the hotheads on the left, though on the evening of the 21st a meeting of prominent radicals at the offices of Ledru-Rollin's *Réforme* decided on a cautious wait-and-see policy. But the street-fighting that broke out on February 22, though related to the banquet crisis, had its own immediate causes, its own inner logic and dynamic. The banquet gave a pretext for the gathering in the Place de la Madeleine on February 22; it provided the revolution with little else in the way of inspiration or issues.

A few demonstrators, the most vocal of whom were students, did show up at the Madeleine on the morning of the 22nd, accompanied by a much larger gathering of curious onlookers. These *badauds* were scarcely what could be called a revolutionary mob. Nearly all accounts agree that they were composed primarily of well-dressed, respectable bourgeois rather than surly lower-class malcontents. Most of them were probably in general sympathy with the opposition or they would not have bothered to venture forth into the steady drizzle that fell upon the capital. No prominent spokesman of the opposition was present. There was at first a good deal of shouting and milling about. One abortive attempt by the students to enter the Palais Bourbon (where the Chamber of Deputies' session had not yet begun) resulted in some minor unpleasantness with the armed guards. All this, however, was aimless and innocuous, entertainment for the spectators rather than serious political demonstration.

Still, the crowd continued to grow throughout the morning, and there is evidence that an increasing number of artisans and working-class spectators helped clog up the Place de la Concorde. It was the combination of this growing crowd and the presence of the Garde municipale, a sort of riot police that was heartily detested in the working-class quarters of the city for its arrogant and occasionally brutal enforcement of order, that produced an inflammable situation. By midday, a good deal of jostling between crowd and Garde was going on, and it was not long until push came to shove. Shortly after noon, the Garde rather foolishly determined to clear out the Place and the first few hundred feet of the Champs-Élysées. It performed this task with some excess of zeal; tempers flared, and there were a few casualties. This appears to have been the decisive provocation; by three P.M., the crowd did begin to disperse, but some of them only to begin the erection of barricades made from paving stones, iron grillwork snatched from buildings, overturned wagons or carriages, and any manner of material that made for a good obstruction.

Violence that night was still scattered and sporadic. The existence of barricades in the working-class quarters of the city indicated that the stage of mere riot had passed, but it would have been difficult to convince anyone that a revolution had begun. The fighting seemed at the time less like a determined insurrection than a release of emotional energy directed against official authority and its symbol, Guizot. It is easy enough to find the motives for such an outburst: the government had turned loose the Garde municipale against the people, the government was responsible for the grave economic deprivations of the last year and a half, the government remained cold to the appeal of that almost magical slogan "reform." Doubtless all these considerations were present in the minds of those who manned the barricades on the night of February 22, though it would have been unusual to find them organized into any coherent statement or uniformly ranked in any order.

If there was any focus for this somewhat diffuse antagonism, it was Guizot rather than the monarchy itself. Guizot symbolized all that was unpopular about the regime, and in the desire for his fall the disorders of the 22nd gradually created a tangible objective. In fact, the cry "Down with Guizot!" signified a serious danger for the throne, for it was a cause upon which working classes and the more well-to-do middle-class reformers could agree. Had the insurgents directed themselves immediately at the destruction of the throne, they would doubtless have frightened off the majority of the bourgeois support they actually gathered.

There were other indications that night that the disturbances of the 22nd would not vanish on the 23rd. For one thing, some of the revolutionary secret societies—caught virtually unaware by the spontaneous outburst of fighting—began to mobilize for combat on the morrow. Such men, though few in number, provided encouragement and even a sort of leadership on the barricades; the initial spontaneity of the rising is beyond question, but these men helped give it an increasingly sharper and more radical character, accelerating the rapid drift toward revolution.

The government may well have expected such developments; it was a common supposition that if an uprising occurred, it would center in the working classes, goaded by case-hardened revolutionaries. What the authorities did not expect, and what constituted by far the most ominous development of the early phase of the fighting, was the threat of rebellion from within the ranks of the propertied classes.

The National Guard was a civilian militia which originated in 1789. The city of Paris had twelve Guard legions, one for each *arrondissement*, with a total of just over 56,000 men in January 1848. What amounted to a property qualification—the requirement that Guardsmen themselves purchase their rather elaborate uniforms and equipment—generally restricted membership to men of some means, though few of the very wealthy chose to serve. During the first decade of the July Monarchy, the Paris National Guard had been an effective force in the service of the regime. It helped put down the republican risings of the early 1830s, and assisted in squelching the secret society putsch of 1839. The ruling elites of the July Monarchy thus had some reason to be grateful to the Guard, but their sense of obligation was not exactly overwhelming. The high property qualification connected to the franchise excluded many of the middle-strata bourgeoisie who comprised the Guard. As early as 1838, some Guardsmen in Paris and a few other large cities began to circulate petitions demanding of the legislature that all members of the Guard in France automatically be granted the vote. The agitation soon ballooned into a full-scale electoral reform campaign, remarkably anticipatory of the one in 1847–48, complete with support from the reformist opposition in the Chamber, a nationwide series of political banquets, and a giant banquet scheduled for Paris which was prohibited by the government and eventually held outside the city limits. In any event, two successive ministries—headed by Thiers and Guizot respectively—led Chamber majorities in defeating the reform proposals. The Paris Guard did not take this setback stoically. A royal review of the Guard in 1840 produced some shouts of "Vive la réforme!" It was the last time Louis Philippe consented to review the Paris legions.

Between this time and 1848, there were no civic disorders in which the loyalty of the Paris Guard could be tested. But there were some disturbing hints. The upper age limit on service of fifty-five meant that veterans of the heroic days of the early 1830s were disappearing from the ranks, to be replaced by younger men who had their minds on reform. The Guard elected its own officers triennially, and a number of these little electoral assemblies of 1843 and 1846 became occasions for political expression of a broader sort, often critical of government policies. Some officers refused invitations to dine at the Tuileries. The government did little to remedy the dry rot that crept through the Paris Guard. In the long period of calm, relative prosperity, and ministerial stability under Guizot, it was not immediately apparent that anything needed to be done. The Guard was hardly a hotbed of revolutionary conspiracies. But neither was it an instrument of authority upon which the regime could rely with confidence.

Unfortunately for the July Monarchy, the principal plan for the quashing of any insurrection in the capital called for just such reliance. Drawn up in 1840 and named for its military author, the so-called Gérard Plan placed considerable responsibility upon the

National Guard and assumed, moreover, an intimate cooperation between Guard and regular troops. It was widely feared by the authorities that the soldiers, many of whom were recruited from the common people, would not fire upon insurgent crowds unless the citizen militia led the way. When the prefect of the capital asked an army officer early in the crisis about his men's morale, he received the reply: "It is excellent. We will march bravely behind the National Guard."

On the evening of the 22nd, a few panicky mayors of the city's *arrondissements* put out the call for the National Guard of their district. The response was spotty and unenthusiastic. The next morning, the general call went out across the city, with results that must have given the government pause. Only one legion, that of the wealthy first *arrondissement*, unequivocally supported the government. Of the remaining eleven, a few were politically divided, and six or seven were belligerently anti-government, assembling with cries in favor of reform, calling for the dismissal and even the arrest of Guizot.

The general attitude of the Guard made effectuation of the Gérard Plan extremely difficult. In some places, the Guardsmen simply refused to take up their assigned positions; in others, they acted as buffers between the troops and the new barricades that went up on the 23rd, refusing to allow the soldiers to fire on the people. In a few instances, the Guard even exchanged some shots with the army. The effect upon the regulars, in more than one section of the city, was disastrous; morale crumbled, and soldiers let themselves be peacefully disarmed by the insurgents. Needless to say, such scenes gave a powerful impetus to the insurrection, as it was by then safe to call it.

By early afternoon on the 23rd, the military situation was, from the government's point of view, beginning to look doubtful. The first minor clashes between troops and people had only spurred on the insurgency. The fever of revolt was spreading, and the people who manned the barricades were becoming increasingly emboldened by the sight of National Guard sympathy. It would take a decisive political gesture to turn the tide, to appease the Paris Guard and to bring down the barricades, thus halting the bloodshed that Louis Philippe so deeply regretted. After much soul-searching and still with great reluctance, the King dismissed Guizot at about two-thirty P.M.

Less than two hours later, Guizot announced the resignation of his cabinet to the Chamber. The majority deputies were stunned and angered; they felt betrayed, and at the same time feared that Guizot's fall signaled a critical admission of weakness, of inability to control the fighting in the streets. Moreover, the King's chosen successor to Guizot was the Comte Molé, a staunch conservative who commanded little confidence in the Chamber. Molé's long career of public service stretched back to the reign of Napoleon I, but his skills lay primarily in administration and political maneuvering. He was not the man to deal effectively with the present crisis, and indeed his conservatism raised the risk that the appointment might cancel out the gains achieved by the regime in dropping Guizot.

Still, it was Guizot's fall that attracted attention in the streets; the news spread rapidly, and there was much rejoicing and parading about. One large contingent of celebrants passed by Guizot's office, located on the Boulevard des Capucines and guarded by troops. A perfunctory exchange of insults ensued, and suddenly someone fired a couple of shots—from which side they came is still unknown. In any event, the troops began to fire into the small crowd, killing perhaps forty persons.

The importance of this famous incident has been a matter of some controversy. To some historians, it marked the critical turning point in the February days, the crucial event that turned a waning (because victorious) insurrection into a revolution. To others, the shooting changed nothing, but only reflected the fact that tension between government and people remained high and was bound to break out in further violence. It is true that the dismissal of Guizot did not bring an end to fighting everywhere, and in some quarters it raged on ferociously. But it is difficult to say whether these pockets of conflict would have cooled down had the Capucines shooting not taken place. What does seem clear is that the incident helped generalize and intensify the fighting, which now gathered a momentum that could scarcely be stemmed by further gestures of concession. Henceforth, abdication became a likelihood, the republic a possibility; the insurgents, with perhaps some assistance from the more doctrinaire secret society men fighting at their side, began to proclaim these as their goals.

It was therefore fruitless for the politicians to attempt, from this point on, to arrest the revolutionary movement in the streets. At best, they could hope that it would ultimately create a situation which they might turn to their own advantage. Yet few of them realized how far the fighting would go. The liberal monarchists hoped that the King would be forced to appoint a Thiers-Barrot ministry. A few moderate republicans began, during the night of February 23–24, to think in terms of Louis Philippe's abdication and a regency under some sort of reformist influence. The radical republicans of *La Réforme* and socialists like Louis Blanc seemed to have no such clear-cut notions of what the fighting would bring forth. In fact, the climax of the February Days dumped power in the laps of the republicans, and the government they concocted was little more than a hasty improvisation born of surprise.

The Comte Molé nonchalantly went about his task of forming a new cabinet with absolutely no sense of urgency, and just as much success. He reported his failure to the King only at midnight, by which time Louis Philippe had very little room in which to maneuver. With great reluctance, the King called upon Thiers, whom he so intensely disliked. At the same time, he named Marshal Bugeaud commander of the Paris troops—the same Bugeaud who, in concert with Thiers, had in 1834 put down an *émeute* in the working-class quarter with a savageness not soon to be forgotten. Had the revolution not already passed beyond the point of no return, the appointment of Bugeaud would probably have provided the necessary push.

It seems pointless to go into great detail here concerning the final day of the revolution. There were sharp clashes across the city, and substantial blood was spilled on both sides of the barricades. But the plans for putting down the insurrection were ill-coordinated, the soldiers' morale was increasingly poor, and most successes belonged to the insurgents. Around midday, they began to scramble over the barricades and take some crucial points of the capital—the Hôtel de Ville for one—and move in on the Palais Bourbon and the Tuileries. Finally convinced that further resistance was futile, Louis Philippe wrote, in two brief sentences, a formal document of abdication. He and a few members of his immediate family fled the capital; they hid out in western France for a few days, and finally arrived—the King and Queen travelling as Mr. and Mrs. William Smith—in England on March 3.

The new King was ten years old; a law of 1842 stipulated that, should he accede during his minority, the Duc de Nemours would serve as regent. But Nemours, perhaps the most unpopular of Louis

Philippe's sons, was now politically unthinkable; the only possible regent was the young monarch's mother, the Duchesse d'Orléans, generally supposed to harbor liberal sentiments. This rather sticky constitutional question faced the Chamber of Deputies as it convened, amidst the chaos of the capital, at twelve-thirty P.M. on February 24.

Insofar as any of the politicians possessed the initiative at this moment, it lay with the republicans of *Le National*. A noon meeting at the *National* offices broached for the first time the possibility of a provisional government, composed primarily of moderate republicans, though whether it would be the ministry of a regency or of a republic remained at issue. It was simply hoped that a government of well-known democrats would have the confidence of the crowds and could bring an end to the fighting. Moving to the Chamber, Marrast and a few others took their proposal to Alphonse de Lamartine, who was destined to be the central figure of the early Second Republic.

Poet, popular historian, aristocrat, Lamartine had made his debut in politics during the 1820s as a staunch legitimist. But he soon found himself caught up in the currents of social concern that swept along so many French artists of his generation. Lamartine began to drift to the left in the Chambers of the July Monarchy, although he refused to identify himself with any faction and created an image of a man above parties. Lamartine broke publicly with Guizot in 1842 over the regency question, when the poet favored the cause of the Duchesse. Since that time, he had been an outspoken critic of the government without revealing in very precise terms just what it was that he favored.

In the Chamber on February 24, the moderate republicans offered to support a regency of the Duchesse with a provisional government composed of democrats and headed by Lamartine. But Lamartine responded that monarchy was no longer possible in France, that he would speak for the republic as the most stable government in the present circumstances.

At about one-thirty P.M., the new King, his mother, and his uncle the Duc de Nemours, appeared at the Chamber. Their rather pathetic presence might conceivably have swung the deputies behind the somewhat irregular regency of the Duchesse. Almost simultaneously, however, the first elements of the revolutionary crowds and some National Guardsmen began to dribble into the galleries of the main hall. As their numbers increased, and their shouts—almost uniformly in advocacy of a republic—continuously interrupted the proceedings on the floor, the entire scene moved very quickly toward pandemonium. The royal party left the floor, never to return.

The mounting confusion rendered speech-making difficult. Barrot was just able to make a plea for the regency heard, but by the time he had finished intruders outnumbered deputies. A National Guardsman leaped to the tribune waving a tricolor, and was accompanied by cries from the galleries of "No more Bourbons!" This was enough for many faint-hearted deputies, who ignored Barrot's plea for sang-froid in favor of more prudent advice: *sauve qui peut*. It was thus to a rump parliament and amidst disorder of truly epic proportions that Lamartine delivered a speech declaring for a provisional government. Although he did not use the word "republic," he did come out flatly against a regency. Names for a provisional government were hastily scribbled on scraps of paper, passed to the tribune, called out from there by various persons, and received the approbation of the crowd. After a few minutes of this, Lamartine—whose name had several times been received with enthusiasm—descended the tribune and led a procession across town to the Hôtel de Ville, where revolutions had earlier been consecrated in 1789 and 1830.

The fighting was rapidly petering out in the capital as the procession made its way through the streets to the city hall, which it found in the hands of the revolutionaries. A large crowd, bristling with weapons, filled the square outside. Lamartine, or any other person there, for that matter, would have been hard put to say exactly who the members of the provisional government were. Roughly half a dozen names had received something like a consensus in the upheaval at the Chamber. Another—a liberal monarchist, Adolphe Crémieux—had somehow been put on the favored list by the crowd there after Lamartine's departure. A short time later, representatives of *Le National* and *La Réforme*, emerging from a joint meeting on the question of a provisional government, arrived at the Hôtel de Ville. They insisted on the inclusion of four more names that had not come up at the Chamber, and the provisional government suddenly numbered eleven members.

Defenders of the July Monarchy like to argue that there was nothing inherently wrong with the regime, that it worked reasonably well while it lasted, acclimating the French to parliamentary government in the process. Only a few relatively minor changes, say these historians, all within the regime's capacity to effect, would have saved it from the revolution and moved France along the path of orderly political development being traveled by the British. One difficulty with such arguments is that they view as open certain avenues of change that were closed off, especially after 1840. Guizot may not have opposed all change in principle, but in fact he increasingly treated even the most modest proposals to reform the status quo as threats to the entire regime. In this rigid conservatism, he and the King reinforced one another. Their attitude came more and more, in the 1840s, to be identified with the July Monarchy itself, though the constitution of 1830 was indeed such that substantial liberal reform was possible within its framework. It may well be true that suffrage extension, which after all was one of the reforms which the July Monarchy began, would have strengthened the regime by absorbing into the ruling elite certain selected groups—the educated, the well-to-do rather than just the wealthy, the National Guard, perhaps even the peasantry. Had the July Monarchy truly been a regime of compromise, of *juste milieu*, as some of its adherents claimed, then it might have endured.

The spontaneous, almost accidental eruption of February 1848 should not cloud the serious discontent that inspired it. The artisans and numerous other occupational groups within the working classes who built the barricades, the students, the small businessmen, the respectable bourgeois National Guard—all represented grievances which the Monarchy had failed to answer, all translated their widely varied resentments into a political hostility which brought down the Monarchy. The grave social tensions which colored the ensuing months of the Second Republic were only made more visible, and not created by, the revolution.

Finally, it has been said in the monarchy's behalf that it did not fail in France, only in its capital, and it is true that the dynasty was not toppled by a nation-wide rising. But Paris was not only the administrative center of France, it was the political heart as well. Discontent in the provinces needed the lead from Paris in order to crystallize into serious political action. Most of the major and middling cities experienced, in the wake of the Parisian rising, some sort of municipal revolution—often but not always peaceful. The provincial urban working classes gave ample evidence of their own dissatisfaction, and there was widespread peasant violence. Such events were clear evidence of the existence of a French—and not merely a Parisian—revolution.

The March Revolution in Vienna

The first news of the Paris revolution seeped into Vienna on February 29, 1848. It touched off intense excitement among the city's reform-minded intellectuals, professional men, and students, and it provided a new occasion for bitter denunciation of the government and its chief symbol, Metternich. Hardly had Louis Philippe's fall become widely known before news of events in the smaller German states began to spread: reformist demonstrations in Baden and Hesse-Nassau, royal convocation of a Diet in Saxony and in Bavaria. At the same time, liberals passed from hand to hand copies of a speech made before the Magyar Diet on March 3 by the radical Lajos Kossuth, a speech which eloquently censured the Hapsburg government and demanded immediate enactment of a constitution. Political ferment in Vienna reached unprecedented heights; yet, in retrospect, the demands of the dissatisfied seem singularly modest. Administrative reform, abolition of censorship, the convocation of an advisory Diet, restrictions upon the political police, recognition of the right of petition—such were the principal elements of the liberal reform program.

What made the situation in Vienna delicate was less the militancy of the reformers than the structure of the Hapsburg regime and the psychology of its rulers. For there existed no legal means into which reformist demands could be channeled, not even a safety valve through which the steam could be released. There was no parliament in which the Viennese liberals could make speeches, much less conduct a vote of confidence upon some responsible official. There were no political journals in which the opposition could denounce the government. All expressions of dissatisfaction, all proposals for reform were, by definition, subversive and seditious. Within a framework where political opposition was legal and where mechanisms for orderly change existed, the government could probably have withstood this agitation, let it run its course, might even have sapped it with a few token concessions. But the very nature of the system helped transmute the reformers into revolutionaries. Concessions were, of course, possible. But the psychology of such governments as this one must always militate against concessions under popular pressure, which were likely to be interpreted as a sign of weakness. Only resistance, the assertion of authority, could maintain the Imperial dignity.

Governmental response to the tension of early March was characteristically obtuse. On March 9, a special commission was established to review the reformist petitions that were beginning to pour in—thus recognizing the existence of the petitions and giving them a vague sort of legal status. This glimmer of a concession was speedily extinguished when the commission advised rejection of the petitions and prosecution of their authors. "Until the very last moment," writes the leading historian of the revolution, "the government was capable of thinking only in terms of force and repression."[2] The authorities reinforced the Viennese garrison, increased the guard at critical government buildings, and generally dramatized their determination to meet any further agitation with armed might.

Such action was drastically to exaggerate the militancy of the liberal movement, within which there was little taste for the building of barricades. The liberals were not organized, they had no recognized leadership. They would have agreed on the abolition of censorship, the removal of Metternich, the guarantee of a few fundamental civil liberties, but otherwise their agitation was diffuse. They had no plan of action, no real sense of where events should lead. There was no political structure to define what their activities might be, no precedents to guide them. Thus they could only continue to pour out petitions, proclamations, statements of grievances, in the vague hope that the court would be forced—like the princes in some of the smaller German states—to enact some program of reform. Only the students, who stood on the left wing of the liberal movement, took any concrete steps to intimidate the government. On the evening of March 12, representatives of the small student secret societies went into the working-class suburbs of the capital, beyond the walls of the old city. They urged the people there to come into the capital on the morrow, probably hoping that their presence in the streets would somehow force the government's hand. Even here, however, the idea was at most to overawe the government, not to overthrow it.

Attention on March 13 centered on the meeting of the Diet of

---

[2] R. John Rath, *The Viennese Revolution of 1848* (Austin, Texas: The University of Texas Press, 1957), p. 53.

Lower Austria, the province that included Vienna. The Diet was a glorious anachronism, a relic of an age of Imperial decentralization and provincial self-rule; it was filled with large landholders and wealthy burghers from the capital, and its powers had long since disappeared. But the Diet, within which there was some sentiment for modest reform, was at least a legal institution through which protest might be channeled. It was rumored that some of its members might present a reform petition to the Emperor, and on the 13th Viennese liberals converged upon the Diet with petitions of their own.

The crowds that gathered before the Landhaus, where the Diet met, that morning were much like those that filled the Place de la Concorde in Paris on February 22: well-dressed, well-behaved, generally sympathetic to the liberals but hardly a revolutionary mob. A large contingent of students was present, but they were doing nothing untoward. Only a handful of workers from the suburbs looked on. A few impromptu speeches were delivered, harmless enough in themselves, but they seemed to embolden the crowd in this daring venture into politics. At the same time, rumors began to fly—members of the Diet were to be arrested, gunfire had been heard, the army was about to break up the demonstration. Some students returned to the suburbs in search of more working-class recruits, this time with better results; droves of workers swarmed toward the inner city. The guards at the several gates successfully resisted their entry, for the most part, but not without violence. The sound of the shots, the word of a rising in the suburbs did not help much to calm the crowd at the Landhaus, which had by noontime spilled out into the areas near the Imperial residence at the Hofburg and the Chancellor's Office.

Throughout the morning, the authorities had displayed an uncommon discretion and good sense, restraining the troops and laboring to avoid a conflict. Had they persisted in this restraint, perhaps the storm would have blown itself out in a few hours. Perhaps the threat of workers battering at the city gates would have distracted the largely middle-class demonstrators from their antagonism toward the government. Or perhaps the government had already waited too long, affording the crowds a chance to develop a dangerous momentum that could only be stemmed with force. In any event, troops were sent into the streets at about one P.M. to restore order.

The total record of the revolutions of 1848 would clearly indicate that, once this order had been issued, an incident was likely, and violence would be difficult to avoid. The incident occurred in front of the Landhaus. Troops attempting to clear the square were tattooed with a hail of rocks and sticks; the Archduke Albert himself, in charge of the Vienna garrison, suffered a nasty gash. The soldiers were not long in replying with gunfire, killing five persons. The demonstrators almost instantly resorted to tactics that recall Paris rather than Vienna. Students draped the victims of the Landhaus clash over horses and paraded them about the city to arouse the populace. Arsenals were raided, barricades erected; there were some sharp exchanges of fire with the troops, although the fighting was far less extensive than it had been in the French capital.

Yet the analogy with Paris may be pressed even further, for the Viennese authorities had also called out the Civic Guard, a citizen militia dating from Napoleonic days, which had since been employed exclusively for ceremonial purposes and which—like its Parisian counterpart, the National Guard—was largely of bourgeois composition. Most of the Guards were inclined to favor reform, and they did little to support the action of the troops. The defection of the Civic Guard was a less severe blow to the Hapsburgs than that of the Paris National Guard had been to Louis Philippe. But it did serve as another indication of the widespread sympathy for reform among the prosperous and respectable elements of the capital.

At this point, however, the Viennese revolution took a somewhat different course from its Parisian predecessor. The troops were reasonably successful in containing the fighting and clearing away a number of barricades. By midday on the 13th, the insurrectionists, if not exactly defeated, had at least been stalled; late that afternoon, they were compelled to accept a cease-fire. Curiously, however, the government drew neither satisfaction nor confidence from these momentary successes, nor were the insurrectionists particularly dispirited by their initial check. Instead, deputations from the Civic Guard and from the University came to the Hofburg insisting upon concessions: the removal of the army from the capital, the dismissal of Metternich, the arming of the students. If the government complied, the Guard promised to ensure the restoration of order in the city; if the government refused, the Guard threatened to assume leadership of the fighting.

The popular insistence upon the removal of Metternich had its counterpart within the Hofburg in the form of a court clique hostile to the Chancellor, though not so much from liberal sympathies as from personal jealousies. As the pressure from these two sources conjoined, it became irresistible; minutes before the truce was due to expire, Metternich laid down the power he had held for thirty-seven years. Simultaneously, the government agreed to arm the students by authorizing the formation of the so-called Academic Legion. The army, while it did not leave the city, did in many places leave the streets and made itself generally inconspicuous.

The fall of Metternich and the government's retreat occasioned general rejoicing within the inner city, but not a return to peace and calm. The momentary flush of victory, the realization that a revolution of sorts had been made, was offset by gnawing suspicion of the government's trustworthiness. Moreover, there was a disturbing complication: the suburbs had erupted into a wild frenzy of violence.

The working-class quarters which dominated *extra muros* Vienna housed both the employees of traditional artisan manufacturers and workers in some of the modern mills which had recently located in the suburbs. Misery did not make such sociological discriminations, however, and living conditions in these quarters were uniformly appalling. There was nothing that could be called a Viennese workers' movement, no leaders or spokesmen to articulate a program, not even a coherent statement of grievances. Yet it was recognized that the workers could be social dynamite. Guards on the city gates nearest the workers' suburbs were customarily heavier than elsewhere; the least whisper of disturbances beyond the city walls was an occasion for flutters of middle-class panic.

The politically-minded University students were the only reformers bold enough to try to shape working-class discontent. For some time prior to the revolution, students had been making forays into the suburbs, trying to convert working-class social and economic dissatisfaction into hostility against the government. Doubtless there was among the students much genuine sympathy for the workers' plight; but there was also a tendency to see the workers as simply a kind of leverage that might be applied against a rigid administration in the attempt to extract some reforms.

The workers, for their part, proved a bit difficult to politicize. Working-class listeners had doubtless been aroused by the student agitators on the night of March 12, but what sparked them to riot were the clashes with the soldiers at the city gates (and perhaps the news of street fighting within the walls as well). At this point, however, the workers turned not upon the monarchy or Metternich or the political police. Their fury was directed against their own habitat. There was, to be sure, a certain amount of rather aimless burning and pillaging. But most of the violence had a more meaningful direction. Food shops were attacked, and the offices of the hated tax collectors were the objects of a special wrath. Workers descended also upon the factories that employed them, smashing the new power-driven machines in one of 1848's more characteristic acts of protest. What was attacked, in short, was property more than political authority. The Viennese workers were still speaking the language of hungry and miserable men to whom the vocabulary of political reform had little meaning.

It was primarily the violence in the suburbs that inspired the demand to arm the students. The Academic Legion and the Civic Guard were concerned with putting down the rioting, or—if that failed—at least with protecting the inner city and bourgeois property against the possibility of a working-class onslaught. Yet the middle-class revolution now had an armed force at its disposal, something which gave it the power and the confidence both to resist any reneging on the part of the court and to demand from it further concessions. Indeed, on March 14, the realization gradually dawned that none of the political reforms which had filled the petitions of the preceding week had yet been wrung from the government. Hastily concocted pamphlets and broadsides began to circulate through the city, calling for freedom of the press, tax and judicial reform, even some sort of popular representation in government. Clearly, the revolution was by no means over.

The government sensed the continuing danger, and that afternoon it publicly proclaimed the abolition of censorship. The concession was well-timed, and by itself might have taken considerable wind out of the revolutionary sails. But, in a stroke of monumental stupidity, it coincided with the announcement that Field Marshal Prince Alfred Windischgratz had been granted full powers to restore order in the capital. Windischgrätz was a flinty reactionary, widely (and correctly) reputed to be spoiling for a chance to teach the obstreperous rabble a lesson. He was the Bugeaud of the Viennese revolution, and his appointment provided the irrefutable justification for popular distrust of the government.

Incredibly, in the early morning hours of March 15, the government repeated this juxtaposition of concession and provocation. There appeared at that time a proclamation signed by the Emperor, promising to bring together representatives of all the Hapsburg realms in order to "advise" him. To liberals, it sounded like the prelude to representative government. But this proclamation was almost simultaneously accompanied by another from Windischgrätz, which announced in ominous tones that he was beginning the restoration of public order. Indeed, this was something of an understatement, for the Field Marshall had been authorized to put the city under a state of siege. Although this information did not appear in the proclamation, the Viennese populace expected the worst nonetheless. The liberals and the students grew even more determined to protect the fruits of their victory, and equally to force the ultimate concession from the court: a constitution.

Probably there was little precise notion in the popular mind as to just what ought to be in a constitution, but the very word had a galvanizing effect. It implied reform of all existing abuses, hinted at representative government, and suggested legal guarantees against arbitrary rule. All throughout the afternoon of the 15th, a swelling crowd surrounded the Hofburg, half hoping that the government would grant a constitution, half expecting it would have to extract one by violence. Finally, at five P.M., the government sent out a proclamation reaffirming the reforms already granted and promising to convoke an assembly representing all the Hapsburg dominions "with a view to establishing the Constitution of the Fatherland." The crowd dispersed in delirious jubilation. It had won.

The Viennese revolution was of course only the beginning of the Hapsburgs' difficulties in 1848. In short order, they were faced with rebellion by their multitude of non-German subjects as well: Magyars, Czechs, South Slavs, Italians. The principal motive behind all these revolts was a desire to be free from Hapsburg/German domination, though their goals ranged from autonomy within the Empire to total independence. In time, the gravity of the nationalities problem overshadowed that of the Viennese problem, as the government faced the prospect of an Empire crumbling in its hands.

The Viennese liberals had hardly anticipated such developments. The question of the subject nationalities did not arise during the March Days, and the liberals never really questioned the existence of the Empire itself. Nor did they ever contemplate an attack upon the dynasty or the throne; republican sentiments were negligible, and the Emperor himself remained popular. Rather, in forcing out Metternich and demanding a constitution, the people of Vienna saw themselves as freeing Ferdinand from the influence of malevolent advisers and placing restrictions upon the arbitrary rule of the bureaucracy.

Political themes dominated the early stages of the revolution. Its supporters, reflecting the social composition of the inner city, were primarily from the propertied classes, though they ranged from modest shopkeepers to wealthy merchants. Their impulses were still primarily political, and it is difficult to see the Viennese revolution as a primordial conflict between bourgeoisie and aristocracy. Nor was it really a product of cooperation between middle-class reformers and working-class radicals, reminiscent of February in Paris or March in Berlin. In Vienna, the middle-class, political revolution took place within the city walls while the working-class, social rising raged outside.

The revolutionaries were, to say the least, dismayed by what their own activities had sparked in the suburbs. From the night of March 13–14, they were really conducting a two-front operation—against the government, but also against the workers. Units of the Civic Guard and of the Academic Legion tried to clamp the lid back on, with only some success. Spasmodic rioting continued through the 15th before finally exhausting itself. Still, the depredations in the suburbs—the wholesale attack on property, the specter of the underclass running amok—was more than the middle-class liberals had bargained for. Their own armed forces conducted wholesale arrests among the workers, and even solicited the aid of the regular police. The Viennese revolution, its makers determined, would remain safe and respectable.

The Revolutions in the German States

It seems clear that the Orléans and Hapsburg dynasties could easily have averted, or at the very least postponed, revolution by merely conceding a few reforms. It was, more than anything else, official intransigence in Paris and Vienna, backed by an inept display of armed force, that left the reformist groups no recourse but to violence. These were mistakes that the princes of the small German states would not repeat. Almost unanimously, they bent with the winds of change, thereby saving their thrones and preserving much of the status quo.

The first German disturbances occurred in the southwest, where special conditions determined that the "revolutions"—if they can be so labelled—would take on a special shape. The states of Baden, Württemberg, and Hesse-Darmstadt were all constitutional governments of sorts. Most liberal opposition was thus legal and respectable, not even vaguely associated with revolutionary sentiment. The principal cities of these states were administrative seats or university towns, not major economic centers which had spawned a large and inflammable working-class population. The social tinder of these regions was located in the countryside, where overpopulation, land hunger, and the existence of a large class of unpropertied agricultural laborers provided the ingredients for a full-scale peasant explosion in 1848.

Urban liberalism and peasant discontent were separate questions; their conjunction was largely fortuitous, though still important in forcing concessions from the princes. The peasantry, goaded by the subsistence crisis of the mid-'40s, began quite spontaneously to riot in late February 1848. Although there was some rather pointless violence, in general the peasants directed themselves to specific grievances—mostly the residual feudal obligations such as periodic labor duties, various sorts of tithes, and certain obnoxious and anachronistic rights preserved by the landlords (hunting rights on tenant lands, and so forth). Peasants throughout the Odenwald and the Schwarzwald—scenes of the famous Peasants' Revolt of the 1520s—descended upon their landlords' castles not to pillage and loot, but to destroy the ancient charters that perpetuated the obligations. The *jacquerie*[3] of 1848 was in no sense a political protest. Its fury fell almost solely upon the large landlords, and on occasion the peasants proclaimed their abiding allegiance to "the Emperor," their slogan for the highest political authority.

Meanwhile, word of the French revolution reached the southwest.

---

[3] *Jacquerie:* French for peasant uprising, deriving from French idiom for peasant ("Jacques Bonhomme," i.e., Jack Goodfellow).

The first repercussions occurred in the Grand Duchy of Baden. The liberal movement there was reasonably well-organized, and as early as February 27 there were large, peaceful public demonstrations for political reform. The government's response was swift and sensible: on the 29th, it promised the formation of a citizen national guard, the establishment of a jury system, the relaxation of press censorship. The Grand Duke was not eager to go the way of Louis Philippe. His concessions also helped deflate the small but vocal radical movement in Baden which was seeking far more sweeping change—even to the point of dispatching the Grand Duke himself. Besides, there was the peasant rising, which did not so much precipitate the reform as it heightened the general tension and climate of anxiety, in much the same way the suburban riots in Vienna affected the political developments within the city. In any event, the urban liberals kept up their own pressure until, on March 2, the Grand Duke dismissed his conservative chief minister of some forty years tenure, and installed a cabinet representative of the middle-class liberals.

The Grand Duke's lead was soon followed by neighboring princes, who did not even wait for opposition groups to demonstrate. Moderate liberal ministries were appointed in Hesse-Darmstadt on March 6, and in Württemberg two days later; the Duke of Nassau, in Berlin at this time, followed suit upon his return. In Bavaria, reform was achieved with less ease. King Ludwig I had been romantically involved with a dancer named Lola Montez, who was therefore widely believed to exercise substantial political influence. This bizarre liason sharpened antagonisms at the Bavarian court, alienated government officials, and put Ludwig in extremely bad popular repute. When the crisis of 1848 struck in the first week of March, the king had little support, and the modest royal concessions announced on March 4 were greeted with suspicion. There was some rioting in Munich, as well as a flood of reformist petitions from liberal groups, municipal officials, and from other cities in the realm. Peasant disorders in northern Bavaria were becoming increasingly serious. Reluctant to concede further royal prerogatives, and determined not to become a mere "signing machine" for his ministers' decrees, Ludwig finally abdicated on March 19 in favor of his son, Maximilian.

The pattern of relatively painless political change established in the south was reiterated in the north: libertarian reform in the Elec-

torate of Hesse-Kassel, reform and the appointment of liberal ministries in Hanover and Saxony and in the free cities of Lübeck, Ham-
burg, and Frankfurt. The liberals achieved victory almost without
exertion, though the princes were doubtless intimidated by the continuing turbulence in the countryside, which soon spread north and
east. Some of the rulers accompanied their political concessions with
such attempts to appease the peasants as the sacrifice of royal hunting rights and the abolition of feudal survivals on crown lands. But
the rural revolt raged on, seemingly operating on a momentum that
was independent of any triumphs gained or any reversals suffered.
It ultimately came to an end, in late March and early April, as
much from exhaustion as anything.

The lesser German princes had acted, if not from deep political
wisdom, then at least from common sense and discretion. For not
only were their countrysides in convulsion, but artisans in their
cities were demonstrating, joining with the liberals in demands for
reform. Few of the petty princes had the coercive resources with
which to repress these movements. Their regimes had functioned by
inertia rather than from broad popular support, and they seemed
to recognize in March that the tide was running with liberalism.
Besides, most of the princes could still work with their new moderate liberal ministries, though they had to give up certain of their
governing prerogatives. In essence, however, the princes had ex-
pediently condoned liberal reform in order to avoid revolution. In
so doing, they may even have helped bolster their badly sagging
popularity.

As of mid-March, Prussia was the only German state of any consequence to have avoided revolution. Even the peasant disorders
were slow in reaching Prussia, though ultimately there was serious
rural violence. Some scattered disorders troubled the Hohenzollern
realm, beginning as early as March 3 with a radical demonstration
in Cologne. And there were, of course, the usual petitions from
middle-class liberals in other provincial cities demanding various
political reforms. But in Berlin, the liberal movement was relatively
weak. Without articulate leadership, it took some time for discontent
to crystallize.

There was some minor agitation among the artisans of Berlin.
Beginning on March 6, workers gathered publicly in parks near the
Tiergarten and gradually formulated their grievances. At first, they
talked mostly of a "ministry of labor" which would cope with their

most immediate concerns: unemployment, low wages, poor working conditions. Their impulses were not in the least revolutionary. Rather, they were simply urging the government to take measures to counteract the worst effects of the current economic crisis, and, more generally, arrest the steady deterioration of the artisanate. On March 13, there was a small skirmish when soldiers—in the absence of anything resembling a police force or national guard—tried to break up such a meeting. The next day, authorities decreed a ban on future public meetings. There followed two days of spasmodic outbursts in the city, mostly at artisan initiative, which consisted mainly of slogan shouting and a little vandalism.

The rumblings in Berlin had yet to take a clearly-defined political turn. It is true that the King was reluctantly prepared to convoke another United Diet, but this was more in response to liberal demands from his outlying territories than to pressure from the capital. It was the news of Metternich's fall, which reached Prussia on March 16, that mobilized the middle-class liberals of Berlin and also helped shape the artisan agitation into a political movement. A few barricades even went up, though there was no street-fighting.

King Friedrich Wilhelm IV was ready as of March 18 to make a few concessions: in addition to reassembling the United Diet, he prepared to loosen restrictions on the press and to form a new ministry led by a moderate liberal aristocrat. But the Berlin reformers, middle-class and artisan alike, had fixed upon yet another demand: withdrawal of the troops garrisoned in the capital and the formation of an armed citizen guard to assume the responsibilities for public order. Setting aside the implications for royal prerogative—the army had traditionally been the King's personal instrument —this was in effect to ask Friedrich Wilhelm to divest his government of all protection and to put himself at the mercy of the armed citizenry. It is not difficult to see why the King refused to go this far; nor is it difficult to see why the reformers insisted that he should. The troops were roundly despised for their history of brutal repression; as long as the King maintained a monopoly on coercion, there could be no assurance that any reforms would be lasting.

Word spread on the morning of the 18th that Friedrich Wilhelm was about to announce his response to reformist agitation. By early afternoon, a large crowd had gathered in the courtyard of the royal palace. The crowd was predominantly comprised, as in Paris and

Vienna, of well-dressed and respectable burghers, with only a sprinkling of working-class onlookers. Friedrich Wilhelm's concessions were indeed announced, but the absence of any remarks about withdrawing the troops was made all the more conspicuous by the presence of a sizeable contingent of soldiers in the courtyard. There was considerable commotion, which only increased when the King ordered General von Prittwitz, commander of the Berlin garrison, to clear the square. The stage was now set for yet another of 1848's ubiquitous "incidents." This time, it took the form of two shots— fired, as usual, by person or persons unknown. As a matter of fact, the shots hit no one, and there were no deaths in the palace courtyard. But the incident was decisive in panicking the crowd, convincing it that the troops were out for blood. Barricades went up again, this time to be used in earnest.

Fighting broke out all over Berlin, involving the propertied middle classes as well as the workers. But it was the artisan craftsmen, and especially the journeymen, upon whom the brunt of the fighting fell; relatively few masters and few factory laborers manned the barricades. The insurgency was not, in military terms, particularly successful. Prittwitz and his troops relentlessly cleared out isolated nests of resistance, and by the 19th had largely succeeded in confining the insurrection to one quarter of the city. He was confident of victory, and ready to bombard the section that continued to fight on. But Friedrich Wilhelm overruled his general. The King was genuinely repulsed by the bloodshed, and could not abide the prospect of wholesale slaughter as envisaged by Prittwitz. In a gesture by no means uncharacteristic of this complex, mercurial monarch, Friedrich Wilhelm issued a proclamation to his "dear Berliners" in which he announced the withdrawal of the army from the capital and the formation of an armed civic guard.

The insurgents, exultant but still suspicious, extracted a further surrender. Late on the 19th, in the palace courtyard once more, they forced the king to don the forbidden red, black, and yellow colors of German nationalism in honor of the something over 200 persons his soldiers had killed. On March 22, the King was made to bare his head at the formal burial.

The victory of the Berlin insurrection did little to calm the rest of Prussia. Rather, it encouraged popular discontent, gave rise to separatist conspiracies in the Rhineland, and was soon followed by rural convulsions in the east. Friedrich Wilhelm had little choice but to move further along the road of concession. On March 29, he removed the moderate ministry of eleven days standing and appointed a new cabinet under the direction of a Rhenish businessman and liberal, Ludolf Camphausen.

It may occasion some surprise that the theme of national unification, so central to German politics later in 1848, was so peripheral at the outbreak of revolution. The immediate issues were those of censorship, constitutionalism, limitations upon royal prerogatives, unemployment, food prices, and agrarian reform. The issue of unification did, of course, arise: Friedrich Wilhelm was responding to real desires when, on March 18, he promised to lead a movement for national unity; the demonstrators in Baden demanded some initiatives toward unification from their government. But, in general, the events of March in the German states were inspired by domestic discontents.

In retrospect, the March revolutions have to some looked very little like revolutions at all. Of the numerous German princes, only Ludwig of Bavaria lost his throne, and at that not really from any popular enthusiasm for revolution. There were changes in ministerial personnel, and a few libertarian reforms; but monarchy and aristocracy remained, though their grip on power had for the moment been undone. The institutional and social structure of the old regime remained fundamentally intact. Only the most unpopular conservative ministers had been unseated, leaving what one historian has described as "a vacuum in which the liberals postured until the vacuum was filled."

The period of liberal ascendancy was indeed short, and the subsequent reversal was impressively decisive—so much so that it is easy to conclude that the old order was only challenged, not revolutionized. Yet it is instructive to view the question also from the vantage point of springtime 1848. Governments which had been shaped by the broad personal prerogatives of the princes now came under constitutional limitations. The ruling elites were no longer composed almost exclusively of aristocratic landlords and titled career bureaucrats; they now included lawyers and writers, academicians and physicians, merchants and bankers and industrialists. The responsibility for public order and law enforcement lay no longer with the regular army—itself usually conceived of as an extension of the

prince—but with citizen guards. The laws themselves were to be
formulated by governments representative in some sense of the
populace and not just of its titled grandees. The press was opened
to free political debate. Monarchy survived for the simple reason
that the liberals were also monarchists; aristocracy, for the reason
that they were not radical egalitarians, though their opposition to
a social system which conferred power and status merely upon noble
birth was plain enough.

It is true that the middle-class liberals in Germany scarcely ap-
proximated the classical models of revolutionaries; they were not
the men to destroy the old regime root and branch. But the states
over which they ruled had changed so suddenly and so substantially
—no matter how tentatively—that it seems pointless to deny to the
whole process the name of "revolution."

The Revolutions in the Italian States

Psychologically, the Paris rising was the first revolution of 1848; it
provided an occasion and even an inspiration for reformist forces
all over the continent. But chronologically, the first revolt occurred
in Sicily, on January 12, 1848. Indeed, Italian rulers clearly sensed
the danger, and either granted or promised constitutions in four
major states before revolution even seemed a threat in France. These
events were greeted with satisfaction by liberals everywhere, but
they touched off none of the intense excitement prompted by the
French revolution. Perhaps European liberals were merely habit-
uated to taking their cue from France. Or perhaps they judged,
correctly as it turned out, that reforms could never be secure in
Italy as long as the Hapsburgs held Lombardy-Venetia and exerted
such potent influence over several Italian princes.

The theme of freedom from foreign domination—principally that
of the Hapsburgs, but later that of Bonapartist France also—is thus
the central one of Italian history in this revolutionary year. For that
reason, the Italian revolts often took on the character of what this
century would call colonial independence movements. This is not
to deny that they had their roots in political aspirations and in
social and economic dissatisfactions. Rather, it is to argue that
political circumstances in Italy determined that virtually all movements—from moderate constitutionalism to radical Mazzinianism—
had ultimately to turn into crusades for freedom from external

control. The brief period of reformism early in the year was one of considerable significance; but the events that really ignited Italy were the revolts against Hapsburg rule in Milan and Venice.

The January 12 revolt in Palermo combined constitutionalism with the powerful urge for Sicilian independence from Neapolitan rule. After a ferocious two-week struggle, the populace had control of the city, and soon of nearly the whole island. When an expeditionary force from Naples was beaten back, King Ferdinand finally agreed to negotiate. But the Sicilians would have none of it. They reinstituted their liberal constitution of 1812, set up a provisional government, and ultimately declared Sicily an independent kingdom with a vacant throne. Meanwhile, Ferdinand's mainland subjects seized the opportunity to make trouble. With revolution threatening, the King suddenly issued, on January 29, a decree promising a constitution and sketching out its principal features. It was an astonishingly liberal system that this most reactionary of monarchs proposed, incorporating a broad range of ministerial authority and a host of libertarian reforms.

The events in southern Italy put tremendous pressure upon the other Italian princes. Demonstrations and rioting in several Tuscan cities were enough to intimidate Grand Duke Leopold II, and on February 17 he published a constitution. Circumstances also forced a decision from Charles Albert in Piedmont. The King had toyed with liberal reformism for some years, but primarily as an arm of his foreign policy. War against Austria was unthinkable without the support of his own Piedmontese liberals, and the liberals insisted upon constitutionalism—which would serve also as a model for the government of the territories to be liberated—as a condition for that support. The King wanted, of course, to postpone the necessary concession until the last possible moment; yet he also wished to give it magnanimously from a position of strength, and not have it extracted under duress. The Neapolitan outburst signaled danger, and early in February Charles Albert granted the *Statuto*, a constitution to take effect the next month.

The remarkable popular enthusiasm which had surrounded Pius IX since his election to the Papacy in 1846 now became a positive liability for him. The expectations generated by his famous amnesty, his administrative reforms, his resistance to Metternich in a minor diplomatic skirmish had all worked to create an almost incurable optimism among the reformers of Rome. On February 10, 1848, Pius issued a statement designed to clarify his position—emphasizing his opposition to constitutionalism and rejecting the thought of war against the Hapsburgs. But this "last despairing attempt to arrest the course of events," as one historian has called it, also contained the phrase "O Lord God, bless Italy." The exhortation was taken by the Romans as a transparent Papal sanction for unificationism, an appeal to nationalist sentiment. It was that sort of interpretation which fitted the popular image of Pio Nono, and which the hopeful chose to remember—though, in context, the remark had no such implications.

Then, on February 12, word arrived in Rome of Ferdinand's constitution; it was followed by news from Tuscany, Piedmont, and France. But the Pope had not yet acted. The contradiction between the public image of Pius and the policies to which he was in fact committed created an impossible situation. It is remarkable that Rome avoided violence as long as it did. Finally, Pius gave in. On March 14, he announced the granting of a constitution, in which, however, the Pope retained an absolute veto power.

The Pope's dramatic gesture, which seemed to confirm once more his leadership of the liberal movement, was everywhere received with enthusiasm. Only one piece of news could have been more electrifying, and it reached northern Italy on March 16: the fall of Metternich. Metternich symbolized Hapsburg oppression far more than did the monarch he served, and Italian nationalists greeted news of his dismissal and flight with wild excitement. Nothing could now restrain Lombard and Venetian insurrection.

The Venetian revolt was a purely anti-Hapsburg affair. Politics in the familiar sense had been so successfully stifled by the Hapsburg administration that no well-defined liberal-constitutionalist movement had developed. Virtually all forms of political expression were translated into protest against foreign rule. Though it is true that official censorship forced circumlocution and euphemism, still even the handful of articulate leaders who made some effort to channel the anti-Hapsburg resentment had no very clear programs. Therefore, when the crisis broke, it very nearly dissipated into aimlessness and incoherence.

The ablest and most respected spokesman of Venetian independence, Daniele Manin, had been imprisoned in January 1848 for public criticism of the government. When news of the Viennese revolution reached Venice on March 17, an excited crowd surged to the prison, clamoring for Manin's release. Refusing to be liberated by sheer force, Manin extracted an official order authorizing his freedom.

With essentially no program, no general agreement upon concessions to be demanded, no sense even of how far the occupying government had been demoralized, the revolutionary movement came dangerously close to faltering. Manin must receive credit for keeping the revolutionary impulse alive by giving it a goal. On the 18th, he demanded of the Hapsburg governor a Civil Guard to be composed of Venetian citizens. The governor, Count Palffy, could hardly refuse, though his authorization limited the number of armed citizens to two hundred. But Manin capitalized upon Palffy's weakness, and enrolled something more than two thousand Venetians into the Guard. The successful defiance of authority, coupled with the possession of arms, should have provided the insurgents of Venice with unshakable confidence. But again, the revolution began to sputter. Few people seemed to realize that the Hapsburg officials had come remarkably close to abdicating their control over the city. Some suggested that Rainier, the Hapsburg viceroy, be transmuted into a constitutional monarch. Once more, Manin crystallized the vague and diffuse impulses of his compatriots. Manin was a republican, though in his context the term evoked none of the resonances of political and social radicalism that it did in France or Germany. Rather, Manin's republicanism was simply an anti-Hapsburg sentiment. His scheme was to build a Venice independent of any dynastic ties and thus free to become part of a united Italy. The goal of a Venetian republic not only gave focus to antagonism for the Hapsburgs; it called forth a special patriotism by evoking memories of the glorious Venetian republic of centuries past.

At the same time, Manin determined to destroy the last Hapsburg stronghold in Venice, the Arsenal. He realized that a vigorous Austrian action from this base could challenge the revolution, and on March 22 he massed forces for its capture. But a revolt within the Arsenal—the three hundred Croats working there murdered their Austrian commander—averted a serious pitched battle. The occupying troops staged only a few rear-guard actions. By the end of the day, the Hapsburg rulers had been sent packing; Manin proclaimed the Venetian republic and assumed the presidency of a provisional government.

It is tempting indeed to suppose that Manin very nearly achieved that historical rarity, a one-man revolution. Manin did perform an invaluable service by repeatedly giving the popular agitation focus and direction. But he was also the beneficiary of circumstances which rendered the Hapsburg administration far less vigorous than usual. The Viennese rising had paralyzed the central government and badly frightened provincial administrators who did not know where to turn for support and guidance. Hapsburg troops in northern Italy were plentiful, but largely drawn from the Slavic peoples of the Empire; with most of the Slavic areas in revolt, Austrian administrators in Venetia were nervous about the reliability of these contingents. Isolated and confused, the Imperial representatives failed to show their customary vigor in repressing acts of insolent Italian nationalism. With the Hapsburg administration thus intimidated, unable to enforce its own laws and uncertain of its own power, the situation was tailor-made for a man like Manin—energetic, effective, but fortunate too.

The Milanese had no Manin, but the temper of the city was such in March 1848 that there was little need for heroic leadership to canalize the revolution. Political discussion, though often driven underground by censorship, was still relatively widespread and also relatively sophisticated. Most of the major political and nationalist persuasions were articulately represented, their programs clearly defined. Again, however, the simple fact of Hapsburg rule made most of this discussion academic, and turned all politics into variations on a single, by now familiar, theme. The senseless butchery occasioned by the tobacco riots of January 1848—a kind of latter-day Boston Tea Party in which the Milanese refusal to consume state-owned Austrian tobacco led to violence—sharply focused and solidified this hatred. To be sure, there were numerous issues, both political and social, for potential strife among the Milanese themselves, and the Hapsburg authorities tried repeatedly to divide the city by stirring up these conflicts. But the Italians showed a remarkable ability to maintain unity in the face of the enemy.

Revolt in Milan was almost a foregone conclusion, and the events of March 18 were clearly more an occasion than a cause of the violence that ensued. The revolution began on the model of those in the great urban centers to the north. News from Vienna stirred up great excitement, and the occupation government voluntarily proclaimed a series of reforms in hope of forestalling revolt. The middle-class liberals countered with a list of further demands, borne to the viceregal palace by a large crowd composed—inevitably, it will by now seem—of well-to-do bourgeois. There was a commotion, the palace guard fired on the crowd, and the revolution was on.

Barricades flew up quickly, and the populace shouldered arms— some of which they pilfered, some of which they had been smuggling into the city for months. A hastily organized coalition of moderates and radicals, under the leadership of the nationalist agitator Carlo Cattaneo, proclaimed a provisional government so quickly after the fighting had begun that it is difficult to claim spontaneity for the revolutionary movement. Radetzky's troops, despite a great superiority in firepower, were at a disadvantage in the cramped quarters of city streets, and they wasted much valuable ammunition against the barricades. Eventually, the soldiers withdrew to just outside the city walls, but even siege tactics had to be abandoned when the insurgents took one of the crucial gates. Wisely, if reluctantly, the old marshal broke off the engagement on March 22 and retreated from Lombardy altogether, taking refuge in the four fortresses in Venetia known as the Quadrilateral. Radetzky had not been defeated, however; he had simply beaten a strategic retreat. He would be heard from again.

The Milanese revolt provided precisely the opportunity that Charles Albert of Piedmont had long awaited. There was some concern, however, that his intervention should look at least vaguely legal, and not until the Milanese revolt had nearly ended did the pro-Piedmontese element there appeal for aid. On March 23, Charles Albert declared war on the Hapsburg Empire, though the delay had put him at a disadvantage by giving Radetzky time to repair to a strong defensive position. Still, Italian nationalism had what appeared to be the irreversible momentum of a revolutionary spirit that had utterly changed the face of Europe in a month.

The whole history of 1848 tantalizes with its similarities, and surely the historian's most difficult task is trying to determine which of them are, in fact, significant patterns. It is clear, for example, that the revolutions all occurred on the heels of an economic crisis. Yet the intensity of the crisis varied sharply from place to place across Europe, as did the classes and the sectors of the economy it affected. One could not discuss the revolutions without discussing the crisis; but its role was too variable to permit very useful generalization.

If one considers for a moment the actual outbreak of the revolutions, as opposed to the more general conditions which made them possible, some meaningful patterns do emerge. For instance, few of these eruptions could not have been forestalled by some prudent and timely concessions to reformism on the part of the old order. In Lombardy and Venetia, perhaps, such concessions would not have helped, since the issue there was separation from the ruling power. Elsewhere, however, the threatened regimes could have easily satisfied most discontent without unduly disturbing the status quo; rarely would it have taken more than the dismissal of an unpopular minister, the relaxation of censorship, perhaps a gesture toward constitutionalism where that was the issue.

The authorities further blundered by resorting to force once reformist agitation reached the streets. Perhaps a more efficient and more ruthless application of force might also have avoided—or, rather, postponed—revolution. But there was surprisingly little efficiency in armed repression in 1848: there were numerous instances of armed force being called in (or threatened) too early, thus provoking popular violence, or elsewhere held off until too late, thus giving an opportunity for barricades to go up. Even more surprisingly, ruthlessness was in relatively short supply; Windischgrätz in Vienna and Prittwitz in Berlin could certainly have cleared the streets of their cities, but their respective governments refused to see the battles through. Besides, by letting the agitation ever get into the streets, the governments seriously enhanced the dangers of conflict, for they were possessed of no very sophisticated instruments of riot control. In the absence of any regular police trained for such duty, governments had to rely upon either civilian militia—which frequently proved in 1848 to be riddled with reformist sentiment—or upon regular troops of the line. The army, however, was rarely trained to do anything more subtle than to crush its opponent with firepower. In these circumstances, and with passions running high on both sides, it was not difficult for events to generate the "incidents" between army and crowd which time after time turned reformist demonstrators into revolutionary street-fighters.

None of this is to argue that profound change could have been averted forever. Indeed, if the ruling elites were correct in their view that any reform would compromise their hold on power—if, in other words, their regimes were that brittle—then surely nothing could have saved them in the long run. Rather, the argument is simply that there was nothing omnipotent and inexorable behind the revolutions of 1848 which meant that they had to erupt when and how they did. The revolutions doubtless had their roots deep in the nature of European society and politics, and the forces for change which they represented could not have been denied forever. But no anonymous historical process brought about the explosions of 1848; they happened how and when they did largely because of human stubbornness and miscalculation.

There is in these arguments another implication, which eventually leads to the question of conditions which facilitated the revolutions. It is that the issues upon which the revolutions originally centered were basically political. This is not to deny that social and economic tensions contributed to sharpening the antagonisms which exploded in 1848, or that they gave to the revolutions much of their subsequent shape. It does suggest that those antagonisms—and particularly those expressed by the radicals and socialists—only began to constitute a serious and immediate danger when they were translated into political terms and thus might coalesce momentarily with liberal reformism. However great the rigidity and incompetence of the authorities, the revolutions would never have taken place without this temporary merger between liberals and radicals, which frequently meant between middle classes and working classes.

It is probably impossible to overemphasize the importance of this largely accidental and unforeseen merger, in which the disparate anti-governmental forces suddenly found themselves cooperating. Everywhere, it was middle-class liberals who gave the popular agitation some form, some goals, even something vaguely like leadership. And everywhere, it was the working classes who did the lion's share of the fighting, spurred on perhaps by hopes for significant social change of a sort the liberals never contemplated. It is inconceivable that the revolutions would have scored their initial successes without these fortuitous—and, as they proved, extremely fragile—alliances.

An explanation of how Great Britain avoided revolution in 1848 probably hinges on just this point. The British seemed to have many of the ingredients for revolutionary discontent. The new industry was rapidly displacing the traditional artisanate, yet not growing fast enough to accommodate the booming population, especially in the cities. Unemployment, that bane to good order, was a serious problem, compounded by the fact that the British working classes were politically aware and active. Any number of movements bid for the workers' support during the 1830s and '40s, but none was more spectacular than Chartism.

Chartism had a broad and diverse following. The product principally of middle-class radicals, it attracted a large number of artisans, some factory workers, some rural laborers. The movement was named for a document, the Charter, which made six demands for reform: universal manhood suffrage, vote by secret ballot, equalization of electoral districts, annual renewal of parliament, removal of property qualifications for eligibility to the House of Commons, and payment of members of the House. Chartist leaders collected more than a million signatures supporting these demands, and presented them to parliament in 1839, only to have Commons refuse to consider them. A new presentation was made in 1842, with what Chartists claimed were more than three million signatures, but with no more success in parliament. Again, in April 1848, their spirits revived by the success of reformists on the continent, the Chartists descended on parliament with yet another petition borne by a large crowd. But police dispersed the demonstration peacefully, and the Chartist movement soon evaporated.

It is interesting that this largest of British working-class movements of mid-century was built on a program of political democracy. Yet the economic tensions that lay beneath the formal demands of the Charter are not hard to find, and historians are fond of noting that the three high points of the movement were also times of serious economic dislocation, while ensuing prosperity tended to take the appeal out of Chartism's political slogans. Perhaps Chartism was mere "hunger politics" and thus doomed to failure. Be that as it may, Chartism still bears some striking resemblances to continental radicalism, and the great demonstration in London of April 1848 was just the sort of affair which served as a prelude to revolution across the Channel.

It is true, of course, that the British authorities showed both firmness and reserve in dealing with the demonstration, that it had a trained and reliable, though still largely unarmed, police force at its disposal, and that the leaders of the demonstration were intent upon avoiding violence. Yet the truly crucial difference between Britain's 1848 and the continent's was that the great bulk of British middle-class liberals flatly opposed the Chartists. The liberals had won their great victory two years earlier when they had forced from parliament the beginnings of tariff reduction. This victory reaffirmed the liberals' commitment to a system which had begun the incorporation of more and more middle-class interests into the ruling elite with the constitutional changes of 1832. Reformers had other items on their agenda, none of which included the sort of democratic upheaval they saw in Chartism. The Chartists were able to generate little middle-class support; an anti-governmental alliance of bourgeois moderates and working-class radicals was not possible, even by accident. That fact, probably more than anything else, spared Britain from revolution in 1848.

Chapter 3

The New Governments

The new ministries and provisional governments of 1848 took office with the assumption that revolution had ended and the task of securing its gains had begun. But revolutions are rarely so easy to stop. The very problems that help create them generally linger on to plague the new regimes. The fact of victory itself tends to arouse hopes and instill confidence in the more radical elements, while counterrevolutionary forces do not easily give up hope of capitalizing upon the confusion and discontent.

It was precisely this perennial squeeze that was applied to the new governments of 1848. In the German states, where monarchy had been shaken but not overthrown, the princes remained in a reasonably strong position while their new ministers were beset by radical threats and increasingly embroiled in the unification problem. The Roman constitution kept the Pope in ultimate command, so that liberals in the new ministry of laymen actually had only limited control over the government and had no way of responding, even if they had wanted to, to the Roman radicals' demands for sweeping reforms. Pro-Piedmontese liberal monarchists in Milan had somehow to contend with both republicans in their city and Marshal Radetzky in the Quadrilateral. The French provisional government had no king to worry about, but the radicals and socialists of the capital threatened to provoke a conservative reaction from the rural provinces.

In these circumstances, the prospects for a speedy return to normalcy were remote, and the new governments faced the difficult task of trying to elaborate their reform programs in an atmosphere of turmoil and conflict. Most of the governments attempted to balance the conflicting forces, to satisfy both sides at once. But such tactics, however common in ordinary times, are rarely successful during a revolution, when all-or-nothing suddenly becomes a popular slogan. Moreover, the new governors themselves made singularly inauspicious revolutionaries. Prior to 1848, most of them had opposed the idea of violent revolution—some from moral scruple, some from the fear of unleashing the masses. Rather, they had advocated orderly change, a few basic political reforms, parliamentary and constitutional government. Only the French provisional government was democratic in sentiment, only the French and Venetian were republican; elsewhere, the reformers remained monarchist.

There were few men here who would use their new powers in a truly revolutionary fashion. There were no Robespierres or Lenins in power in 1848, no one who would ruthlessly destroy all opposition and all vestiges of the old regime. The governments of 1848 resorted not to executions and banishments, but to amnesties. One of the first acts of the French provisional government was to abolish the death penalty for political crimes. Perhaps, as Alfred Cobban wrote of France, the new leaders would have been "less despised by historians if they had been more bloody-minded."[1]

By and large, these men bitterly opposed radicalism and socialism, something it would be easy to explain as an outgrowth of class fear. The new governors were men of property, drawn primarily from the professional classes and from business, with a rather large contingent of landowning aristocrats among them. But their hostility sprang as much from temperament as from social status. Though often painted as rather doctrinaire ideologues, they tended in fact to be empirical, skeptical of all panaceas, gradualists who despaired of effecting profound social change by decree. Besides, they had struggled for years to free their countries of what they saw as the stultifying influence of state control. Now, as they were on the verge

---

[1] Alfred Cobban, *A History of Modern France*, 2nd ed. (Baltimore: Penguin, 1965), II, 140.

of achieving this goal, the social radicals were demanding what looked disturbingly like just another form of statism.

The men elevated to power in 1848 were clearly surprised by events and unprepared for their new roles. They had always supposed that, when their moment came, they would be enacting their reforms in a time of calm and order. They had no program for action in a revolution and at bottom no real sympathy for revolution, which they saw as a threat to the realization of their aims. Their efforts were therefore divided between reform and the attempt to harness the revolution, all the while juggling the conflicting forces which threatened their political position.

Order and Reform

From the very beginning the French provisional government was reminded of its dependence upon the revolutionary crowds of Paris. As the government met in the Hôtel de Ville on the night of February 24 and tried to gather its wits, a large throng filled the square outside and much of the building as well, occasionally bursting into the government's own room and shouting radical demands. There was noisy insistence upon formal proclamation of a republic. The government, betraying a certain legalism, wanted to wait until the election of a constituent assembly representative of the entire nation before taking this step. But there was no putting off the crowd, which soon heard an announcement that the provisional government "wants the REPUBLIC, pending ratification by the people." The crowd was momentarily appeased, though on the 26th it forced an unqualified statement from the government.

Proclamation of the republic on the 24th had not emptied the square, which now echoed with cries of "the organization of labor." No slogan was more popular with the Parisian working classes, none meant so many different things. Delegates from the crowd who repeated the demand to the government were hard put to say what they meant by "the organization of labor," but insisted upon its enactment in any case. The government finally responded in kind, accepting the crowd's demands in a bewilderingly vague decree. On the next day, the organization of labor began to take some concrete form with the establishment of the "National Workshops." The name evoked the "social workshops" proposed by Louis Blanc (now a member of the provisional government) in his book *L'Orga-*

nisation du travail, but did not in any other way resemble them. The National Workshops were not workshops at all, but public work contingents open to unemployed workers. Those enrolled—their number at one point exceeded 100,000—were given a small wage for some trivial ground-clearing and terracing and an even smaller dole when no such busywork could be found. Just to make sure that nothing more radical emerged from this program, the government put it under A.-T. Marie, the new Minister of Public Works and a notoriously conservative republican.

The National Workshops were not a social reform, but a political sop, an attempt by the moderate majority in the government to satisfy popular demands with show rather than substance. The Workshops represented no one's preferred solution to the problems of working-class unemployment and misery. Still, they were widely taken in the rest of France as indicative of socialist influence upon the provisional government, providing reactionaries with a convenient issue. It was precisely this sort of situation that the provisional government hoped from the outset to avoid. As long as the Paris crowds could force the government into even pseudo-radical measures, the more conservative provinces were likely to view the republic with suspicion. Obviously, the government would have to gain control of the streets of the capital; more specifically, certain crucial administrative positions would have to be confided to the moderates, and not to more "advanced" republicans like Ledru-Rollin, generally (if incorrectly) assumed to be in fundamental agreement with the revolutionaries.

The moderates were not entirely successful in this early power struggle which anticipated later rifts within the republican camp. The prefecture of police had been captured during the February fighting by a small band of revolutionaries led by Marc Caussidière, who immediately designated himself the new prefect and could not be rooted out by the government. And as the new executives chose, on the evening of the 24th, the ministries they would direct, they had to be conscious of the crowd outside, and thus reluctantly gave the critical Ministry of the Interior to Ledru-Rollin. Only the office of mayor of Paris, among the critical posts in the capital, passed into moderate hands.

As it turned out, Caussidière came increasingly to think of himself more as a police chief than as a revolutionary, and he put his men at the service of the government rather than the crowds. The government also controlled the National Guard, membership in which was now democratized; within a few weeks, the ranks of the Guard swelled from 50,000 to nearly 200,000. In addition, the government created the *Garde mobile,* yet another armed force; the *Gardiens de Paris,* an unarmed unit supposed to patrol the streets and prevent the inflation of minor incidents into major explosions; and a special group of eight hundred soldiers to guard the Hôtel de Ville. Finally, the government fairly bristled with spy systems, most of which tried to infiltrate radical circles and gain advance notice of any revolutionary conspiracies. Such networks of informers operated—separately, and sometimes in rivalry—out of the Ministry of the Interior, the Paris mayor's office, the Ministry of Public Works, and even the Foreign Ministry under Lamartine. By such means as these, the provisional government steadily gained the upper hand over its turbulent capital. But it was a slow process, and as late as mid-March the government lacked the confidence to reject radical demands when an organized mass demonstration presented them.

Not all reforms, however, had to be extracted from the provisional government under popular pressure. On March 5, the government extended the franchise to all male citizens twenty-one years of age and older, in what proved to be the most significant and durable reform of the Second Republic. Moreover, the government abolished censorship and the newspaper stamp tax, lifted all legal restraints upon the right of assembly, reduced the maximum working day to ten hours in Paris and eleven in the provinces, legalized the formation of labor unions, abolished slavery in the French colonies, and decreed a whole list of lesser social reforms. These decisions were made not under intimidation, but out of genuine commitment and often in response to urgent needs. Some of the moderates were also nervous about the legal authority of the government to make such sweeping changes and preferred to leave the disposition of major issues to a popularly elected assembly. Others worried less about questions of authority than about a conservative reaction from the provinces on election day.

No new German government faced the same sort of left-wing threat as did the French. Since, with the exception of the Prussian, the liberal governments had come to power without violence, there were no ready-made armed urban mobs to intimidate them. There was a republican movement of some vigor in Baden, which attempted a rather sad little putsch in April. But otherwise, radical forces were relatively slow to group together and make themselves heard.

There was, however, the peasantry, whose rural depredations continued, regardless of the liberal victories. For all their own diatribes against feudalism, the liberals could not have been more out of sympathy with the peasants. Liberals roundly denounced the violence and destruction of property, and where the princes had been inclined to respond with some concession, the liberals tended to employ troops. Yet neither conciliation nor force seem to have been sure-fire solutions to the peasant rising, which ultimately simply exhausted itself. When it had done so, the liberals could then turn to the tasks of reform.

Few of these reforms were remarkable; they consisted primarily of an implementation of promises made by the princes in early March. Constitutions were drafted, parliaments were created, representation defined so as to include well-to-do burghers along with the titled nobility, and ministries were usually made responsible to these bodies. Some of the original excitement and significance attached to constitutionalism on the local scale began to wane, however, with the increasing likelihood that a German national parliament would be convened to write a constitution for a unified nation. Still, taken all together, the extent of orderly political reform in the lesser German states was reasonably impressive.

But the fate of reform in the smaller states turned in large part upon the success of the revolution in Prussia, where the liberals were being squeezed in the familiar vise. Berlin had a large working-class population, now both embittered and emboldened by the violence of March. The King and the army had suffered humiliations not soon to be forgotten. The aristocrats of the east, accustomed to a leading role in the affairs of state, watched power pass to the middle-class businessmen of the Rhineland, who—in the persons of Ludolf Camphausen and David Hansemann—dominated the new government.

The Prussian United Diet reassembled on April 2, to confirm the royal concessions granted in March and to arrange for the election of a constituent assembly. The Diet was the same one that had met in 1847 under royal auspices, and tended to be the expression of conservative landed interests. There seemed little choice for these Prussian squires but to acquiesce in the liberal reforms; yet the sentiments of one young Junker, Otto von Bismarck, were doubtless widely shared:

> The past is buried; and it is a matter of more poignant grief to me than to many of you that no human power can raise it up again, since the Crown itself has thrown the earth upon its coffin. But if, constrained by force of circumstances, I accept this, nevertheless I cannot end my activity in the United Diet with the lie on my lips that I rejoice at what at the very least must be considered a mistaken course.

While waiting for the constituent assembly, scheduled to meet in late May, Camphausen found himself in a difficult position. His government was not yet strong enough to undertake a thorough housecleaning in the bureaucracy. He expected reinforcements in the form of a majority in the new Diet; but in the meantime, he was forced to depend upon the cooperation and support of the existing state machine. This situation need not have been disastrous, and indeed, when it came to dealing with the critical economic situation, liberal ministers and conservative officials worked together successfully. But it did produce one peculiar and dangerous situation.

There was considerable apprehension in Berlin that the increasingly vocal radical elements would incite the workers into further violence, apprehension which occasioned something of a middle-class exodus from the capital. Camphausen shared these fears, and doubted that the citizen guard created in the March Days could handle such an explosion should it come. Late in March, therefore, he authorized the return of several regular army units to Berlin. The effect of his decision was not only to undercut the *Bürgerwehr*, the Berlin counterpart to the National Guard, and eliminate the likelihood of further popular pressure upon the crown. It also helped maneuver the forces of reaction into a position from which, in time, they could strike at the revolution. It was Friedrich Wilhelm's momentary loss of control over his capital that had brought the liberals to power, and now the liberals helped to give the city back to the King.

The German liberals, with their toehold in government, had some base from which to accomplish the swift and rather impressive transition from absolutism to constitutionalism. The Viennese liberals had won no such government positions in their revolution, only promises of reform and a certain leverage through the citizen militia and the Academic Legion. The incompleteness of the revolution seems almost to have made future upheavals inevitable.

One of the early Imperial concessions had been the establishment of a National Guard, superseding the older Civic Guard and incorporating the Academic Legion. In fact, the student group—which soon included professors and non-academics as well—preserved its own identity and gave the Guard a political cutting edge. The Legion kept up the pressure—mainly verbal, but always implying the threat of another rising—for the authorities to enact the promised reforms. When the government announced its new press law on March 31, a proposal which maintained many restrictions upon free expression, quick and forceful Legion complaints resulted in revocation of the law and eventual drafting of a new and far more permissive statute.

The revolutionaries, then, had a reasonably confident and effective organization; the government, by contrast, demonstrated only demoralization and disarray. The events of March 13–15 had made it unwise for the most stiff-necked reactionaries to remain visible. Yet there was no dynamic figure to fill the void. The reorganized ministry was entirely composed of career bureaucrats, of whom only Baron von Pillersdorf might have passed for a moderate liberal. Pillersdorf, who directed the crucial Ministry of the Interior, favored relaxation of the most obnoxious governmental controls; but his desire to conciliate liberal reformers was accurately read by radical elements in the Legion as a sign that he could be pushed around. The forced withdrawal of the press law can only have confirmed this impression.

The new ministry was thus at a loss to cope with events in Vienna. As if that were not enough, however, it quickly faced revolt throughout the Empire. In other major Austrian cities, there were riots

which subsided only after municipal officials agreed to the formation
of civic guards. The Magyar Diet proclaimed a series of drastic
reforms which amounted to the creation of an independent Hungary
joined to the Empire in name only, and the Croats voiced similar
demands for autonomy. Lombardy and Venetia violently evicted the
Hapsburg garrisons. There were riots in Lvov, in Hapsburg-con-
trolled Galicia, in Dalmatia on the Adriatic, in Transylvania. A
group of Czech nationalists petitioned the government for changes
that would both have liberalized their government and given their
province considerable freedom within the Empire. At first, the central authorities tried to delay, but on April 8 they suddenly accepted
the entire petition.

Official ineffectuality only gave further confidence to the Viennese
left, which now broadened its organizational base. Radical members
of the National Guard joined with the Academic Legion and a few
outsiders to form a Central Committee of Citizens, Students, and
National Guards. Democratic rather than liberal, the Central Committee also betrayed some signs of social awareness and became
something of a spokesman for working-class grievances. The students
had maintained their contacts in the suburbs and had built up a
considerable following there. By the end of April, the left was
therefore in a position to bring the working-classes into the streets
once more, though now with some leadership to give them political
direction.

The important concession of the March Days had been the
promise of a constitution, which was to emerge from a joint meeting
of all the provincial Diets. But the Diets had never met. The
government hesitated to convoke such an assembly, for fear that the
rebellious provinces would vote the Empire out of existence; but
neither could it delay the granting of a constitution for much
longer. The solution, such as it was, came in the form of a govern-
ment-authored constitution issued on April 25.

Most liberals were content with the document, even though it left
the Emperor an absolute veto. But the democratic left was dissatisfied, in part because of the constitution's substance—there were
property qualifications on the vote, and an upper legislative house
was to be composed of nobles, large landholders, and various Imperial appointees—but even more because the constitution had been
written by the government rather than by a representative assembly.
The new radical press, given birth by the abolition of censorship,

attacked the constitution and the government; the Legion and the Guard organized frequent demonstrations. On the night of May 3, a large crowd, including workers, invaded the office of the chief minister, Count Fiquelmont, and forced his resignation. Two days later, a student committee petitioned the government to decree a completely democratic suffrage. Pillersdorf, now Minister-President, responded with a franchise law which still virtually barred wage earners and stipulated indirect voting. But the democrats both supported the principle of popular sovereignty and wanted working-class support in any future election. The Central Committee prepared for a vigorous protest campaign, and the situation in Vienna became extremely tense once more.

At this point, the government suddenly imagined it had a back bone, and tried by decree to prohibit the National Guard from political activity. Pillersdorf supposed there was sufficient Guard dissatisfaction with the radicalism of the Central Committee that he could split the organization wide open. Conservative Guardsmen were ambivalent, but the radicals were organized. Publication of the decree touched off still more demonstrating, and the democrats brought their working-class troops into the city to surround the Hofburg. The menacing crowds brought yet another ministerial capitulation, which extended also to the suffrage question, and served to announce that the government had completely lost its grip on Vienna.

Throughout these turbulent weeks, Emperor Ferdinand's reputation had been only slightly tarnished. Republicanism remained negligible, and few of the revolutionaries blamed the monarch for the deeds of his ministers. But the court could take little consolation in this. It was by no means clear that the surrender of May 15 would satisfy the radicals, and the Imperial inner circle did not wish to wait and find out. On May 17, Ferdinand and several other members of the royal family slipped out of Vienna; two days later, they reached Innsbruck, tucked safely in the sleepy Tyrol. The Emperor then addressed a manifesto to his subjects, announcing that "an anarchical faction," inspired by the Academic Legion and National Guard, had tried to deprive him "of all freedom of action, in order to enslave the loyal inhabitants of my capital and the provinces." He promised, however, to remain open to proposals of reform (as long as they were not "extorted by arms") and even to forgive the "lost" children of the capital who had wandered into error.

The flight of the Emperor, taken primarily for reasons of safety, turned out to be a shrewd political move. It dramatized just how far the revolution had gone, and it linked the growing fear of radicalism with veneration of Ferdinand. It turned public opinion in Vienna against the left, which suddenly found itself on the defensive. The Central Committee now agreed to cease its political activities; the National Guard and Academic Legion even submitted themselves to the jurisdiction of the local military commander. This spontaneous reaction, given time to mature, would almost certainly have wiped out the left as an effective political force. But the government could not resist tampering. Although the students too had agreed to withdraw from politics, the ministry tried to push things along by closing the University and collecting the arms of all non-Viennese members of the Legion as a prelude to its dissolution.

The Legion, however, refused to go that far, and it did have its own reservoir of popularity upon which to draw, especially in the suburbs. Nor did the government help matters by calling the military to its aid, for the March Days had left a residue of bitterness in the city which now worked in the students' favor. Barricades went up on May 26, and the Academic Legion—reinforced by large working-class contingents—sat behind them, insisting that the ministry reverse itself. Characteristically, the government caved in and agreed to retain the Legion.

Meanwhile, the left now reorganized. Elements of the old Central Committee reformed into a group popularly known as the Security Committee and began immediately to act like both a revolutionary council and a legal authority. The Security Committee arrested government officials whom it held responsible for the events of May 26, started to issue statements which had the tone of decrees, and in short moved into the void left by ministerial capitulation and Imperial flight.

The victory of the left in Vienna was in large part circumstantial, stemming from the weakness and fumbling of the authorities. But it came also from organization, from the fact that the democrats had banded together, defined their aims, and built up a following upon which they could call. The movement had very nearly floundered after the departure of the Emperor, and a prudent and patient government would have let it collapse under the weight of public dissatisfaction. But now the left was in a stronger position than ever. The revolution would continue.

Italian domestic politics naturally took a back seat to the war with the Hapsburgs.[2] The new ministry in Naples, run by moderate liberal aristocrats, was being egged on by radicals, held back by conservatives, and crippled by administrative chaos. Provincial risings were common and taxes almost impossible to collect, so that the simple operation of the state machine—much less the consolidation of reforms—was a Herculean labor. In Venice, Manin carried through a broad reform program, instituting the usual political freedoms, liberalizing the press laws and legal system, and convoking an assembly. But the war and the unification question consumed his city, and one of the first acts of the new assembly— much to the republican Manin's grief—was to merge Venice into the Kingdom of Piedmont-Sardinia.

In Rome, the new government was not of particular importance, and attention remained centered on the Pope. Pius IX had authorized a unit of the Papal army to proceed to the northern border of his territories and guard the frontiers against any possible Austrian invasion. But the general in charge, Giovanni Durando, was a Piedmontese, anxious to throw his troops into action on Charles Albert's side. Durando tried to cover himself by broadly hinting that he was acting under Papal inspiration, precisely the sort of thing most Italian nationalists were ready to believe.

War against the Hapsburgs was the last thing Pius wanted, and he took the occasion for a general pronouncement that was designed to end misinterpretation of his position once and for all. His Allocution of April 29 stated flatly his opposition to the "extremist" movements that were everywhere challenging authority, his refusal to declare war on the Empire, his disavowal of any intentions to lead a unification movement in Italy. The shock of disillusionment was monumental. Scarcely ever has the public estimate of a man undergone such an instant and total reversal. Roman radicals turned their wrath from the Austrians to Pius, and began to talk of a provisional government that would to all intents and purposes sup-

---

[2] For a discussion of the war, see Chapter 4.

plant the political authority of the Pope. The enthusiasm which had greeted the constitutional reforms evaporated, and the newly-elected parliament could not even summon a quorom at its first session. Pius juggled ministries, to the contempt of radicals in the newly-formed political clubs. In September, he appointed Count Pellegrino Rossi, a Tuscan who had lived in France and served as Louis Philippe's ambassador to Rome. A competent and determined administrator, Rossi was ready to challenge the left in hopes of stabilizing the situation in Rome. But he was murdered by radicals on November 15, before his government could summon sufficient forces to assert its authority. There were defections in the army and the police, and Pius suddenly found himself at the mercy of the clubs. He was forced to appoint as Premier, Giuseppi Galetti, a Mazzinian democrat. On November 16, the Pope suffered a riotous invasion of the Quirinal itself. Having lost control of Rome, Pius left it to the radicals and fled to Gaeta in the Kingdom of Naples. Premier Galetti proceeded to operate Rome as a republic, which it was formally proclaimed to be in February 1849.

The Urban Poor and the Social Question

1848 has been widely heralded as the year that witnessed the emergence of the working classes as a political force, anticipating the militant proletarian labor movements of later generations. It is true, of course, that certain conditions of the mid-'40s—the increasing concentration of workers in the cities, the general poverty and misery sharpened by the economic crisis—began to create some vague sense of common interest among the urban poor. It is equally true that workers were more concerned about unemployment than about ministerial responsibility, that they occasionally banded together in 1848 to force some amelioration of their condition. But the danger here is in going too far, in ascribing to the social discontent of 1848 a scope and a sense of purpose that it did not have. "The working class," writes one historian, "were out to turn the political revolution into a social one." In fact, most of the workers' demands were highly specific and localized, directed toward working conditions, wages, and a host of individual abuses peculiar to their own situation and not even cumulatively amounting to a revolutionary program.

In some places, the social question was never even a live issue.

The Venetian poor seem to have been satisfied when Manin simply reduced the salt tax. The workers of Vienna could be mobilized into political activism, and they were miserable enough to strike out at machines and tax offices. But their idea of a social revolution seems to have encompassed little more than a moratorium on rents and an extension of the dole. Even the more mature working-class movement in the German artisanate cherished an ideal—slightly over-simplified, the preservation of the guild system—which it is a little difficult to think of as a program for social revolution. Only in France, where socialist notions fused with an older revolutionary tradition to gain some currency among the workers, were there groups that consciously and deliberately attacked such fundamental social institutions as the distribution of property. But even here they were not dominant; the heterogeneity of the urban poor and the varieties of their wretchedness were reflected in demands for particular remedies rather than broad and coherent programs of social renovation.

In general, then, the working classes were too internally fragmented, too politically and ideologically unsophisticated, to produce any significant movement for what may fairly be called social revolution. But they were also too hungry and miserable, too desperate, too excited by the revolutions themselves, to sit still. The very fact that they had the temerity to enunciate aspirations panicked the propertied classes, who exaggerated any complaints about working conditions into an attack upon property itself, and thus created (along with some of the more excitable radicals) the myth of the workers of 1848 bent on systematic social renovation and the creation of the new utopia.

The scattershot social reform program of the French provisional government reflected the demands of its beneficiaries as much as the mentality of its authors. It is true that most of the republican leaders favored piecemeal social reform at best. Even Ledru-Rollin had failed to go beyond a fuzzy sort of minimum wage scheme, and only Louis Blanc had any well-thought-out program for what might be called social revolution. But the demands for amelioration that poured in from the Paris poor generally sought only remedy of specific abuses: reduction of food taxes, a maximum on the working day, prohibition of cheap prison and convent labor, restrictions on immigrants—mostly Belgians and Italians, who were taking jobs away from Frenchmen—and relaxation of the penalties on debtors.

Perhaps the most menacing demand was for a Ministry of Labor, a special government agency designed to represent and protect working-class interests. The proposal implied that there was a sense of solidarity among the workers, and that they fully intended to unite for the realization of their aims. The demonstration of February 25 in front of the Hôtel de Ville, in favor of the republic's adopting the red flag as its own, suggested a commitment to revolutionary ideals that must have given pause to the timid.

The provisional government was able to resist the red flag, by force of Lamartine's dazzling oratory, and at least to deflect the demand for a Ministry of Labor. Instead, it authorized a sort of congress of Parisian workers—with no official powers—under the presidency of Blanc, to thrash out grievances and proposals. The so-called Luxembourg Commission, taking its name from the palace in which it met, drew together delegates from all the Paris crafts, which is to say that it was primarily an artisan congress. Its meetings provided an occasion for a great deal of working-class protest and criticism, and it also became a focus for the social fear and hate of other classes throughout France. As a matter of fact, the Luxembourg was not such a hotbed of radicalism. The delegates to the Commission remained in the older, corporative tradition, and their ideal was roughly akin to a monopoly of the guild system— though the guilds were to be somewhat streamlined, with internal inequalities eliminated by a more democratic organization. The government would regulate markets and prices, but ownership would remain private and individual--not a very "socialistic" program. The Luxembourg Commission was an enemy of the status quo, but not of private property.

The more dangerous socialist agitation actually took place not in the Luxembourg, but in some of the nearly two hundred political clubs that sprang up in the new climate of freedom. Not all the clubs were on the extreme left, but the ones led by prominent social revolutionaries—Blanqui, Proudhon, and various secret society alumni—tended to be the most visible. The club movement gave the left-wingers a forum, an opportunity to expound in regular meetings their social critiques and panaceas to a substantially working-class audience. It was through the clubs that radicals and revolutionaries tried to structure their political activity—the preparations for elections, or the organization of mass demonstrations designed to pressure the government into more advanced measures.

If there was any conscious and concerted effort in 1848 to turn the political revolution into a social one, it came from these Parisian clubs. They publicized their radical aims through the hundreds of new Parisian newspapers, themselves thriving after the abolition of censorship and the expensive stamp tax, but they did not spend all their time propagandizing. They made some effort to coordinate their activities through a central body of delegates from each individual unit, the Club des clubs, and they put a great deal of energy into the election campaign.

The club movement, then, had a certain revolutionary potential, as the provisional government well recognized. The republican authorities were clearly worried by this activity to their left, though they were never quite sure how to deal with it. Their responses ranged from infiltration with paid informers and attempts to buy off club leaders with minor government positions to petty harrassment, usually in the form of making it difficult for clubs to find a meeting place. Yet the clubs never proved to be either as dangerous or as effective as many persons expected. The intense rivalry between various club leaders frustrated any meaningful and durable unity, and the government was constantly laboring to build up its powers of resistance to club pressure. More important, though the clubs claimed to represent the people and to be the spokesmen of the masses, it became increasingly clear that in fact the more militant clubs stood considerably to the left of most Frenchmen, rich and poor alike. When the election to the National Constituent Assembly verified this situation for all to see, the moral foundation of the club movement—and the morale of its membership—became visibly shaky.

The common theme of virtually all working-class social protest was a desire for state intervention, and government responsiveness was now all the more expected since it was presumably a government of the people. The provisional government shared this view to some extent, and was not averse to a sort of qualified interventionism, of which the decree on the length of the working day was the most dramatic instance. It declared illegal certain kinds of managerial exploitation, in one instance threatened to sequester a privately owned mine unless the owners met their employees' wage demands, and it even flirted with price regulation by establishing a maximum for railroad tickets. The majority position in the government was perhaps best put by Hippolyte Carnot, the Minister of Education:

> We reject [the theories of socialism] as erroneous and dangerous, at the risk of being accused of pure liberalism, because in our view they make of man a slave to the state; but, in our turn, at the risk of being called socialists, we want the state to act as a *paterfamilias* with regard to all its children, to give them education and assistance, and we beseech our fellow citizens not to haggle over sacrifices in order to achieve this result.

The moderate majority in the government was willing to have the state tinker with specific social difficulties, but it never supposed that such action would solve the profound, long-range problems of working-class poverty. The state might now and then intervene to bring up wages and even try to improve working conditions. Otherwise, the moderates saw poverty primarily as a factor of unemployment. The important thing was to get the workers working and off the "artificial" state dole; to do this in 1848 involved a resuscitation of the stricken French economy. What these moderate republicans really wanted was not an increase in welfare measures, but the creation of a prosperous economy that would render welfare unnecessary.

The provisional government, which had no very sophisticated understanding of economics, tended to think in functional rather than in structural terms. Its object was not to reshape the economy, but simply to get it operating again. The task was formidable, for two reasons. To begin with, the revolution had seriously compounded the economic crisis of the mid-'40s. The apprehensions and dislocations that accompanied the upheaval had forced many businessmen, manufacturers and merchants alike, to close down. Revolutions are not propitious times for investment, and credit for working capital was virtually non-existent. The Bourse, always a barometer of economic confidence, had registered uniform decline in late February and early March, especially in the ordinarily popular government bonds. To make matters worse, the government was in no position to help. The republicans had taken over a state treasury which, to their astonishment, contained only about sixty million francs. In addition, political circumstances forced them to relinquish two substantial sources of revenue—the indirect tax on food and the periodical stamp tax—while assuming a sizeable new expense, the National Workshops. The difficulties were so formidable that the first republican Minister of Finance resigned after less than two weeks in office. His successor, Louis-Antoine Garnier-Pagès, one of the eleven provisional governors, had some familiarity with the technical esoterica of government finance, but he also clung stubbornly to the fiscal orthodoxies of his time. Confronted with the suggestion that he make a declaration of state bankruptcy and default on bond payments, he answered: "To suppress, by law and by force, a freely contracted debt is to steal. Theft is a vile crime." The more acceptable measures were still niggling—a 1 per cent tax on mortgage income, a sumptuary tax that included pet dogs, the melting down of the royal silver plate.

Something more drastic was clearly necessary to forestall total calamity, and Garnier-Pagès finally hit on the idea of a national system of Comptoirs d'Escomptes—that is, commercial credit banks. Funds for the sixty-seven Comptoirs eventually established were to be supplied on a basis of one-third from public subscription, one-third from local taxation, and one-third from the central government. The Comptoirs were essentially a socialist inspiration, adherent to the dictum that the state ought to provide cheap credit. The provisional government resorted to them as a means of stimulating the economy, providing the credit that would get business back on its feet and thus create jobs for the workers. Still, the government had to come up with its one-third of the funds. Indirect taxes were slow to come in, and were unpopular with the urban poor besides. Thus the only alternative appeared to be increased direct taxation. The government therefore added a 45 per cent surtax onto all direct taxes—what came to be known as the "forty-five centimes."

This decision, designed ultimately to deal with urban poverty, opened up a whole new dimension of the social question. For the French tax structure, based largely upon land and dwellings, determined that the forty-five centimes would fall principally upon the peasantry. Historians have traditionally ignored the peasants of 1848; usually they appear only as an anonymous vote-casting mass, monolithically conservative, jealously guarding their little plots of land. In fact, the countryside seethed with discontent, arising from sources already designated: overpopulation, land hunger in some places, labor shortages in others, dependence upon capricious market conditions, the decline of rural industry, already high taxes, and everywhere the absence of credit and the prevalence of usurious interest rates. Since many agrarian laborers and small farmers doubled as part-time cloth spinners, the shrinking market and un-employment of the economic crisis also affected them. In the wake of the Parisian revolution, there were numerous peasant distur-bances—demands for grazing rights on what had once been common land, food riots, demonstrations against such feudal remnants as the hunting rights on tenant land preserved by estate owners, protests against the loss of wood-gathering privileges in formerly common forests. In short, there was discontent in the countryside that could have been exploited to political advantage by men less urban-centered than the republican leaders. The provisional government passed not a single agricultural reform and scarcely acted as though it supposed any were needed. Instead, it forfeited the peasants' support by noticing them only in taxing them.

The surtax ought to have brought in nearly 200 million francs; instead, by the end of July, only about 96 million francs had been collected, and that not without serious difficulty. Northern France— where the surtax fell on the middling and large landowners who dominated the area—paid most of its assessment without difficulty, though without enthusiasm too. But in the overcrowded and under-developed center and south, where peasant smallholdings were more prominent, most *départements* paid only a tiny fraction of their obligation and much of that had to be extracted by force. The sleepy little *département* of Lot alone suffered disturbances which required the intervention of the army nine times. Garnier-Pagès had indeed included in the decree clauses providing that persons unable to pay would not be taxed. But provincial administrators, probably anxious to build up an impressive record with the central office, often insisted upon an "integral" application of the surtax.

For all this, one wonders what would have happened had the government not chosen to fund the Comptoirs d'Escompte (and the surtax probably was the quickest available means of raising the money). The Comptoirs did not exorcise the economic crisis, but they did keep the economy from total collapse. The tax revenues also gave the government a sort of collateral with which it could negotiate a 150 million franc loan from the Bank of France. In short, the measure bought time for the republic, though at the cost of accelerating the urban-rural conflicts that eventually helped under-mine the republic.

Historians have not often noticed that the provisional government spent, for another purpose it considered essential, a large amount of money which might have gone toward economic recovery and averted the necessity for a surtax. During the July Monarchy, the republicans had been united in their criticism of what they considered a flaccid and unworthy foreign policy. They howled at every instance of cooperation with monarchical Britain, and worried that valuable energies were being wasted in conquering Algeria when they should have been concentrated in Europe, preparing for a revision of the treaties of 1814–15. Moreover, the republicans, who knew their history, fretted that the advent of a republic in France would evoke a military response from a coalition of conservative European powers. One of their primary concerns after February 24, therefore, was to build up the army. Almost 114 million francs went into this enterprise between late February and early May—that is, two-thirds of the provisional government's total expenditures aside from the surtax revenues put into the Comptoirs. Seen within the total context of economic and social demands, it was an allocation singularly difficult to justify. Oddly enough, no one asked the provisional government to do so.

The existence of the Parisian club movement points to an independence and self-reliance among French workers that took some time to develop east of the Rhine. German artisans demonstrated a strong inclination simply to place their case before the government and trust in official sympathy. On the level of emergency welfare measures, the governments proved trustworthy: there was a flurry of public works projects and emergency relief programs in March 1848, mostly inspired by a desire to get the unemployed off the streets and provide them with some minimal means of subsistence. But the artisans were also hopeful that the new governments would help them reestablish the protections and advantages they associated with the old guild system. Here the authorities were unresponsive.

Obviously, not all German workers were interested in restoring the guild system. The demand was simply irrelevant to the large numbers of perennially unemployed unskilled laborers, and it was of little appeal to the smaller group of factory workers, whose primary concern was some improvement in working conditions. Nor could the artisans themselves agree on what they wanted restored. There were differing demands from different crafts and from different locales; journeymen sought certain liberalizations in their relations with masters, while most masters wanted to see their own ranks made more exclusive.

In spite of these internal divisions, the artisan movement thought it had enough common ground on which to unite. Without anything approaching consensus, there was still broad support for a return to the system of regulations on production, prices, and employment that had characterized the era of the guilds. There was even broader support for the notion that advocates of such regulations would have to come together, to build organizations that would give some cohesion to their agitation. Gradually, the artisans realized that they would have to rely on themselves to extract from indifferent or frankly hostile governments the reforms they sought.

There were a few German radicals who yearned to divert this impulse toward more revolutionary ends. The students who edited the new Berlin newspaper, *Der Volksfreund,* called for the complete destruction of capital. Friedrich Held, another Berlin journalist, treated the guild system as an anachronism and tried to interest the workers in more up-to-date reforms. Karl Marx, running the *Neue Rhenische Zeitung* in Cologne, largely ignored social questions and tried to enlist workers in the radical democratic movement. Though Marx made no pretense about his contempt for mere political democracy, neither did he deem it wise to try to outdistance history. Any purely working-class revolt, he felt, would necessarily fail at that stage of German social and economic development; he thus devoted his efforts to the political revolution. As his collaborator Friedrich Engels explained:

The working-class movement itself never is independent, never is of an exclusively proletarian character until all the different factions of the middle class, and particularly its most progressive faction, the large manufacturers, have conquered political power, and remodelled the state according to their wants. It is then that the inevitable conflict between the employer and the employed becomes imminent, and cannot be adjourned any longer; that the working class can no longer be put off with delusive hopes and promises never to be realized; that the great problem of the nineteenth century, the abolition of the proletariat, is at last brought forward fairly and in its proper light.

It is not surprising that these radical spokesmen attracted hardly any following. "Proletarian" was a name the artisans dreaded; it was the very status they were trying desperately to avoid. What artisans wanted first of all was to stabilize a deteriorating situation, not to create a new one. Their interest in political questions was increasingly subordinated to their drive against industrial freedom—that is, the laissez faire regime of free competition and free markets. They saw this freedom as precisely the cause of depressed wages, unemployment, and the other forces that seemed to be pulling them down from the respectable artisanate into the proletariat. Any would-be leader of the working classes would have to preach on that text if he wanted much of an audience.

The German workers had initially expressed themselves in humble petitions to the authorities or in sporadic outbursts of violence —machine breaking, bread rioting, vandalism of various sorts. By early April, however, working-class activities had become more purposeful. The right of free assembly, recognized in Prussia on April 6, spawned a large number of political clubs and mutual aid societies. At the same time, workers turned from aimless violence to more deliberate action in the form of strikes. There had already been a few nearly spontaneous work stoppages; but as the strikes spread from craft to craft, they exhibited increasing organization, especially among the more highly skilled artisans, such as printers. The strikes were almost uniformly directed against low wages, and on one level expressed a simple desire to make more money. In broader terms, however, they indicated a growing independence in the working-class movement, and were themselves a factor in creating a desire for greater working-class organization so that further goals could be realized. Most major German cities witnessed attempts to form a single workers' association—usually, like the Paris Club des clubs, made up of delegates from the various clubs. A few of them achieved the illusion of unity, but in most places the internal divisions of the artisan movement kept such organizations weak and of little use for direct action—something which was in any case not frequently contemplated. Where these proto-unions were dominated by journeymen, the masters often united against them. Nor was it unusual for factory workers to establish separate, and more moderate, organizations of their own, further dramatizing the splits within working-class ranks.

Still, the demand for "organization"—which became a captivating slogan with all the appeal and much of the fuzziness that accompanied the "organization of labor" in Paris—was irrepressible. In the early summer, various crafts organized regional congresses, anticipating even more broadly-based meetings to come. In mid-July, a First German Handworker and Industrial Congress opened in Frankfurt, just a few doors away from the National Assembly. Ostensibly a gathering of working-class representatives from the entire Confederation, the Frankfurt Congress was actually dominated for most of its one-month duration by master craftsmen from the north and central states. The sessions tended only to publicize and even intensify the conflict between master and journeyman. The masters were content to see the old guild system restored without much in the way of reform, and if anything the position of the master made more absolute and more difficult to attain. The handful of journeymen, who had reluctantly been admitted to the Congress as non-voting observers only, finally walked out in disgust on August 4.

Ironically, then, the drive for unity and organization had helped to divide the artisan movement. The attempt to organize a national artisans association had only hastened the showdown between masters and journeymen. The journeymen organized their own congress, which also met in Frankfurt from late July into late September. Although this meeting eventually tried to draw together workers of all pursuits, whether from the artisan crafts or not, its chief importance lay in its statement of the journeymen's program. It called not for the restoration of the guilds but for the establishment of a new system, democratically organized in order to break the masters' grip. The journeymen's demands concentrated on working conditions and wages, both to be regulated by the government. On the other hand, guild traditionalism remained strong, and there were appeals for controls upon factory competition with which the masters' congress could not have disagreed.

In retrospect, the German artisan movement has about it an air of futility. Though artisans seemed to glimpse the future when they sought freedom of association (that is, the right to form labor unions) and the right to strike, still most journeymen and masters alike clung to a system of production—and indeed a whole organization—doomed by forces over which they had little control. And yet, by 1848, those forces had not sufficiently demonstrated their power to convince the artisanate of their irreversibility. The whole situation would seem to confirm Marx's prediction that a truly revolutionary movement among the working classes awaited the replacement of the artisan guild economy by the new factory industry.

The artisans had staunchly supported the March revolutions. But the liberals to whom power had passed in March were intent upon an economic regime of freedom, of diminished state interference, of free trade and free competition. Even after some heroic efforts at compromise, their outlook could never be harmonized with the artisans'. When this conflict became clear, the artisan movement did not turn upon the middle classes and move leftward to a more revolutionary position. It maintained its commitment—however internally variant—to some form of the guild ideal, operating under government protection. Curiously, it found that the only persons willing to grant that demand were the conservative representatives of the regime against which the revolution had been directed.

If the urban poor were not "out to turn the political revolution into a social one," they were at least out to assure that the politicians did not forget the social question, that something was done about working-class poverty. In one sense, they were successful: virtually every revolutionary center which experienced lower-class discontent in 1848 countered it with some reforms. Strikes, political agitation, the threat of further upheaval, or simply philanthropic sentiments—all combined to bring some wage increases, reductions of the working day, or extension of welfare relief. Indeed, it could even be argued that these minor gains hurt the working-class movement, sapping militancy with the illusion of victory. If this is true, it only demonstrates once more the relatively modest, and surely unrevolutionary, goals of most of the urban poor.

The chief weaknesses of the social movement, however, were its disorganization, its lack of leadership and of widely-shared goals, and the fact that its numbers were so few. Urban misery was surely the most visible social evil of the 1840s; but relative to the rest of the population, the urban workers constituted only a rather small fraction. They could hardly expect to dominate a conservative, agrarian population on election day; they could not even control by force the cities in which they were concentrated. Internally, the movement was divided—in its composition and in its aims. The members of Europe's heterogeneous working classes shared the experience of poverty, but they shared so little else that it was difficult to find a basis on which to unite.

Elections and Assemblies

Europe in the summer of 1848 presented a spectacle that must have warmed the hearts of those liberals who, for a generation, had been preaching the gospel of constitutionalism and representative government. A French National Constituent Assembly, elected by universal manhood suffrage, was at work on a new republican constitution. In Frankfurt, a National Assembly representative of all the German states had been empowered to write a constitution that would produce a unified Germany, and a Prussian constituent assembly was also busy with the task of reform. In Vienna, an elected Reichstag composed of roughly equal portions of Slavs and Austrian Germans was about to set aside the constitution given them by Imperial fiat and construct a new one. And in nearly all the other areas touched by the revolution—Hungary, Rome, Naples—assemblies toiled over the reform of absolute and arbitrary government.

As impressive as this sight may have been, the new Assemblies were not everywhere of paramount importance. It is true that the Constituent Assembly became the new locus of power in France. The Reichstag, however, was a rather ineffectual body, and the real struggle in the Empire took place outside its walls. Where the monarchs still controlled the army, as in Prussia or Naples, the liberal assemblies lived a rather precarious existence. The Frankfurt Parliament had little coercive authority over the German state governments, a critical factor in the ultimate frustration of its work.

It was perhaps a fatal error on the part of the liberals to mistake the existence of parliaments for the triumph of parliamentarism. Too often, they set about the business of operating a representative government without ensuring that its foes were unable to destroy it—yet another indication of the liberals' unrevolutionary mentality. Moreover, they demonstrated questionable political judgment when it came to the elections that produced the assemblies. In France and Austria, proponents of a democratic franchise overlooked the possibility that the predominantly rural electorate might look askance at urban radicalism. Prussian liberals, on the other hand, found that voters returned more left-wingers to the Constituent

Assembly than they would have expected. And the German liberals at Frankfurt supposed that they could keep the vote from the lower classes with political impunity.

For such reasons as these, the parliaments of 1848 turned out to be something less than the bastions of a new era of liberalism. Within a year, all of them save the French had disappeared, and most of their constitutional accomplishments had been undone. Only two will receive attention at this point, the French National Constituent Assembly and the Frankfurt Parliament, whose origins and composition are matters of some importance.

The first free democratic election in European history took place in France on Easter Sunday, April 23, 1848. The balloting went on without serious incident, attracted over 80 per cent of the registered voters, and produced a National Constituent Assembly that must have prompted conservatives to wonder why they had ever opposed universal suffrage.

The Parisian club radicals were of course disappointed by this outcome, but they really ought not to have been surprised. It had been their position from the beginning that provincial France was not ready for elections, that the peasants labored under serious misapprehensions about republicanism and needed an extended period of education in the virtues of democracy. The clubs argued for an indefinite postponement of the election—which had originally been scheduled for April 9—so that they could set about the conversion of the countryside.

The provisional government, already nervous about the legitimacy of its rule, took the opposite position. It feared that postponement would only give conservative forces, badly demoralized by the revolution, a chance to regroup and threaten the republic. Moreover, the provinces were liable to interpret delay as an attempt to extend the "dictatorship" of radical Paris, a fear voiced in the numerous petitions against postponement sent to the government in early March. The government faced a genuine dilemma: it badly needed a counterweight to the clubs in the form of solid backing from the provinces, but it also ran the risk of tipping the balance too far to the right.

The clubs forced the issue. On March 16, a small group of conservative National Guardsmen demonstrated in protest against the democratization of the Guard. The next day, on the pretext of supporting the government, the clubs staged a massive demonstration. This show of strength was accompanied by further demands for postponement of the elections. The government did not yet feel prepared to challenge the clubs; a few days later, it postponed the election for two weeks. This token gesture obviously provided insufficient time for an "educational" campaign in the countryside. But it did satisfy the clubs by dramatizing that they could still exert decisive pressure on the government—a fact that did not go unnoticed in the provinces.

Perhaps speedy elections would have aided the provisional government. There were initial traces of enthusiasm for the republic—though they may have been more an expression of satisfaction at the fall of the widely unpopular July Monarchy—and an early vote might have avoided other disadvantages. The peasants would not have had much chance to feel the burden of the 45 per cent surtax, and the government might not have suffered from the adverse effects of further radical turbulence in Paris (there was another club demonstration on April 16). Still, there is good evidence to suggest that the clubs' estimate of the provinces was correct: there was little republican sentiment to be found there, and even where there were potential sources of support, there was little in the way of local leadership to exploit them.

Dynastic rivalries aside, the great bulk of Frenchmen in 1848 were still monarchists, and their monarchism thrived on anti-republicanism. The republic was still widely associated with Jacobinism, and now the "terror of the Terror" was reinforced by wild tales of anarchists and communists who supposedly controlled Paris. In the spring of 1848, provincial France was in the grip of something approaching anti-radical hysteria. Numerous candidates in the election ran on a platform pledging the "defense of property, family, and religion," though in retrospect it is hard to detect a serious threat to any of those three institutions.

Besides this fear, and of course the continuing economic crisis with which the republic was now identified, two forces shaped the election. First, there was an intense localism, expressing both the fear of radical Paris and the tendency in times of upheaval to turn toward familiar faces and traditional leaders. Almost eight hundred of the new *constituants*—that is, nearly 90 per cent—were elected by *départements* to which they were native or in which they resided. Departmental electoral committees usually tried to put forward one candidate from each local sub-district, all the while remaining cool to outsiders, especially Parisians. Next, and obviously related, was the influence of the local notables—the large landowners, the magistrates, the mayor, the upper clergy, in some cases even substantial businessmen. These men—sometimes aristocrats but sometimes commoners too—had constituted the political class of the July Monarchy, dominating not only the parliament but also the departmental and municipal councils. In 1848, localism, traditionalism, and fear of radicalism all worked to the notables' advantage. It is true that few of the most prominent supporters of Guizot were elected on April 23. But still the electorate produced an Assembly with a majority of well-to-do, conservative, monarchist notables.

Curiously, most historians of 1848 have supposed that the election resulted in a victory for those moderate republicans usually identified with *Le National*—the middle-class political democrats who stopped short of any sweeping social reforms. It is hard to see how, in the circumstances already described, even the moderate republic could have received a vote of confidence. And indeed, recent reexamination of the evidence indicates that only about 280 of the 900 seats went to candidates endorsed by *Le National*, with another 70 or 80 to left-wing republicans and socialists. The remaining well over 500 seats went to monarchists. The republic did not, however, immediately disappear. The monarchist majority was by no means a coherent bloc; it numbered liberals and conservatives, Orléanists and Legitimists. Besides, a monarchist restoration—of whatever dynasty—was for the moment so far beyond hope that most monarchists resigned themselves to a few years of the republic. The Assembly majority's most immediate concern was that the republic be safe and sane, which meant eliminating any threat from the radical left. Since the moderate republicans shared this concern, the majority was willing to join with them in coalition against the left and to support republican governments for the rest of the year.

Lamartine alone among republican leaders understood that to ignore the left totally could endanger the republic itself, and, as of early May, he alone had the prestige to force his will on the Assembly. In the foregoing two months, Lamartine had towered above his colleagues in the provisional government and had nearly become the human symbol of the republic. Yet his stature was the result less of any great positive achievement than of avoiding trouble. As foreign minister, he had issued a manifesto to Europe which reaffirmed France's position as the cradle of European democracy while at the same time it quieted any fears of French missionary activity. At home, he tried to keep both left and right happy and balanced, frequently mediating disputes, exploiting his image as a man above political factions and devoted only to the republic. Both this posture, and the enormous publicity it earned him, made Lamartine the best-known and most popular man in France by election time. April 23 was a spectacular success for Lamartine: he was elected in ten different *départements* with a total of over a million votes.

As the Assembly convened on May 4, however, Lamartine insisted that the new government which was to be formed include Ledru-Rollin—again, as part of his policy of equilibrium. The demand incensed conservatives and moderate republicans alike, who presumed that the election had consigned the radicals to political oblivion. The Assembly could not deny Lamartine, but his ultimatum virtually exhausted his credit. The new government, known as the executive commission, included both Ledru-Rollin and Lamartine; but it also numbered three moderate republicans, and in any case the Assembly itself kept the executive commission on a tight leash.

These maneuverings should not disguise the fact that April 23 was a crucial turning point. Legitimate authority now resided in the Assembly, elected on terms laid down by the republicans and not the monarchists. Club radicalism now lost its moral foundation, its argument that it represented *le vrai peuple*. The Assembly, if not exactly "a living protest against the pretensions of the February Days," as Karl Marx saw it, was at least an unmistakable repudiation of the radical left. Little was to be expected of the Assembly in the way of significant social reform, and the mood of the Paris left now shifted from cautious optimism to a much more dangerous frustration and despair.

April 23 occasioned a decisive shift in political power, from progressive Paris to the conservative provinces. The longstanding republican demand for universal suffrage rested on an assumption that the great mass of Frenchmen were themselves republican, though in fact democratic sentiments existed in only a few regions of the countryside. The republican fallacy was clearly demonstrated on election day. "In establishing universal suffrage," wrote Alexis de Tocqueville of the republicans, "they thought they were summoning the people to the assistance of the Revolution: they were only giving them arms against it."

The German liberals were careful not to make the same mistake. Far from viewing the masses, both urban and rural, as a potentially conservative force, they feared them as a source of social and economic radicalism. Liberal doctrine firmly linked the right of franchise with the status of "independence"—that is, economic independence, which usually meant a certain level of education as well. One prominent liberal put it succinctly when he argued that "the right to elect and to be elected ... should be granted to every citizen who is engaged on his own account (not in the service of another) either in commerce or in some trade or in agriculture."[3] In effect, this would give the vote to businessmen, but not to their employees; to master craftsmen, but not to journeymen; to landlords, but not to peasants.

Discussion of the franchise was of course preceded by discussion of what was to be elected. On March 5, a self-appointed committee of fifty-three south German reformers had met in Heidelberg to discuss, somewhat abstractly, various schemes for national unification. Simultaneously, events were elevating liberals to power throughout the south, and the Heidelberg committee suddenly found that it could engage in more ambitious and more concrete efforts. It therefore issued invitations to more than five hundred prominent German liberals to gather in Frankfurt as a Vorparlament, or Preparliament, in order to begin the process of national unification.

The Vorparlament convened on March 31, utterly without legal authority of any sort. But it had a sort of political legitimacy, born of the revolutions, and it seemed to offer some hope of consolidating the liberal victories of March. The Vorparlament was dominated by moderate liberals, advocates of constitutional monarchy, who were determined to keep the revolutionary tide in check. They consistently voted down proposals put forward by the more radical, democratic minority, and placed their stamp of cautious reformism squarely upon the Vorparlament's four-day career. There was a

---

[3] Quoted in Theodore S. Hamerow, "The Elections to the Frankfurt Parliament," *The Journal of Modern History*, XXXIII, No. 1 (March 1961), 22.

small radical walkout, followed on April 12 by an abortive republican putsch in Baden, the dismal failure of which can only have contributed further to the liberals' confidence and self-satisfaction.

The Vorparlament's most important decision was to convoke and prepare the mode of election of a German National Assembly which would meet in Frankfurt on May 18 and be empowered to write the constitution that would unify the German states. It was obviously important to give the Assembly a broad mandate, but still the liberals were anxious to guard against the presumed dangers of democracy. They began by ruling out direct elections, on the ground that indirect elections would be more likely to produce electors of substance and sane political views, like themselves. Next, they resolved that "every independent citizen who has reached his majority is eligible to vote." These proposals were quickly endorsed by the old Diet of the German Confederation, so that they attained some legal status. In fact, the details of electoral organization were left to the individual German states, themselves mostly governed now by liberal ministers.

The Vorparlament's proviso regarding "independent" citizens was not lost on these ministers, most of whom effectively disenfranchised what they supposed to be the radical and irresponsible elements of their citizenry—in short, the poor. Some states denied the vote to any persons on the public relief rolls (there were three-quarters of a million such persons in Prussia alone). Others insisted upon a residence requirement, thus excluding transient journeymen and unskilled workers who roamed about in search of employment. Others still barred persons "in the service of another" from the polls. Bavaria even went so far as to stipulate a property qualification. Most states adopted the suggestion of indirect election, further insulating the results from any taint of lower-class influence. More unsavory tactics were not unknown, and some states required oral voting or signed ballots.

The liberals were unable to exclude all workers and peasants by law or other means. But the transparency of their efforts to do so produced a widespread disgust which led to rather high abstentionism. Equally important, the peasantry had relapsed into apathetic silence by the end of April. The turnout in most states was therefore low; in all probability, the Assembly rested on the votes of substantially less than half the adult male population.

Beyond question, the election was a resounding victory for the middle-class liberals. Of the something more than eight hundred deputies who sat in the Paulskirche in Frankfurt there were less than one hundred aristocrats, only four artisans, and but a single peasant. The liberals had not entirely succeeded in filtering out all the advocates of democracy. Nearly one hundred democrats were returned, though they disavowed any sympathy with social radicalism and soft-pedaled their republicanism. The liberal majority included men from the professions, government service, and a number of liberal aristocrats. The Frankfurt Assembly has long been castigated as the Professors' Parliament, an ineffectual debating society, the living embodiment of the Revolution of the Intellectuals. In fact, only forty-nine professors were elected to it, as opposed to over two hundred jurists—and the legal profession is not noted for its abstractness and impracticality. In short, moderate liberal constitutionalism overwhelmingly dominated the Assembly, and the liberals rarely had to worry about losing a vote to the left or the right. What they should have worried about—but again, rarely did—was the extent of their majority in the nation itself.

The elections for a Prussian National Assembly, in the meanwhile, had failed to extricate the liberals from the fatal squeeze being applied by left and right together. A reasonably democratic franchise law and high rural abstentionism helped produce an Assembly with a large contingent of democratic radicals. The left's noisy and insistent spokesmen, returned mostly by the larger Prussian cities, created a serious dilemma for the new ministry of David Hansemann, a Rhenish liberal who succeeded Camphausen at the end of June. If Hansemann made concessions to the radicals, he would only further energize the forces of reaction; if he resisted, he would be doing the reactionaries' work for them. For the most part during these tense summer months, Friedrich Wilhelm IV wisely kept his distance, allowing the liberals to sap their strength in conflict with the radicals. The spectacle of disorder and disunity on the left could only fortify the royal cause.

Chapter 4

The Crisis of Liberal Nationalism

When the Frankfurt Parliament gathered in late May to address itself to the question of unification, it soon discovered that no question was thornier than the one which asked: what was to be unified? There was no neat geographical entity with which to work, as in the case of the Italian peninsula. Any attempt to draw the map of the new Germany on purely linguistic lines would not only entail interminable border disputes; it would also result in a state which sprawled all over central Europe with wildly irregular and probably indefensible frontiers. Some deputies suggested using the existing German Confederation as a basis. But this would have been to accept an already intolerably arbitrary arrangement which, for example, excluded some important Prussian territories and included some sections of the Hapsburg Empire.

The two most popular solutions were the so-called *grossdeutsch* or Greater German proposal and the *kleindeutsch* or Lesser German scheme. The *grossdeutsch* plan was simply to create a giant central European nation out of all the German states of the Confederation plus German Austria and Germanized Bohemia. The *kleindeutsch* position was that such a state was too large and unmanageable, that a more reasonable procedure would be to keep the Imperial territories out of the new Germany. Most liberals finally came around to the *kleindeutsch* camp, and the idea has since frequently been identified with liberalism. But in fact, probably the majority of liberals began in 1848 by supporting some version of the *grossdeutsch* scheme. In the first flush of the revolutionary spring, nothing seemed impossible, not even the *mitteleuropean* colossus stretching from the Baltic to the Adriatic envisioned by Great German nationalists. Besides, it then looked as though the Hapsburg Empire was about to disintegrate, so that stability in central Europe counted on its virtual replacement by a large German national state. It was for such reasons that the liberal-dominated Vorparlament invited both Austria and Bohemia to hold elections for delegates to the Frankfurt Parliament, implying that they would eventually be part of the new state. It was only the pressure of events which forced *grossdeutsch* liberals to seek more modest goals. When the conservative recovery began in the Empire, it became clear that Greater Germany was an impractical ideal; liberal nationalists thus turned to the *kleindeutsch* solution as the only available one.

The Frankfurt Parliament sought early to assert its legitimacy as a unifying agent and at the same time to begin the process of unification. In late June, the Parliament called Archduke Johann of Austria to assume the executive power of the new German state, with the title of Imperial Vice-Regent, and charged him to form a provisional government. The very fact that Johann was a Hapsburg only further muddled the already confused relation of Austria to Germany, and surely there were more capable men around. But none of them combined the prestige of a Hapsburg grandee with mildly liberal propensities and German nationalist sentiments.

Besides, Johann was an agreeable and politically harmless man, and his responsibilities were not that great. He was never much more than a symbol of the unification that was desired but yet to be achieved. The Frankfurt Parliament remained far more important than the new provisional government. The individual states must surely have recognized the relative insignificance of the appointment, for they accepted it without objection. But when Johann attempted to make appointments to his government that could have curtailed the powers of the states, such cooperation was not forthcoming. There was serious resistance, for example, when he named a Minister of War; several states—Prussia and Austria foremost among them—simply refused to surrender control of their military forces to Frankfurt.

The fact that individual states could defy with impunity the provisional government (and, by implication, the Parliament) pointed up a central paradox in the German political situation. The Parliament had, beyond its electoral mandate, no legal authority over the individual states until it could formally unify them under a single constitution. But the Parliament was at the same time unlikely to achieve that constitutional unification unless it could force the individual states to accept its authority. In other words, the issue of unification, like most political issues, was rapidly resolving itself into a question of power. Events in the summer of 1848 were to show unmistakably that power still lay with the individual states, with their rulers whom the March Days had failed to unseat, and with their armies.

The dispute surrounding Schleswig-Holstein was an excellent example of the Parliament's inability to bend the individual states to its will. Schleswig and Holstein, lying at the base of the Danish peninsula, were possessions of the King of Denmark. The population of Schleswig, however, was only about half Danish; Holstein was almost totally German and a member of the old German Confederation. In early 1848, the new Danish King, Frederick VII, tried to change the status of Schleswig from a province attached to his kingdown through personal union only to an integral part of Denmark. But the German population in Schleswig and Holstein leaned toward separatism and incorporation into Germany. When Danish troops marched into Schleswig, both provinces rose in revolt and appealed to the Confederation for support. Coming on the heels of the March uprisings in the German states, the events in Schleswig-Holstein attracted much attention. Here, after all, were Germans who asked nothing more than to be a part of Germany. The Diet of the Confederation authorized the intervention of neighboring Prussia in Schleswig-Holstein, an act later enthusiastically sanctioned by the Frankfurt Parliament.

Friedrich Wilhelm IV of Prussia did not share that enthusiasm. It is true that if Schleswig and Holstein could be detached from Denmark, they would probably, given their geographical location, have come under strong Prussian influence. But the risk being run by Prussia in this little war seemed far greater than such profits warranted. For Russia and Great Britain gave strong diplomatic support to Denmark. Neither of these great powers was anxious to see Prussia ensconced on the North Sea; both wished to see weaker Denmark control access to the Baltic. Besides, it seemed to Friedrich Wilhelm a bad time to be challenging the rights of another legitimate monarch, and he disliked acting on behalf of the Frankfurt Parliament. Thus he had never prosecuted the war very vigorously, and in late August—without consulting the Parliament—he concluded an armistice on terms generally favorable to the Danes.

The Parliament had seen the war as a perfectly justifiable, and indeed desirable, liberation movement. The armistice of Malmö provoked shrieks of protest in the Paulskirche, and a majority of deputies at first refused to recognize it. But the Parliament had no real means of reversing the *fait accompli*. The King of Prussia remained the supreme commander of his army; the Parliament had scant means with which to resume the war on its own or to force Prussia to do so. Once again, the weakness of the Parliament was plain for all to see, and the revelation could only engender confidence among the anti-Parliamentary forces.

Perhaps if the Parliament had moved quickly and decisively to the question of German unification, it would have been more successful. In early summer, the old regime was still demoralized, its leaders in disarray. The liberal victory in the May elections provided a momentary moral force of considerable importance. But instead of turning immediately to the question of unification, the Parliament spent most of the summer involved in its own internal organization and in foreign policy—Schleswig-Holstein, Poland, Bohemia, matters only tangentially related to the root issues of unification. Only in October did the deputies formally take up the drafting of a new German constitution and, it must be recalled, they equated the process of unification with the process of writing a constitution. But by October, the situation had changed. The tide was beginning to run against liberal nationalism, and the prospects for unification seemed far less bright. Conservative forces were unmistakably reviving in Prussia and the Empire, and the Frankfurt liberals discovered that if they had ever had a chance to unify Germany, it had passed them by.

As long as the liberals thought of unification in terms of constitution-making, they never really had that chance. That, at least, was the position of the British historian Sir Lewis Namier, author of an influential essay on 1848. "States are not created or destroyed," wrote Namier, evoking Bismarck, "and frontiers redrawn or obliterated by argument and majority vote; nations are freed, united, or

broken by blood and iron, and not by a generous application of
liberty and tomato sauce; violence is the instrument of national
movements." The Frankfurt Parliament, however, had neither the
will nor the wherewithal to employ violence. The liberals accepted
war as a means of liberation, as in Schleswig and Holstein, but not
as a means of unification. But even if they had, they lacked the
forces with which to fight one. The only troops they might conceivably have summoned to battle were the poor. But then the liberals
were unwilling to risk a revolutionary war, and the poor were increasingly uninterested in the struggle for unification.

This may seem sheer determinism, a rationalization for the Bis-
marckian solution which argues that the way in which Germany
was unified was the only way in which Germany could have been
unified. Yet there is another implication, one which points up the
peculiar nature of the German revolutions of 1848. The revolutions
were, by most standards, oddly halfhearted affairs which brought
the old regime to its knees momentarily but did not destroy it.
Perhaps this outcome was accidental. Or perhaps it reflected upon
both the leadership and the rank-and-file of the revolutionaries,
none of whom were prepared—if for different reasons—to destroy the
old regime. Unification might have been achieved in 1848 had the
revolutions been more radical, had there been more democrats in
Germany, had the old regime been more systematically removed
from power. All that, of course, would be to suppose that Germany
was a far different place than in fact it was in 1848. Violence might
have achieved unification. But in 1848, conditions produced no
major nationalist group so ardently dedicated to unification that it
would resort to violence.

The Frankfurt Parliament had problems enough trying to find
some way to unify Germans; its tasks were badly complicated by
the question of what the relation of the Slavic peoples to the new
Germany would be. Critics of the *grossdeutsch* solution complained
that to accept the breakup of the Hapsburg Empire was to cut
adrift millions of Slavs, thus creating not stability but dangerous
political uncertainty in central Europe. The *grossdeutsch* liberals
never gave a satisfactory answer to this criticism, but simply went
ahead with their plans to bring the Austrians and the Czechs (but
not the Empire's other southern Slavs) into unified Germany. The
Czechs resisted, and refused to take part in the Frankfurt Parliament; the Germans' reactions alternated between gruff talk and

blandishments about autonomous status. The recovery of pro-dynastic forces in the Empire, which is to say enemies of German unification, soon rendered all such talk academic.

The Polish question would pose the liberals far greater difficulties, and incidentally bring down upon them a storm of abuse from posterity. The liberals have been flayed for a cynical and hypocritical betrayal of their principles when it came to their Polish policy. Sir Lewis Namier claimed to see a malevolent "national egotism" beneath the fine liberal rhetoric and argued that "these German 'Liberals' [were] in reality forerunners to Hitler" in their treatment of the Slavic peoples.

In the tumultuous and confused days of March, the Polish national movement experienced another of its spasmodic eruptions. There were disturbances throughout the Prussian Polish territories, and exiled leaders of the Polish cause returned to their homeland to assume command. The German Vorparlament generally sympathized with the Poles, perhaps out of genuine concern, perhaps because it was attracted by the idea of an independent Poland acting as a buffer between the new Germany and archconservative Russia. In any case, the Vorparlament formally resolved its support for the restoration of an independent Poland.

The resolution was yet another reflection of the Vorparlament's heavy overrepresentation of the south and west and underrepresentation of the north, which is to say mainly Prussia. The Prussian government, while professing concern for Polish independence, was by no means anxious to divest itself of its large holdings in the territory of Posnania. Radicals in the newly-elected Prussian Assembly favored outright Polish independence, but the conservatives could appeal to German national feeling. There were large numbers of Germans in Posnania who were now clamoring loudly for protection and who, conservatives argued, could not simply be sacrificed to Polish nationalism. The Hansemann ministry inclined characteristically toward a compromise in the form of a partition of Posnania— then a part of East Prussia—which would protect German nationals and their property while still making some concession to Polish independence.

In the best of times, a compromise may have been possible. Polish leaders were not averse to negotiation. But amidst the tensions of 1848, they found it difficult to restrain the Polish peasantry, which had borne generations of exploitation by Prussian landlords. There were violent attacks on German property and something like a small-scale *jacquerie*. The Prussian military in Posnania welcomed the opportunity for an (unauthorized) response, which was conducted with an enthusiasm notably absent in the Danish war. The resultant clashes inflamed Prussian nationalist feeling, and played directly into the hands of conservatives loath to make any concession to the Poles. With the initiative passing to conservatives in the bureaucracy and military, Prussia went through the charade of partition in the late spring. An enormous slice of Posnania stayed under Prussian control and only a negligible fragment went to the Poles.

In late July, the Polish question came before the Frankfurt Parliament. As Namier himself observed, few persons believed that the Parliament could or would nullify the partition. The attacks on German property in Posnania and the anguished appeals of Germans there had decisively set German opinion against the Poles. Moreover, the partitions had been accomplished and were defended by the Prussian army, a force the Parliament could hardly hope to match even if it wished to. Yet the Poles were far from being without defenders at Frankfurt. The small democratic bloc, which argued for a return to the Vorparlament's principle of a restored Poland, was able to prolong debate for three full days, even though it was ultimately outvoted.

Many commentators have given special attention to the speech of Wilhelm Jordan, a Berlin democrat. Jordan delivered a remarkable address to the Parliament which in most respects anticipated the callous *Realpolitik* of a later generation. He extolled the Prussian partition in terms of the "right of conquest," and insisted that "mere existence does not entitle a people to political independence." Jordan's speech has been seen as evidence for a massive sellout of the left to nationalism, indicative of the cynicism and brutality that underlay the German unificationist movement. In fact, Jordan's views should not have come as much of a surprise. He had been praising "national egoism" for months, and much earlier in the year had cautioned his fellow democrats that "the golden age of the fraternity of nations has not yet come." Moreover, the rest of the left at Frankfurt refused to follow him, and Jordan's fellow Berlin democrats in the Prussian National Assembly remained staunchly against the partition.

In examining the majority's justifications for its reversal of the

Vorparlament's stand, it is difficult to discover much that smacks of Hitlerism, however unfair the partition was to the Poles. Some deputies spoke in terms of a benevolent German paternalism: the Polish peasantry was manifestly unprepared for self-rule, and in any case was better off under enlightened German care than under the cruel Polish aristocracy. Others feared international repercussions. A large independent Posnania could only further provoke Russia, already at odds with Germany over the Danish war (which was still sputtering along in July). Others still wished to avoid a confrontation with Prussia, which represented the Parliament's only hope for a successful outcome in the Danish war. And the Frankfurt majority did, for what it was worth, vote "unrestricted national development and equal treatment with respect to church affairs, education, literature, internal administration, legal matters, and language" for all non-German peoples to live in the new state.

Again, the central issue in the Polish question was not the enslavement of Poles, but the protection of Germans. The Parliament revealed less a streak of hypocrisy than a strain of consistency. Just as it endorsed the Danish war in order to free the Germans of Schleswig and Holstein from foreign rule, it refused to contemplate the sacrifice of a large German population to Polish rule.

Surprisingly, perhaps, in Italy, as in Germany, there were disagreements as to what would constitute the new Italy. The Italian peninsula would seem to have provided a convenient and coherent geographical basis, and it was in just such terms that the Mazzinians thought: all Italy brought together, with a reborn Rome as capital of the republic. The Piedmontese had different ideas. Like *kleindeutsch* nationalists, they feared that such a large state would be difficult to govern, hard to keep stable. They thought instead of Piedmont expanding its rule over some larger portion of northern Italy, though the extent was debated—Lombardy and probably Venetia, but perhaps Tuscany too. Such a state might not include all Italy, but at least it could control all Italy. It would be economically and militarily strong enough to hold off Hapsburg influence, and it would have been founded on safe, liberal-monarchical principles.

The Mazzinians were obviously not anxious to see unification take place under these auspices. But the Piedmontese had an army, and the republicans knew that the eviction of the Austrians stood first on the agenda. As for Piedmont, nationalists there had no desire to be stampeded into a war which might simply be serving the republican cause. Even so, there is some evidence that the exact timing of the declaration of war of March 22 on the Empire was related to attempts to placate republican agitation in Genoa. The relations between these two political blocs were to remain complex and delicate throughout the year.

With the Piedmontese declaration of war, the struggle for unification in Italy became largely military. While it is true that the fighting was restricted to Lombardy, the military outcome would clearly have repercussions throughout the peninsula. Italian unification turned largely on the balance of military might, and the year between March 1848 and March 1849 was dominated by the war of liberation against the armies of Marshal Radetzky.

Thus King Charles Albert and his Piedmontese army bore the burden of the nationalist cause. Yet the head of the House of Savoy was not really equal to the task. Charles Albert was not a bold leader who could inspire much confidence among his followers. He had only reluctantly granted liberal reforms in his own kingdom, and he approached the war with Austria hesitantly and with serious misgivings. He was hardly the sort of dynamic figure to whom nationalists in central and southern Italy could rally with enthusiasm, and indeed, the King himself showed little interest in the revolution outside of northern Italy. Moreover, Charles Albert's apprehensions about the war were well-founded. The Piedmontese army was small and sadly inexperienced. Even when joined by small contingents from the Papal States and the Kingdom of Naples, the liberation armies were hardly a match for Radetzky.

Nor was the shaky little Italian coalition destined to last. The Papal and Neapolitan regimes had rested primarily upon Hapsburg support. Pius IX revealed the connection once more in late April when he effectively removed Papal troops from the war. Just two weeks later, King Ferdinand of Naples followed suit. After a swift military counterstroke had defeated and dispersed the Neapolitan rebels, the King withdrew his country's troops from the north and prepared for an assault upon the Sicilian separatists. Again, Naples anticipated developments elsewhere: the January rising had been the first eruption of 1848, the May counterrevolution the old regime's initial recovery. The Piedmontese were now left to go it virtually alone.

At first, the authorities in Vienna despaired of their chances for maintaining a hold on Lombardy, the key to their power in Italy. The Viennese revolution, the expulsion of Imperial troops from Milan, the successful rising in Venice—all seemed to spell the end of Austrian control over the peninsula. A dark pessimism swept over the Imperial Court. There was talk of writing off Lombardy and using Radetzky's troops to save Venetia, or perhaps even bringing them back to hold together the Empire in central Europe. The government dispatched a representative to Lombardy in early April to seek negotiation with the Piedmontese and to argue the wisdom of peace to Radetzky.

Had it not been for Radetzky, liberation might have been handed to Lombardy free of charge. But Radetzky opposed any concession to Italian nationalism, and he evaluated the military situation more coolly than his superiors in Vienna. The Marshal never doubted that he could prevail. Moreover, he had the advantage of being almost the only high Imperial official left in northern Italy—those not expelled had been incarcerated—and could thus pursue his policy of resistance with relative freedom. He did have some sympathy from Fiquelmont, the new foreign minister, who believed that the Empire could manage sufficient foreign diplomatic support to maintain the Austrian presence in Lombardy. But Fiquelmont's efforts were complicated by the despair in the upper ranks of government.

There was one more important element in the Italian situation which was of great potential influence: the attitudes of the two great powers which had traditionally taken a close interest in Italian affairs, France and Britain. The new French republican government was torn between domestic preoccupations and a long-standing sentimental commitment to Italian independence. The new foreign minister, Lamartine, was full of goodwill for the Italian nationalist movement. But he understood only too well the perils of intervention at a time when the Second Republic had by no means consolidated its own government. Besides, as Lamartine's envoy in Piedmont made clear, Charles Albert was as nervous about involvement with French republicanism as he was about fighting Radetzky. The Piedmontese moderates had no desire to see the French radicalize their war, and, perhaps, turn it into a Mazzinian crusade. Lamartine's successor of mid-May, Jules Bastide, appeared to take a more forward position. At the time of the first serious military engagement between Piedmont and the Hapsburg troops, the French massed nearly thirty thousand troops on their Alpine border with Piedmont. The purpose of this maneuver has never been entirely clear. Perhaps Bastide meant seriously to propose intervention, either out of pro-Italian altruism or in an attempt to appease the radical, anti-Austrian left in Paris. Or perhaps the French troops were merely meant to provide the muscle behind Bastide's offer to mediate in the Piedmontese-Hapsburg war. In any case, French intervention never materialized, and serious disorders in Paris during June temporarily postponed French availability for action in Italy.

British policy was even more difficult for contemporary observers to puzzle out. Foreign affairs were in the hands of Lord Palmerston, whom the Hapsburgs had long considered an enemy of their presence in Lombardy. In fact, Palmerston's objections were less to the Austrians' presence than to their methods. He disliked the Hapsburgs' repressive regime, and felt that liberal reforms would be more efficient in forestalling upheaval in Italy. At the same time, he was dismayed at the prospect of French intervention in Italy, which struck him as the overture to a new outburst of French expansionism and general dislocation on the continent. Both Austria and Piedmont, however, were unclear as to British policy, which itself was complicated by the general pro-Italian sentiments of the rest of the Cabinet. When Palmerston observed in the spring of 1848 that the loss of Lombardy could do no irreparable damage to the Empire, it appeared that British influence was tipping toward the Italians. But, at the same time, Palmerston's emissary in Vienna was giving Fiquelmont some cause for optimism. Probably, the British Foreign Secretary was less interested in *who* won the war than he was anxious that *someone* win it quickly. Whoever the victor, a swift conclusion of hostilities would end the risk of French intervention.

Given the absence of French support, which Charles Albert did not in any case want, the principal Piedmontese hope lay with the defeatists in the Imperial government. At the end of May, the Piedmontese engaged a Hapsburg force at Goito. The Italians actually won the battle; but, by failing to pursue the enemy, they missed an excellent opportunity for a far more significant victory. Radetzky's troops had a chance to regroup and recover, and the Marshal still held the critical four fortresses of the Quadrilateral. Nonetheless, the battle of Goito seemed to confirm the worst fears of the cabinet in Vienna. Fiquelmont had by this time left the foreign ministry under pressure from the left, and hardly a voice remained for resistance to the Piedmontese. Once more, the government insisted that Radetzky negotiate a truce and planned to offer independence to Lombardy.

With the Piedmontese armies apparently in control of most of Lombardy, Charles Albert's prestige was at its zenith. His victories kept the French at bay, and seriously weakened Italian republicans. The Milanese provisional government agreed to fusion with the Piedmontese monarchy. In early July, the infant republic of Venice followed suit. Republican leaders like Mazzini and Manin were seemingly powerless in light of Charles Albert's impressive military accomplishments. Ironically, it was Radetzky who altered the political balance in the republicans' favor.

Radetzky was not only disgusted by the defeatism in Vienna; he had never liked central government interference in his affairs. His response to the demand that he negotiate was thus entirely characteristic: he simply refused to receive the envoy from Vienna. Instead, he demanded reinforcements and determined to continue the war. Radetzky also had a new ally of some importance. Prince Felix zu Schwarzenberg had been the Imperial ambassador to the Kingdom of Naples in 1848. With the outbreak of revolution in Italy he went north, joined Radetzky, and in effect served as the Marshal's political advisor. Schwarzenberg, like Radetzky, remained confident that the Hapsburgs could reestablish their control throughout the Empire—in Lombardy, and in Austria as well. He insisted to authorities in Vienna that Radetzky could retake Lombardy, and he seems to have helped create some will to resist. He was aided by the liberals, who did not view the loss of Lombardy lightly. Liberal opinion in Vienna had never opposed the idea of the Empire, only the way in which it had been ruled. In mid-summer, reformist spokesmen began to support the war in northern Italy.

In brief, Radetzky and Schwarzenberg ultimately won some backing for their policy of resistance, and Radetzky swiftly showed the policy's wisdom. The Piedmontese forces were stretched far too thinly across northern Italy, increasingly distant from their supply bases. Charles Albert's troops were none too well-equipped to begin with, and by July their supplies were in a deplorable state. This was the moment that Radetzky, now somewhat reinforced, chose to emerge from the fortresses of the Quadrilateral. In the last week of July, he decisively defeated the Italians at Custozza, and Charles Albert was forced to withdraw all the way to Milan. But the King soon discovered that he could not even hope to defend the city. In early August, the Piedmontese withdrew ignominiously from Lombardy and marched safely behind their own borders. Radetzky naturally did not pursue them farther, since invasion of Piedmont would surely have brought French intervention. The Marshal was, however, in control of Lombardy once more, and accepted an armistice from Piedmont on August 9. His victories left only Venetia still in Italian hands, and the Austrians now proceeded to regain territory around Venice and blockade the city itself.

Radetzky's virtual rout of the Piedmontese dealt a severe blow to Charles Albert's prestige. He had momentarily united northern Italy under his flag. But the first session of the new government took place when Radetzky was once again back in Milan and Venice was under blockade. With monarchist leadership suddenly in eclipse, the republicans' moment seemed to have arrived. Manin recovered his authority over Venice after the brief interlude of pro-Piedmontese enthusiasm, and the Roman left began to agitate. It is not entirely clear, however, what the republicans expected to achieve. The unification question, more than ever, remained soluble only by military means. The republicans talked enthusiastically but still vaguely of a "peoples' war" against the Austrians, but in fact a *levée en masse* was no more than a wishful dream. With the Hapsburgs once more in control of Lombardy, with republican Venice's days clearly numbered, and with the liberals soundly defeated in Naples, the republicans can hardly have hoped to gain any meaningful political advantage. Perhaps it was sheer revolutionary idealism, or perhaps it was the frustration of certain defeat, which inspired the Roman radicals in particular. In any case, as already described, they forced the moderates from power and drove Pius IX from Rome. On February 9, 1849, the Papal States became the Roman Republic. But while these months gave republicans a brief taste of power, there was not and could not have been any change in the politics of Italian unification. That issue had been decisively settled, for the next decade, at least, on the battlefield at Custozza.

In case anyone supposed that Custozza had been a fluke, Radetzky offered a repeat performance the next year. In accepting the armistice of August 1848, Charles Albert had been led to believe that he might still receive Lombardy by diplomatic means. But later that year, Schwarzenberg formed a new government in Vienna, and thereupon stoutly refused any territorial concessions. A vocal war party in Turin pressured Charles Albert to resume hostilities, and indeed the king was casting about for some means of reestablishing his badly shaken prestige. On March 12, he declared the armistice void, and marched back into Lombardy. But in less than two weeks —and just a year and a day after the original declaration of war— Radetzky thoroughly defeated the Piedmontese at Novara. It was the end for Charles Albert, who abdicated in favor of his son, Victor Emmanuel.

The battle of Novara seemed to leave Italian nationalism just about where it had been before the revolutions of 1848 divided, frustrated, if anything weakened by its defeats. Mazzinians and pro-Piedmontese were as bitterly opposed to one another as ever. Liberals were horrified at the republican experiment in Rome, and more than ever determined to keep any larger Italian state to a size they could control. The republicans lost all faith in Piedmontese leadership; rather than turn elsewhere for military assistance in the future, they built their own popular force, relying on dedicated nationalists and a republican myth built at Rome in 1849. But Piedmontese leaders learned a military lesson too. Obviously, expulsion of the Hapsburgs demanded war, and 1848 proved that a successful war was going to require foreign assistance.

Finally, the revolutionary year did simplify somewhat the alternatives open to Italian nationalists. The options had clearly been cut from three to two. Papal leadership of any unification campaign was now out of the question, at least as long as Pius IX ruled at the Holy See. Indeed, the Papacy soon became one of the leading spokesmen in Italy—and indeed, in Europe—for the status quo and against any movements intent upon upsetting it.

German and Italian nationalists in 1848 were concerned to unify their politically fragmented peoples into a new state. But in the Hapsburg Empire, Slav and Magyar nationalism represented centrifugal rather than centripetal forces. The issue there was not unification, but decentralization at the least, and dissolution of the Empire at the extreme.

As always, the nationalist forces were internally divided. Moderates sought primarily a recognition of their cultural identity, which typically amounted to more extensive use of their native language rather than German. The more advanced groups went further, demanding some measure of political autonomy along with the usual liberal reforms—constitutionalism, parliamentarism, freedom of the press and of assembly, and so forth. As of early 1848, only a relative handful of radicals went so far as to demand complete independence for their respective peoples. Moreover, ethnic conflicts separated the various anti-Austrian groups. While Magyar nationalists sought some loosening of Imperial centralization for their own benefit, they could not support far-reaching independence for the Slavs. For Hungary itself included a large Slavic minority whom the Magyars were accustomed to treat as essentially subject and inferior peoples.

The gentry provided the cutting edge of the Magyar nationalist movement, operating from its strong base in the lower house of the Hungarian Diet. The very existence of the Diet gave the nationalists an opportunity to organize and to articulate a program. By the end of 1847, it will be recalled, a coalition of reformist magnates and gentry led by Francis Deák had gathered around Deák's so-called Ten Points, which combined liberalism with virtual Hungarian autonomy within the Empire. A more openly separatist position was upheld by Kossuth, the landowner turned political journalist whose stinging attacks upon the Imperial government helped energize the Viennese reformers at the time of the March uprising.

The Viennese revolution all but paralyzed the central government, and suddenly Deák's moderate proposals seemed too mild. The Emperor Ferdinand accepted the Ten Points, which thus became equivalent to a skeletal constitution. But the ease of this victory served to strengthen the radicals' position rather than the liberals' and encouraged the radicals to demand more. Kossuth commanded an extraordinary prestige. By April he was insisting that Hungary become a virtually independent kingdom, joined to the Empire only through personal union with the Emperor. Like the Ten Points themselves, this demand had by no means the full support of the Diet. Many of the landed magnates who controlled the upper house, and who had long ago made their peace with the Hapsburgs, opposed Kossuth. But the radicals had the initiative, and Ferdinand meekly accepted the proposal.

Independence and constitutionalism put the Magyars in an even stronger position within Hungary. Formerly, the Imperial government made at least nominal efforts to protect the large Hungarian Slavic population from the worst instances of Magyar oppression. Indeed, it had been in the Austrian interest to make certain that no one of its subject peoples became too strong, and even to play them off against one another. The Croats and the Transylvanians, for example, had their own provincial governors and their own provincial Diets—not particularly powerful institutions, perhaps, but providing at least some measure of insulation against the Magyars. The events of March and April changed all that. The new Hungarian government abolished the Transylvanian and Croatian governors and Diets, Magyar became the official tongue even for Hungary's Slavic minorities.

In the spring of 1848, there were revolutionary and nationalist spasms in nearly all the Hapsburg's Slavic lands—in Polish Galicia, among the south Slavs along the Dalmatian coast and the Serbs in the Voivodina, and in Transylvania. The two most notable movements, however, occurred in Bohemia and Croatia. In Bohemia, the familiar pattern which saw cultural nationalism linked to liberal reformism emerged once more. Few Czechs of note talked seriously of outright independence. Attention centered rather on schemes for various degrees of autonomy within the Empire, for putting the Czechs on an equal footing with Magyars and Austrian Germans.

Czech nationalists were less well-organized than the Magyars, besides being less shrill. They had no Diet which could channel nationalist energies; their leaders tended to be intellectuals and professional men. Foremost among them was Francis Palácky, whose *History of Bohemia* had done much to stir the Czech sense of cultural identity and pride in a glorious past. After the revolution struck in Vienna, Palácky and the Czech liberals demanded only the promise of a constituent assembly for Bohemia, with the understanding that the assembly would proceed to organize some degree of political and cultural autonomy. The Czechs in fact had no good reason to desire total independence, which is also to say the disintegration of the Empire. Liberal leaders declined an invitation to have Bohemia participate in the election to the Frankfurt Parliament—on the ground of separate Slavic identity, to be sure, but also because acceptance might endanger the integrity of the Empire itself. "If Austria did not exist," said Palácky, in one of his less original turns of phrase, "it would be necessary to invent her, in the interests of humanity." Czechs understood that dissolution of the Empire would actually leave them weaker than would autonomy within the Empire. Totally independent, they could not depend upon Austria for protection against the hostile Magyars, nor could they count on the substantial economic benefits of union. Submerged within a new German state, they would have no leverage to bargain for autonomy.

The task of Czech nationalism was thus a delicate one. It had to assert Czech identity and build a viable form of autonomy without going too far and threatening the Empire itself. It would have been a difficult job, but as it happened the Czechs never really had a chance to try. In early June, Prague played host to a Pan-Slav Congress, bringing together delegates from all the Slavic peoples of the Empire. Czechs dominated the gathering. But there were also representatives from Slavic groups living in Hungary, so that the Congress constituted a challenge—at least in theory—both to Austrian centralism and Magyar superiority in Hungary. Palácky hoped that the Congress, which dwelled mostly on matters of Slavic cultural identity and pride, would generate self-confidence and solidarity among the Slavs, thus confronting both Austrians and Magyars with a force that would have to be recognized—preferably by some degree of autonomy. Still, he made clear again and again that his goal was a kind of federalism, not Slav separatism. "Vienna," he said, "is the center which is competent and called upon to assure and protect the peace, freedom, and rights of my people."

Given the sharp and increasing tension between Slav and Magyar, the central government might well have used the Congress to its advantage, allying with the Slavs against Hungary. Some months later, the Hapsburgs hit on this solution with regard to Croatia. The Czechs themselves were clearly willing to play the game. They were frightened by Viennese radicalism, and even more by *grossdeutsch* talk of breaking up the Empire and incorporating Austria and Bohemia into a new Germany. When the disturbances of late May in Vienna led to the establishment of the Security Committee, the provisional governor of Bohemia refused to recognize the Committee's authority—an unmistakable signal of Czech loyalty to the concept of the Empire, but one which the Hapsburgs chose to ignore.

In any case, Prince Windischgrätz, commander of the Imperial garrision in Prague, did not appreciate such political subtleties. In mid-June, with the Congress still in session, he used the pretext of some popular disorders (in which his wife was killed) to bombard Prague, disperse the Congress, declare martial law, and take control of the city. It was the first serious setback in central Europe for the forces of change, the first indication there of resurgence on the part of the old regime.

The Croatian situation was complicated by the confusing policy of the Hapsburg government. Naturally, nationalists in Croatia-Slovenia used the March crisis to extract a measure of provincial autonomy from the central government. Accompanying this concession came the appointment of Baron Josef Jellachich as governor of the province. But these decisions almost directly contradicted simultaneous concessions to the Magyars, which entailed the virtual absorption of Croatia into Hungary. Throughout April and May, the Hungarian Diet insisted the Emperor annul his concessions to the Croats and give formal sanction to the Diet's own abolition of the Croatian provincial governorship. Jellachich, for his part, led the Croatian-Slovenian Diet in a formal refusal to recognize Hungarian authority over the province. The Magyars remained in the commanding position, however, and the Hapsburgs as yet failed to see the advantage of a close working alliance with the Slavs. In mid-June, the Emperor suspended Jellachich from office.

Events during the summer of 1848 presented the Imperial court with the idea and the opportunity of attempting a new policy. Windischgrätz's demolition of the Pan-Slav Congress and Radetzky's reconquest of Lombardy gave the Hapsburgs new confidence that the revolution might be rolled back. At the same time, the new Reichstag, in which Slavs slightly outnumbered Germans, was demonstrating a distinct preference for maintaining the Empire intact. Besides Viennese radicalism, the most serious threat to the old regime was Magyar nationalism. The one force that could be used against both was the Slavs, in particular Jellachich and the Croats.

Almost alone in 1848, the Austrian and Magyar radicals could countenance the total disintegration of the Empire with equanimity. If the Austrian left could have found some means of ensuring that it would not be buried in a Greater Germany, it would have been ready to join up, taking the Bohemians along, and leaving Slovakia, Transylvania, and Croatia-Slovenia to Hungary. It was a vision, needless to say, that the Magyars found attractive. Against these disruptive forces, the Hapsburgs had only Slavic fear of being swallowed up to use. In early September, therefore, the Hapsburgs turned to the Croats, and reinstated Jellachich as Governor. This act amounted to a direct challenge to Hungarian independence. In case the Magyars had any doubts as to its implications, Jellachich provided the ultimate clarification two weeks later by mounting an invasion of Hungary. Early in October, the court formalized the alliance by naming Jellachich commander of the Imperial forces in Hungary.

Liberalism and nationalism had joined in the revolutionary offensive of March. In the autumn, Magyar and Viennese radicalism, Hungarian and Great German nationalism found themselves together on the defensive. For in October, the Hapsburgs also decided they were strong enough to turn on the revolutionaries in their own capital. Clearly, the old regime had begun a concerted counterattack.

1848 has generally been viewed as the first stage of Slavic nationalism, anticipating the great movements of the late nineteenth and early twentieth centuries which culminated in the breakup of the Hapsburg Empire. From one perspective, that view may be correct. But it should be recalled that it was not the Slavs who tried to force a disintegration of the Empire in 1848. Almost uniformly, the Slavs sought to retain the Empire as a protective framework; their goal was not independence, but autonomy. The German rulers of the Empire may have missed a great opportunity for continuing stability in central Europe when they refused to honor the Slavic demands. Cooperation would of course have meant some compromise on the Austrians' part: the sacrifice of absolutism to constitutionalism, the sacrifice of administrative centralization to decentralization. The Hapsburgs chose to make none of these compromises in 1848. Yet some concessions to the nationalities question were clearly inevitable. They came twenty years later, when the Austrians decided rather to cooperate with the Magyars against the much more numerous Slavic peoples. Once that arrangement had been completed, Slav nationalism could be expected to intensify, and be less satisfied with mere autonomy.

Chapter 5

The Triumph of Counterrevolution

Historians have often reflected on what they took to be the fleeting, ephemeral character of the revolutions of 1848. The counterrevolutionaries of 1848, however, found the revolutions far more tenacious; outside of Naples, reaction was nowhere accomplished with a single stroke. When Windischgrätz controlled Prague, Palácky and the Czech nationalist leaders repaired to Vienna and tried to use the new Reichstag as their forum. When Radetzky rolled over the Piedmontese army, revolutionaries appeared in Rome. The Frankfurt Parliament was still meeting in April 1849; France remained a republic, at least in name, until the end of 1852.

The problems of recovery for the old regime were as much psychological as they were political and military. The swiftness and comparative ease with which the revolutions had triumphed delivered a stunning blow to the confidence of the old elites; the Hapsburg panic which nearly surrendered Lombardy without a fight had its counterparts elsewhere in Europe. The restoration of that confidence took some months, and was probably the most important factor in the old regime's recovery. In the Empire, it was the stern resolution of Windischgrätz and Radetzky which demonstrated that all was not lost. In Germany, the Frankfurt Parliament steadily revealed its weakness, and at the same time the petty rulers came to realize that their anti-unification sentiments had support in popular particularism. The conservatism revealed in the French election of April gave right-wing politicians a pleasant surprise.

The role of economic changes during 1848 is rather more difficult to assess, since they differed from one country to the next. In France, for instance, the revolution choked off the incipient economic revival of early 1848, and converted the inflationary subsistence crisis into a serious depression. The business community lacked both capital and confidence, so that production and trading moved at far less than their normal rate for nearly three years. Similarly, agricultural prices plummeted to barely remunerative depths. In the German states, however, 1848 brought a sustained upswing from the nadir of 1847: consumer prices tapered off to a more reasonable level, jobs opened up again, and the "hungry forties" came decisively to an end. While such factors must obviously play a part in the study of individual countries, however, it is hard to know what to do with them in a more general analysis. Economic depression would seem to have hurt the Second Republic's chances for stability and public confidence. As one French historian has written, "Before February, the economic situation worked in favor of the revolution; after February, against it." But in Germany, economic prosperity did not entail a successful revolution, and some historians have argued that prosperity took the sharp edge off popular protest and removed the element of desperation that incites men to destroy an entire social and political order. In these circumstances, it would be a bit silly to generalize about *the* economic factor and the fate of the revolutions.

Much attention, in explaining the triumph of reaction, has centered on the breakup of the so-called revolutionary coalitions, an issue about which it is important to be especially clear and precise. For coalition may easily call to mind, for example, the coalition governments of different political parties not uncommon to mid-twentieth century Europe, yet very much unlike the kinds of political arrangements that obtained in 1848. The revolutionary coalitions were in most cases purely tacit alliances. They brought together, from one place to the next, liberals and radicals, monarchists and republicans, aristocrats and bourgeois and urban poor —in short, groups whose interests often diverged sharply, but who found themselves acting together out of force of circumstance, or even sheer coincidence. Moreover, the nature of these coalitions changed over time, or at least they should have changed. It takes no formal contract for such rival groups to cooperate in the earliest stages of a revolution; they need only share deep hostility to a regime in order to find themselves together behind the barricades, trying to overthrow it. On the day after the revolution, however, all that changes. First of all, the issue is no longer destroying a government but building one. Moreover, the common foes of the defeated regime have suddenly become, by the simple fact of their victory, competing power blocs. But revolutions made by coalitions usually depend for their perpetuation upon the durability of the coalitions, which must become something more than coincidental liaisons, must forge some agreement on matters of future policy. The groups involved have to feel that protecting the revolution's accomplishments and sustaining its life are more important than their mutual differences, even though a faction might cooperate with its rival only in hope of ultimately seizing total power. Unless, for some reason, there is an explicit and powerful will to keep these political marriages of convenience alive, the revolution is bound to falter.

That will was conspicuously absent in 1848. Liberals grew too easily frightened by their radical partners, radicals were too impatient with liberal caution. In France, for instance, the radicals cost the republic crucial support from reformist elements in the middle classes, who became increasingly responsive to the call for order. In Germany, on the other hand, the liberals' moderation cost the revolution the support of large segments of the masses, who demonstrated little interest at the time of a showdown between revolution and reaction. Perhaps the coalitions would have lasted longer had there been some external stimulus to unity, something like the foreign invasion which held together a number of bitter rivals during the France of the 1790s. But in any event, they proved too fragile to bear the stress of extensive cooperation. The broad revolutionary fronts of February and March dissolved into feuding factions and isolated grouplets which could not recover their unity enough to battle the counterrevolution.

One more general feature of the European reaction deserves notice here. It is not quite correct to refer to the recovery of the old regime, since in several cases what recovered was not the old regime at all, but a refurbished version of it. If the revolutions accomplished nothing else, they forced a reordering of the elites. The men who had in fact presided over the old regimes disappeared; Metternich and Guizot were gone, never to return, not even in the form of their closest associates. The threatened monarchs turned to new men, more resolute and sometimes more ruthless, who would not make the mistakes committed by their predecessors of February and March. The new governors were frequently characterized by a willingness to try new measures. In place of ineffectual resistance, they employed efficient repression, sometimes mixed with timely compromise.

Everywhere, however, this general pattern was complicated by more or less unique circumstances. The revolutions themselves had broken out in remarkably similar fashion; the old regimes they had shaken each found a different path back to power. The progress of reaction was, moreover, halting and uneven across Europe, though hardly unrelated from one country to the next. The two states in which the reaction preeminently affected revolutionary destinies elsewhere were surely the Hapsburg Empire and France.

Reaction in the Empire

The Hapsburg recovery was signalled by the successful assault on the subject nationalities—the bombardment of Prague, the reconquest of Lombardy, the alliance with Jellachich and the Croatians against Hungary. The recovery was as much psychological as military. Victories in battle wiped out the ministerial panic in Vienna, and helped create a will to resist by demonstrating that resistance was possible. At the same time, the ruling elite experienced a significant turnover. The bureaucratic artifacts of the Metternich era began to disappear, replaced by a tougher breed of conservatives and also by a few liberals who had been involved in the March reform movement.

The most interesting of these latter was Alexander Bach, made Minister of Justice in the late spring. Bach was a genuine liberal, devoted to constitutionalism and civil liberties, but equally loyal to order and to the maintenance of an Austro-centric Empire. The events of late May—the creation of the Security Committee, the Italian victory at Goito—seemed to him to signal that revolution had gone too far. He now threw his prestige behind moderation, lest radicalism jeopardize the fundamental gains of the revolution. Where liberal doctrines might, in the abstract, counsel reductions in the power of the central authority, Bach now supported administrative centralization as a means of preserving the Empire against the disintegrative forces of nationalism. Commentators critical of mid-century liberalism have tried to argue that Bach's position was not new at all, but rather characteristic of the basic moderation that had always been implicit in liberal doctrine. As far as political theory goes, this may be true. But on another level, Bach's conversion was genuine, and it typified that of an important faction of Viennese liberalism.

In March, liberals like Bach had no idea where their reformism would lead them. When they got a glimpse of the future, they were forced to reevaluate their politics, to make some choices as to how far they wanted to go and what they wanted to preserve. Such liberals wanted an end to arbitrary and absolute government, not to the Empire itself. They would not at first have identified themselves as supporters of a return to Hapsburg rule. But Viennese radicalism and Hungarian separatism forced them ever closer to that position. These men were of course a minority group; many other reformers continued to favor some decentralization of the Empire. But the conversion of the Bach liberals represented an important victory for the counterrevolutionary proponents of restored Hapsburg authority.

Viennese radicalism had been bubbling steadily throughout the summer, trying to pressure both Reichstag and ministry into more sweeping reforms. The Academic Legion remained strong, the workers—still widely unemployed—a constant threat to order. At the end of August, the ministry forced the issue by deciding to decrease slightly payments to public works laborers (analogous to those enrolled in the French National Workshops) at precisely the moment when these same workers were demanding an increase in wages. The students supported the workers, though largely because it was rumored that the government also planned to disband the Academic Legion. Yet the students well realized that agitation could be carried too far, that bourgeois support for the revolution was easily alienated. They stood with the workers only reluctantly, and they retired when the ministry vowed that it had no designs against the Legion. But the workers pushed forward, and on August 23 their noisy demonstration exploded into a clash with the National Guard. It was an incident remarkably like that in Paris during June, though on a smaller scale. The Guard waded into the workers with a vengeance. In a few hours, the demonstration was totally dispersed, and the workers, who suffered heavy casualties, had lost. The students did not intervene. The forces of order had won another victory, and the specter of independent lower-class action had been dissolved. Some radicals recognized the political implications of August 23, and conducted a prudent retreat; later that month, the Security Committee voluntarily disbanded.

As summer turned to autumn, the Viennese left began to discover—somewhat to its surprise—that its own fate was connected with the war being fought in Hungary. To many in Vienna, Jellachich's invasion of Hungary seemed at first an independent act of Croatian nationalism in which the extent of Hapsburg complicity was vague at best. But in late September, word began to leak out regarding covert government support to Jellachich. There was great uncertainty as to how to treat this news. The large Slavic delegation in the Reichstag was torn between opposition to Hapsburg centralization and opposition to Magyarism. Some liberals feared that a Croatian victory would embolden the Hapsburgs to concentrate their energies against political reformists, and yet also understood that a Magyar victory might spell dissolution of the Empire, which the liberals equally wished to avoid. The Viennese radicals wavered less, however. They screamed that the war was a clear-cut confrontation between revolution and reaction, and they were able to energize the various left-wing elements which had been somewhat demoralized by the setbacks of August. The radicals directed their fury against the man formally responsible for the war policy, Count Latour, the Minister of War. On October 3, a mob of radical students and workers invaded Latour's office and brutally murdered him.

An unusually vigorous government might have taken this occasion to apply the *coup de grace* to Viennese radicalism. Instead, the authorities panicked. Most members of the Reichstag simply left the city; much of the government and important segments of the bureaucracy followed suit. The radicals were probably more surprised than anyone to find themselves in control of the capital. But they were also isolated and conveniently concentrated for attack. The government now authorized Windischgrätz to undertake an attack on Vienna and root out the radicals once and for all.

There is no reason to go into lengthy detail here on the investment of Vienna. The radicals were quite isolated, received little more than moral support from their handful of counterparts elsewhere in Austria, and had only one faint hope of assistance. The

Hungarian Diet had vested much of its own defense effort in Kossuth's hands, and by early October the Magyars had blunted the first Croatian thrust and were pursuing Jellachich across the Austro-Hungarian border toward Vienna. The radicals began to imagine that the Magyars might break Windischgrätz's siege from the rear, as the two revolutionary movements of the Empire would link up on the battlefield. It proved a vain hope; the Magyar contingents were not prepared for a major offensive engagement, and the Imperial armies turned them away without much difficulty. Thereupon, Windischgrätz moved into Vienna, where he found resistance stiff. Casualties on both sides were heavy: the rebels lost perhaps 5,000 men, the soldiers nearly 2,000. But by October 31, Windischgrätz controlled the city, whereupon he conducted a thorough and relentless repression which decisively broke Viennese radicalism.

The liberals welcomed the demise of radicalism, to be sure, but they did not at the same time give up their commitment to reform. There was still a Reichstag charged with giving the Empire a constitution; the gains of March still had to be secured. The difficulty was, of course, that the Hapsburg conservatives were now in a very strong position from which to resist reform. Moreover, the conservatives had found new leadership in the person of Prince Felix zu Schwarzenberg.

During the siege of Vienna, Windischgrätz had employed Schwarzenberg, who happened to be his brother-in-law, as his chief political deputy, and meanwhile urged the court at Olmütz to name Schwarzenberg head of a new ministry. The court complied, and Schwarzenberg formed his government in November. Its composition was indicative of a new tone in Hapsburg politics. Schwarzenberg paid little heed to the political antecedents of his ministers, and called on both liberals (like Bach and Count Stadion, a liberal who headed the sensitive Ministry of the Interior) and conservatives. The new prime minister sought only two things in prospective cabinet members: high technical competence, and dedication to a unified and centralized Empire. He had no qualms about working with bourgeois liberals, and left no doubt that as far as he was concerned the days of exclusive dominance by the nobility were over. He was not even averse to permitting, eventually, some measure of local autonomy for the various nationalities. But he insisted that such concessions should in no way compromise the authority of the Hapsburg family. He had no sympathy for constitutionalism, which only placed checks upon rulers, and was clearly determined from the outset to free the Emperor from these fetters.

Besides choosing a new ministry, Schwarzenberg insisted within court circles upon one more critical personnel change—that of the Emperor himself. Schwarzenberg was eager to rebuild Hapsburg strength on new foundations, and for this he needed a new ruler. He understood that the Imperial throne had to be a vital force in its own right, and could not depend upon vigorous ministries alone. Ferdinand was obviously not the man for such a job, but there was a candidate at hand, one whose availability was attributable chiefly to the efforts of the Archduchess Sophie. Sophie was well aware that Ferdinand's abdication might have political advantages; her husband, Archduke Franz, would have been successor to the throne, but she persuaded him to step aside in favor of their eighteen-year-old son, Franz Josef. Schwarzenberg and Franz Josef agreed on Imperial policies, and the experienced politician and the tough-minded, intelligent young prince constituted a formidable alliance. The abdication took place on December 2, 1848.

The consolidated and rejuvenated forces of Hapsburg centralism were now ready for a confrontation with the Reichstag. The Reichstag had never been able to insinuate itself into the center stage of Imperial politics during 1848, yet it made some important contributions to the revolution. Surely its greatest moment came at the end of August when it abolished all serfdom and peasant servitude, with only partial indemnification payments to noble landlords. Like the advent of universal suffrage in France, this was the Austrian revolution's single most important and most durable reform. Interestingly enough, it came without serious opposition or protracted struggle. Most interest groups accepted the liberal argument that serfdom was not only unjust but costly and inefficient, and the landlords put up concerted resistance only over the indemnification question. Many historians have added at this point that the Reichstag's decision so satisfied the peasants that they were effectively removed from the revolution. In fact, the peasants had never been an important political force in the revolution, and could therefore hardly have been removed from it. Rather, the abolition of serfdom tended to neutralize that part of the Reichstag itself which represented petty landed property and which defined the revolution as an opportunity for liberation.

During the siege of Vienna, the Reichstag had been adjourned to the small town of Kremsier in Moravia. There, relatively removed from the public eye, but also somewhat cut off from political developments, it worked out a constitution for the Empire. A majority coalition drawn from the Slav delegations and including a number of Austrian liberals put together a document of which the most critical sections dealt with the administrative organization of the Empire. The constitution called for substantial decentralization and local autonomy, institutionalized in local Diets, for all the major ethnic groups. Furthermore, in provinces with large ethnic minorities, those minorities would have their own representative bodies with rights of appeal directly to the Imperial Reichstag. The difficulty was, of course, that the appearance of Schwarzenberg on the political scene rendered the delegates' efforts largely futile. The Reichstag had no leverage with which to force acceptance of its constitution, and it was clearly not the sort of draft Schwarzenberg was going to accept voluntarily.

It is difficult to evaluate the so-called Kremsier Constitution, since Schwarzenberg never gave it a chance to work. Perhaps it would have served to institutionalize and perpetuate ethnic factionalism and dissension. Perhaps federalism was only an attenuation of Imperial disintegration. Or perhaps it offered an opportunity for genuine stability on a liberal basis in southcentral Europe. The Kremsier Constitution, with its recognition of cultural identities and its protection of them through the checks and balances of a federal system, may well have been the key to the difficult nationalities problem of the Empire.

In early March 1849, a few days after the deputies had voted approval of the constitution, the prime minister dissolved the Reichstag and shortly thereafter proclaimed the ministry's own constitution—a document hastily concocted by Stadion, and featuring more generous Imperial prerogatives and a tight administrative centralization. The one concession to decentralization was in a provision for relatively broad powers for municipal government. There would also have been a central, representative parliament to which the ministry was responsible. But there was a catch. The ministerial constitution was to be held temporarily in abeyance, not to go into effect until the national emergency had come to an end (which proved to be a euphemism for never). In the meantime, the Emperor himself would rule.

A good many liberals were understandably furious at the suspension of the Kremsier constitution; yet there was very little that they could do. In their minds, an appeal to the people ran the risk—in fact, not very great—of reactivating radicalism. An important liberal faction within the government argued that the best means of reform was support of the government against revolutionaries and separatists. The Magyar war stirred Austrian and pro-Imperial patriotism and made talk of decentralization sound a little treasonous. The public seemed weary of politics; liberals could detect no surge of popular support for a Kremsier-style Empire. The government's coup—unthinkable a year earlier, when the reformist surge seemed omnipotent—put an unmistakable end to the Austrian revolution.

Schwarzenberg now had but one piece of unfinished business: the Hungarian war. Announcement of the new centralist constitution had pushed Magyar radicals to the wall. In mid-April, the Diet—meeting in Debreczen with Imperial troops in control of Budapest—proclaimed Hungary a republic and named Kossuth "responsible governor-president." These were empty gestures. Hungary's fate turned not upon political forms, but upon military might. Surprisingly, the Magyars prolonged the war beyond most expectations. The Hapsburg victory at Kapolna in late February had cleared out most of western and central Hungary and .the besieged Magyars were further troubled by annoying uprisings among local Slavs. Still, by summer, the Hapsburgs had been unable to deliver the knockout blow. The longer the war dragged on, the more dangerous it became for the Empire. It was not so much that the Austrians feared defeat, which seemed unlikely. But total reestablishment of Hapsburg authority demanded a return of order and tranquillity; besides, the successful resistance of the tiny Magyar force was bad for Imperial prestige.

Finally, in June, Franz Josef and Schwarzenberg swallowed their pride and accepted a Russian offer of assistance tendered by Czar Nicholas. The decision made good military sense. Hapsburg supply lines were stretched thin across Hungary, and the Magyar armies were concentrated in the east, close to the Russian border. From Nicholas' point of view, intervention had its advantages. He was the only major continental monarch whose domain had escaped upheaval, and he was anxious to suppress the revolution's last spasms. Besides, Hapsburg indebtedness could be convenient in the future—though as Nicholas had occasion to learn only a few years later, the Hapsburgs had short memories. In any case, Russian assistance decisively turned the tide. Within two months, the chief Magyar general, Görgei, surrendered and Kossuth and his radical colleagues were forced to flee the country.

A year and a half after the first tentative demands for liberal reform in Vienna, political peace returned to the Hapsburg Empire. The revolution had been defeated, but it also left its mark. It cost Ferdinand his throne. It displaced the aristocracy from its exclusive control of political power. It raised to prominence the nationalities issue which henceforth became the central, and seemingly insoluble, question of Imperial politics. If anything, the revolution also intensified administrative centralization by bringing to power its most efficient proponents. Schwarzenberg shared many of Metternich's aims—centralization, bureaucratic control, Imperial prerogative. Indeed, during the early months of his ministry, Schwarzenberg maintained a correspondence with the deposed Chancellor who was languishing in England. But Schwarzenberg's style was totally different, and it reflected the impact of 1848. More ruthless and more vigorous, blessed with a more useful sovereign, he finally mastered the revolution which had sent Metternich packing.

Finally, the restoration of Hapsburg power had a profound impact beyond the Imperial frontiers. The destruction of Viennese radicalism put an end to Great German nationalism in Frankfurt, and narrowed the German liberals' range of choices. Henceforth, only a *kleindeutsch* solution to the problem of unification would be possible. Moreover, unification would be increasingly difficult now that German particularists could turn for support to Austria. The new Emperor and his government could hardly be expected to be any more sympathetic than their predecessors to the idea of a strong unified power on their northern border. And, obviously, Hapsburg resurgence spelled disaster for the last flickering hopes of Italian nationalism.

France from Civil War to *Coup d'État*

The revitalized Hapsburgs thus posed tangible political and military threats to revolutions elsewhere. The progress of reaction in France had a more varied international impact, since it extended over a longer period of time and was different in nature. In general, conservative successes in France did not so much threaten the cause of the left elsewhere as they demoralized other European radicals. The Parisian workers in particular were widely thought of as the heroic vanguard of revolution; when the workers were crushed in the streets in June, their admirers across the continent could hardly have felt confident about their own future. But it was still not until mid-1849 that France became formally involved in international counterrevolutionary repression.

The February revolution had dispatched the Orléans dynasty once and for all, and there was never a serious threat of restoration. Indeed, in the early months of the Second Republic, it appeared as though the conservatives were hopelessly divided and leaderless. But continuing radical agitation helped bind them together and the April election gave them a chance to organize. The heavy peasant vote for conservative candidates showed that they had popular support, and the new primacy of the National Assembly gave conservatives an excellent opportunity to influence policy.

There were, then, no serious efforts to overthrow the Republic because there was no viable alternative available. Attention centered rather on social radicalism, on the presumed challenge it raised against the existing social structure and against property, and on its potential for generating further revolutionary outbursts. The panicky expressions of concern about the sanctity of property which had loomed so large in the electoral campaign were reiterated on the floor of the Assembly. Specifically, the conservatives focused on the Republic's most visible concession to social radicalism, the National Workshops. In mid-May, the Assembly's right wing, with the Comte de Falloux, a Legitimist, in the forefront, launched a campaign to put an end to the Workshops.

While monarchists and anti-democratic reactionaries conducted their assault on social radicalism, the radicals and moderate democrats were involved in their own struggle. Between February and April, neither group had been able definitively to consolidate its power. The moderates dominated the executive commission, selected by the Assembly. The radicals had the clubs, demoralized by their poor showing at the polls, but still a potentially powerful force. Paris radicalism had made the revolution at the barricades, and it had forced postponement of the election with its great demonstration of March 17. The key to the defeat of radicalism was by no means the dissolution of the National Workshops, but rather, as the moderates in government understood, reestablishment of government control over the capital. As elsewhere, that required above all the recovery of self-confidence.

The fact that the government did indeed have the resources with which to control the capital came as something of a surprise to most of its members. The provisional government feared the worst from another radical demonstration scheduled for April 16. Yet the demonstration was rather easily dispersed by National Guardsmen. The Guard's loyalty and the clubs' inability to force further concessions from the government were important boosts to government confidence. A week later, in the general election, Paris voted lopsidedly for moderate republicans over radical republicans like Ledru-Rollin and Flocon, not to mention the socialists Blanc and Albert (all of whom were doubtlessly badly hurt by high working-class abstentionism).

As it happened, the first violent confrontation with the radicals came not in Paris, but in the Rouen-Elbeuf complex, where textile workers went to the barricades at the end of April. The National Guard of the city crushed the rising and once more events seemed to testify that the authorities retained adequate force with which to repress radicalism. The lesson was not lost on the Paris clubs. In early May, one left-wing faction in the capital began to organize a demonstration in support of the Polish insurrection, wistfully hoping to see France go to war for Polish independence. But the leading radicals were almost uniformly lukewarm about the idea; they feared that a demonstration could easily get out of hand, and that the government could use the occasion of even minor disorders to destroy the clubs. Yet it is difficult for radicals to preach moderation in time of crisis, difficult for them to ignore a flanking movement by ambitious rivals. The cause of embattled Poland was extremely popular with the club rank-and-file. Leaders of the club movement, like Blanqui, Armand Barbès, or François Raspail, could not ultimately avoid participating in the demonstration, which took place on May 15. As it turned out, their apprehensions were entirely justified. For some of the lesser club leaders saw May 15 as the occasion for something like a *coup*.

When the large crowd advanced on the Assembly, most of the slogans shouted and banners carried concerned Poland. Ostensibly, the plan was to present the deputies with a petition in support of the Poles. Although the crowd encountered only token resistance at the door of the Assembly, emotions were high, and there was a forward surge. The demonstrators spilled into the main hall, and began to disrupt the session. A number of club leaders spoke from the tribune, including Blanqui, whose speech on Poland drifted into demands for social reform. Amidst the confusion, a club leader named Aloysius Huber leaped to the rostrum and declared the Assembly dissolved. The crowd rapidly evacuated the hall—some returning home, some heading towards the Hôtel de Ville in the fashion of their predecessors of February. From nowhere, handbills proclaiming a new provisional government of decidedly left-wing complexion suddenly appeared. Somewhere within the club movement—just where is still unclear—there lurked a conspiracy to make a great deal more of May 15 than simply support for Poland. But the conspirators apparently counted on mass support which failed to materialize. There was a half-hearted assault on the Ministry of the Interior, easily repelled by the regular guard. The troops guarding the Hôtel de Ville offered no resistance, and simply waited for reinforcements. They arrived soon, and easily took in hand the would-be revolutionaries, some of whom had entered the Hôtel de Ville and were even going through the motions of establishing a new government. But the great majority of the demonstrators treated the intrusion upon the Assembly as a lark, and simply failed to take Huber's cry seriously. No barricades went up on May 15.

But the government took the events of the day seriously, at least to the extent that they justified more vigorous action against the clubs. The authorities rounded up a number of club leaders and held them for trial. Moderates now forced Caussidière's resignation, since the Prefect of Police had done a poor job of keeping the peace.

May 15 marked the beginning of reaction, and at that almost by chance; the clubs had gratuitously presented the government with a golden opportunity. But the reaction was by no means complete; arrests struck mainly the leaders of the clubs, and only a dozen of them. Conservatives and moderate republicans alike realized that Paris radicalism was far from dead. There was widespread talk of a confrontation. Some deputies began to carry pistols to the Assembly. Extreme conservatives were openly spoiling for a fight, and Falloux now began his offensive against the Workshops.

At first, the debate over the Workshops took place on a financial level. Conservatives insisted that the operation simply cost too much, especially now that enrollments had mushroomed to well over

100,000 persons. The administration had been improvising economies for months: the dole on non-working days was reduced, and the number of working days was reduced to one out of every four. Probably everyone would have considered the expense of more than 100,000 francs a day a bargain if it kept the unemployed workers of Paris out of trouble; indeed, the Workshops' membership had stayed out of the left-wing demonstrations of March 17 and April 16. But a few contingents had shown up in the May 15 parade (though they had not become involved in the invasion of the Assembly), which so irritated the government that it fired the Workshops' director and tried to impose tighter internal control over the workers' political activities. But the May 15 business gave Falloux some political fuel with which to stoke his financial fire.

What was basically at stake in the debate over the Workshops, of course, was a matter of principle. For both the left and the right, the Workshops had become the central symbol of the "social republic." They represented the republic's acceptance of the right to work, of the public responsibility to provide employment. For thousands of Parisian workers in no way dependent upon the daily dole, the Workshops were an ideal, and one they were determined to defend. Falloux understood this, and his program of dissolution was almost surely an attempt not merely to rid France of what he considered a detestable social experiment, but also to provoke the workers into some sort of demonstration which would justify a more thorough official repression. Yet he hardly expected the holocaust which ensued.

While the government would have been happy to be done with the expensive Workshops and the pestiferous clubs, the idea of a violent showdown gave it pause. The executive commission spent a great deal of its time in the five weeks after May 15 organizing military detachments in and around the capital (and did, as events bore out, none too efficient a job of it). But at the same time, the government resisted pressure for dissolution of the Workshops, and countered prods from the Assembly with promises of further economies. Yet the executive commission was unable to deflect the movement toward violent conflict. It was the sort of job which Lamartine might have undertaken in days gone by. But Lamartine's electoral successes marked the zenith of his political effectiveness. He had squandered most of his political credit when he forced the

Assembly to vote Ledru-Rollin into the executive commission, and now, as crisis approached, Lamartine was pathetically powerless, and generally ignored.

The impulse toward a showdown was not confined to conservatives. The Parisian workers were defensive about the Workshops, but they were also frustrated by the course of events. The majority of Frenchmen had decisively rejected the idea of a social republic, and the Assembly was devoting itself to carrying out the voters' mandate. Orthodox political action seemed futile, and the mystique of revolution was thus all the more attractive. Moreover, the conspicuous troop movements around the capital did not intimidate working-class radicals, but angered them. Rumors flew that the government was preparing to massacre the people. Naturally, such attitudes thrived in a city wracked with unemployment, in which depression-level wages made physical subsistence a daily struggle for thousands upon thousands.

On June 21, the government finally buckled under pressure from the Assembly and dissolved the National Workshops. The decree left those enrolled in the Workshops the options of employment on provincial public works projects, army service, or unemployment. It took nearly forty-eight hours for radical opinion to formulate a response, and they are forty-eight hours about which historians know embarrassingly little. On the evening of the 21st, a group of former delegates to the Luxembourg Commission called for a giant protest demonstration on the following day. The demonstration was in fact rather small, and did little else besides troop around the city all day. That evening, a permanent denizen of the radical clubs by the name of Pujol suggested another demonstration for June 23 at the Place de la Bastille, in the heart of the working-class district. It was after this gathering on the 23rd, where Pujol apparently extolled the virtue of revolt in the most violent language, that the crowds dispersed and began to build barricades all across the city. Just what spark set them off is still impossible to say, though clearly the flammable material was there.

For three days Paris experienced widespread and bitter fighting before the government finally crushed the rebels. The Assembly turned over full powers to the minister of war, General Eugène Cavaignac, who coolly waited while the insurrectionists concentrated themselves before launching his attack. Government figures claimed that two thousand rebels were killed, almost certainly an underestimate. Another fifteen thousand persons were arrested, although here many were dragged in on suspicion alone and doubtless had no connection with revolt. With such imprecise materials describing the rebels, it is difficult to say with much confidence who they were. It does seem clear that they were by no means exclusively working class, nor were the anti-rebel forces solely from the ranks of the propertied. A few National Guard units supported the rising, most opposed it. For all the bourgeois radicals who cropped up on the rebels' side, however, the uprising was still primarily a working-class affair. The National Workshops themselves do not seem to have contributed many men to the barricades, perhaps because of the government's decision to continue paying Workshop wages during the insurrection, an interesting commentary on the issues behind the fighting which supposedly broke out over the dissolution of the Workshops. Since Paris was primarily an artisanal city rather than a factory town, it is natural that mostly artisans of one kind or another show up in the ranks of the arrested. But it is also fascinating that such an extraordinarily high proportion of workers from the new industries, and particularly from the railroads, show up on these lists.

Contemporary observers of all political persuasions were united in an evaluation of these events that horrifies historians concerned with making fine discriminations about the social composition of crowds. For contemporaries saw the June Days as class war, pure and simple. The idea has its attractions: just what specific goals the rebels had, if any, have never been clear, but they made their hate for property-owning bourgeois society perfectly plain; the supporters of order were equally direct in their expressions of disgust for the lower classes and their determination to protect the current structure of society and distribution of property. Scholarly research may well prove the contemporaries wrong, yet the very fact that their evaluation was so widely shared is an indicator of the prevailing intensity of social stress and even of class hatred.

It is easy to mistake the June Days for the last gasp of social radicalism in France, since the defeat of the insurgents was so decisive. Indeed, many historians have virtually terminated their accounts of the revolution of 1848 with the defeat of the Parisian insurrection. But this approach will not do. Even a glance at French history of the next few years clearly reveals that the forces which inspired the revolution were far from dead, though for the rest of

1848 they were certainly in abeyance. Both liberals and radicals continued to exist. In some places they thrived, and conservatives were far from ignorant of their presence.

The familiar picture of France during the early months of the Second Republic is one of Parisian turbulence and provincial concern for order. To some extent, this is accurate. The provinces indubitably gave a mandate for order in April. When news of the June Days reached the provinces, a number of spontaneously-organized armed contingents prepared to march on the capital and put an end to Parisian radicalism once and for all. But rural and small-town France were at the same time undergoing changes which few Frenchmen could have perceived, much less understood. Perhaps the best way to characterize those changes is with the concept of "politicization." The great masses of Frenchmen were coming to political awareness, were starting to realize that their hitherto purely local concerns had national significance, starting to grasp the fact that their grievances were in some way related to other persons' grievances elsewhere and related also to the way in which political power was being exercised on a national scale.

Surely the critical factor in the process of politicization was increased communication. The newly-freed press, the lifting of restrictions on assembly, the electoral campaigns of 1848 and 1849 all served to intensify communication and to keep political issues constantly before the French people. In some cases, politicization only fortified natural conservatism; but elsewhere, it amounted to radicalization. The process took time—indeed it was not fully completed for a generation. Still, by the election to the Legislative Assembly in May 1849, the provinces were demonstrating both a political interest and, in some pockets, a degree of radicalism that were clearly new. In these circumstances, conservatives could hardly afford to rest easy after the June Days.

In the other revolutionary countries of Europe, it is reasonably easy to assign something like a terminal date to the revolutions, to pinpoint rather closely the triumph of reaction by the military defeat of the rebels or some such decisive event. In France, this is much more difficult to do. The danger of revolution remained a live issue in France as late as 1852. Thus, it is almost impossible to disentangle the story of the struggle between reaction and revolution from the story of the developments which led to the establishment of the Second Empire.

It is true that, in the last half of 1848, radicalism went into momentary eclipse. There was a noticeable lag between the destruction of Parisian radicalism and the development of a provincial counterpart. Politics in the meantime settled down to a contest within the Assembly between the conservative majority and the moderate republicans. When General Cavaignac had crushed the revolt, the Assembly discovered that it had no one to replace him. There was no conservative who could yet play the role of strong man, so that there was little choice but to charge Cavaignac with the formation of a ministry. Cavaignac's brother, who died a few years earlier, had been one of the leaders of radical republicanism and a friend of Ledru-Rollin. The General, however, was squarely in the camp of *Le National,* a firm opponent of radicalism and socialism, and he drew his ministry largely from the ranks of the moderate republicans. The moderates thus controlled the government for over five months, serving at the pleasure of a predominantly conservative and monarchist Assembly. It was a peculiar situation, arising both from the notion that Cavaignac was the only strong executive who could keep the lid on social radicalism and from the fact that the monarchists were not yet ready to bid for control of the government. There were serious dissensions within the conservative camp, and with a monarchist restoration out of the question, there was a problem of leadership on the right. As it happened, Cavaignac proved to be something of an annoyance to the conservatives. He did indeed suppress the left-wing clubs and newspapers, but he choked off some of the reactionary journals as well. His government even put forward a program of mild social reform. To have voted down all these reforms would have run the risk of provoking Cavaignac's resignation, and as yet the right was not ready to move in.

The Assembly's principal charge had been to draw up a new constitution, and in November it completed its work. The monarchists had little alternative but to go along with a republican form, though they were able to resist such concessions to radicalism as a constitutional guarantee of the right to work. In general, however, they acquiesced to a predominantly democratic constitution, featuring universal suffrage and such republican trademarks as a unicameral legislature. The majority's position with regard to the constitution is not entirely clear. Perhaps it felt strong enough to offer concessions to political democracy as long as social order could be maintained. Or perhaps, as Thiers remarked a decade later, they did not take the constitution seriously at all and assumed that it was an "ephemeral" document.

One of the most controversial constitutional provisions was that for popular election of the President of the Republic. Critics of the provision have maintained that it set up a counterforce to the parliament, complete with popular mandate, without at the same time establishing means for resolution of a conflict between the two institutions. But the concern for order was strong in the Assembly, and it was generally supposed that order could come only (in the absence of a monarch) from an executive legitimized by popular election and with some independence from the legislature. Opponents suggested instead appointment of the President by the legislature itself, but the centralization of virtually all power in the Assembly was widely feared. Amidst grumblings that the constitution could bring a new revolution if President and legislature came into conflict, the provision on the executive power was passed by a large majority.

Discussion of the presidential election entails the introduction of an entirely new theme, the sudden rise to prominence and power of Prince Louis-Napoleon Bonaparte. Nephew and heir to Napoleon I, Prince Louis-Napoleon made two abortive attempts to overthrow the July Monarchy, in 1836 and 1840; the last cost him several years in a French jail before escaping to England. The utter failure of these ventures led him to depend henceforth upon legal means in his single-minded quest for power; the events of 1848 gave him his opportunity. In the June 1848 by-elections, while he was still in England, Louis-Napoleon was elected to the French Assembly by four different *départements*. Republicans and monarchists alike feared the implications of his election, and raised some furor. From his exile, the Prince resigned his seats, for which he had not in any case campaigned formally (though Bonapartist agents had conducted a small effort on his behalf). But in the by-election of September, he was elected for five different constituencies, and this time he decided to accept.

Once French politicians got a look at Louis-Napoleon, they may have been slightly embarrassed that they had ever taken him seriously. At forty years of age, he was of a totally unprepossessing physical appearance, and in his first remarks before the Assembly he spoke haltingly and with a rather pronounced German accent.

Small clusters of sympathizers were cranking out mountains of Bonapartist propaganda, evoking the glories associated with the Empire. But it should also be recalled that the Prince was at first the object of numerous jokes, cartoons, and general ridicule.

Once the constitution had been voted, on November 4, all attention turned to the presidential election, scheduled for December 10. There were no less than four republican candidates: Cavaignac, representing the moderates; Ledru-Rollin, the radicals; François Raspail, the socialists who had broken with Ledru-Rollin; and Lamartine, representing his faded hopes of the summer. The conservatives were anxious to unite behind a single candidate. They had even momentarily considered Cavaignac, who refused their conditions and emphasized once more his fundamentally republican convictions. Thiers himself was a possibility, but there was concern about his identification with the discredited July Monarchy. Surprisingly, Louis Napoleon seemed the only acceptable candidate with a good chance of victory. He openly courted the support of the conservative organization, the Réunion de la rue de Poitiers, and accepted its conditions; he even discussed the possibility of naming Odilon Barrot to form a government. In several meetings, he dispelled the image of himself as a political clown, though the conservatives still expected to control him at their will. Legitimists and Orléanists had to struggle with dynastic scruple, but the Prince had two strong things in his favor: he was clearly on the side of order, and his popularity was undeniable and growing.

In his campaign, Louis-Napoleon made an appeal which offered something for everyone, but most for the forces of order. Yet at bottom, as historians have time and again been compelled to conclude, his greatest (and perhaps sufficient) political virtue was his name. It evoked French greatness, stability, and a guarantee of revolutionary gains without the disadvantages of revolution. An elaborate Napoleonic myth had been developing for more than a decade, and Louis-Napoleon cashed in on it. He received 5.3 million votes, and all his supporters combined drew less than 2 million. Cavaignac gained majorities in only four of the eighty-six *départements*, and Ledru-Rollin received less than 400,000 votes.

But the staggering size of Louis-Napoleon's mandate can easily be misleading; in many respects, it represented a vote for a legend, and did not accurately reflect the strength of the various political persuasions represented by the other four candidates. Democratic radicalism had no chance against a name like Bonaparte, but in other circumstances it could command far more than the 400,000 votes given Ledru-Rollin and Raspail together. Politicized dissatisfaction was growing rapidly in much of provincial France, and the radicals were working hard to regroup. *Solidarité républicain,* Ledru-Rollin's campaign organization, remained intact. Indeed, it grew stronger, while preparing for the election which was anticipated upon dissolution of the Assembly and which provided a convenient pretext for an exaggerated left-wing scare. The government therefore dissolved *Solidarité républicain,* but not the forces it represented.

The strongly pro-Church Legitimists were an important part of the rue de Poitiers group, and one of the conditions they laid down to which Louis-Napoleon agreed was to maintain the temporal power of the Papacy. This power had of course been challenged by the December revolution in Rome and the subsequent establishment of the Roman Republic. While the question of temporal power concerned the conservatives, the prospect of an Austrian repression of the Roman Republic also raised fears about Hapsburg influence in Italy. The way was thus eased for the government's decision in April 1849 to intervene in Rome on the Pope's behalf. Naturally, the announcement touched off outrage among the republicans; but French nationalists thirsted for some foreign venture, and were excited at the prospect of reestablishing French influence in Italy. Moreover, French troops lost their first engagement with the Italian republicans so that the expedition now became an affair of honor. Conservatives could claim in the election campaign that radicals who opposed intervention were unpatriotic.

Still, the charge carried little weight in some important sections of French society. The May election revealed to what a surprising extent democratic convictions had taken hold. In broader terms, it showed a clear process of polarization, one which was virtually extinguishing the moderate republicans. Of the 750 seats at stake in the new Legislative Assembly, moderates gained less than 100. The conservatives took over 450; even Odilon Barrot estimated that, as a group, they tended to be to the right of him. The "demo-soc" contingent, the so-called Montagnard radical democrats and the various socialists, showed astounding strength with roughly 200 seats. Indeed, the demo-soc showing was so strong that many conservatives—in spite of their own substantial majority—were plunged into depression. The radicals had drawn much support from rural and small-town France, areas which had voted for conservatives in April and for Louis-Napoleon in December. The impact of mass politicization was now beginning to be felt on a national level.

During the next two and a half years, two general issues dominated French politics: the "red scare" and, less visible at first, a growing struggle between President and Parliament. Ultimately, the issues became one, as Louis-Napoleon used the fear of left-wing revolution to consolidate his personal power at the expense of the legislature's. At first, however, attention centered on resurgent radicalism.

In the May 1849 election, Ledru-Rollin had been elected by five *départements* with a total of two million votes. This sort of support emboldened him to exaggerate the strength of the left, and he seems to have thought that he could intimidate the government with a mere show of numbers. On June 13, he planned a large (though peaceful) demonstration in Paris; but his description of it had the ring of an announcement of revolution—Ledru-Rollin was frequently given to such mercurial oratorical performances—and some of his overheated disciples supposed that the moment of truth had arrived. There was a handful of what hardly seem like more than scuffles in the capital, mostly involving left-wing National Guardsmen, while Montagnard leaders stood by stunned. Ledru-Rollin was as surprised as anyone that his remarks had caused trouble, though he proclaimed of the troublemakers: "I am their leader. I must follow them." This pathetic little affair gave the authorities an excellent excuse for action. There were large-scale arrests in Paris, and Ledru-Rollin himself fled into exile; in the provinces, the government took the opportunity to act against republican organization. Moreover, the repression continued for more than two years. Authorities undertook a campaign of prosecutions against radical newspapers, and the government steadily weeded out bureaucrats who had been appointed in 1848. In mid-1850, the Assembly qualified universal suffrage by putting a three-year residence requirement on the franchise, thus striking against the usually transient (and presumably radical) urban poor; the new law disenfranchised nearly three million voters. Political clubs, already under strict controls dating from the Cavaignac regime, were now virtually abolished, even during the election campaigns.

The fact that such vigorous repression could not destroy republicanism is further testimony to the impact of 1848 upon France.

Government and legislature alike labored to break the back of the radical movement. But the left continued to return a few candidates to the Assembly at each of the periodic by-elections for vacated seats, only further frustrating and frightening the right. Partly, of course, severe repression only prompted the left to close ranks and work all the harder. But also, the conservatives were looking in the wrong place. The core of the republican movement was not to be found in clubs or newspapers or among petty bureaucrats. It lay rather in deep-seated social and economic grievances among large masses of people in big cities, in small towns, and even in the countryside. The grievances were diverse—bread prices, land hunger, usury, unemployment, working conditions—and often purely local in origin. In one sense, they had little to do with republicanism and democracy, and indeed they often occurred among people who had voted for conservatives in April 1848. But the politicizing processes of the revolution gave those aggrieved people new channels for their protest, and new symbols against which to direct it. Thus it took often a left-wing, and certainly an anti-governmental, direction.

As the radical menace stubbornly refused to disappear, conservatives began to fear a new upheaval. They even thought they could date its eruption: it would be in 1852, the year in which the terms of both the President and the Legislative Assembly would expire. Article 45 of the constitution forbade consecutive terms by the same President. It seemed a tailor-made opportunity for a new radical offensive. This odd quirk of events began to obsess the supporters of order, and yet many of them resisted the suggestion put forward by Louis-Napoleon himself: that is, simply change the constitution. Conservative deputies, many of them Orléanist liberals, had a genuine commitment to parliamentarism, even though they stopped far short of democracy. They had watched Louis-Napoleon gradually aggrandize executive power—principally, beginning in October 1849, by appointing a new ministry of men devoted first of all to himself —and they suspected that in the back of his mind was a new Bonapartist regime, a second Empire. Given that prospect, many of them preferred a conservative republic. While the President's proposal won a simple majority in the Assembly, it fell short of the three-fourths vote required for constitutional revision.

Louis-Napoleon's parliamentary defeat may have been a blessing in disguise for him. Conservative segments in society at large, badly rattled at the prospect of a new revolutionary surge, were less jealous of parliamentary prerogative in the face of a more serious threat to the status quo. When the Assembly blocked legal revision, and seemingly the perpetuation of a strong executive dedicated to order, many persons were probably increasingly prepared to have order by whatever means. The President himself disliked the idea of extralegal means; it meant altering the image that he had carefully constructed for three years. But he saw no future in the existing constitutional structure, and he sincerely believed that a more powerful executive could bring France both order and liberty. Republican legend has painted the *coup d'état* of December 1851 as a crude power grab, pure and simple. But the evidence strongly suggests that Louis-Napoleon actually undertook it only with reluctance, and in the last analysis only because dictatorship seemed to him the sole alternative to rampant disorder.

The *coup* of December 2, 1851, began with a proclamation announcing the dissolution of the Assembly, the restoration of universal suffrage, and the promise of a new constitution to be submitted to the nation for approval by plebiscite. Many persons who could hardly be described as Bonapartist accepted it as preferable to what they saw as inevitable revolution. Yet the *coup* did not go uncontested; indeed, it provoked what may well have been the largest single popular protest of nineteenth-century France.

The national response to the *coup d'état* has not yet found its historian, so that it is difficult to generalize about it with any confidence. In Paris, the government was reasonably well-prepared for protest, much of which it anticipated by rounding up potential troublemakers—including nearly two hundred deputies—before they could do much damage. There was some attempt at violent resistance among the republicans of the capital, but the government crushed it with overwhelmingly superior forces. In the provinces, however, the government was less well-organized, and forces hostile to the *coup* were able to mount what easily passed for an insurrection, and incidentally seemed to give added justification to the *coup* itself.

Provincial resistance seems to have been of two kinds. On the one hand, there were left-wing militants, concentrated largely in the cities, who were fighting political extinction. On the other, there were peasants and small-town artisans, who had been feeling the squeeze of economic conditions, whose motives were less clear and for that matter probably varied widely from place to place. Perhaps they were simply translating this economic dissatisfaction into the most convenient political terms—a protest against authority. Perhaps they represented genuine converts to democratic republicanism. Or perhaps the predominance of traditional craftsmen and of small-town businessmen in the ranks of the insurgents suggests that their protest may have been against the centralizing, modernizing tendencies of which the *coup* was broadly representative. Such men still looked back to the traditional society in which their existence had been more secure and stable, to a time before urbanization, industrialization, and centralization threatened that existence.

One thing is certain, however: the scope of the protest points to very serious and deeply-rooted discontent. About 100,000 men struck out violently against the *coup,* and the government was forced to arrest over one-fourth of them in the course of its repression. In many places, the insurgents were able to capture and hold briefly the local town. On occasion, they even established their own municipal governments, showing clearly that the revolts were far from being aimlessly apolitical. The government ultimately prevailed, though only after the commitment of sizeable troop detachments to the provinces. Once the mopping up had been completed, roughly 20,000 were convicted, of whom half were shipped off to Algeria. For the time being, the republican movement was broken; within a generation, it demonstrated remarkable powers of recovery, though with a largely new personnel from top to bottom.

By 1852, the revolution of 1848 and the repercussions it set off were well in hand; but they were not in the hands of a revivified old regime. It is true that the political class of Louis-Napoleon's new Empire, formally proclaimed at the end of 1852, included a good many Orléanists. But structurally, the Empire represented some substantial changes over the July Monarchy, especially in the relative power of monarch and parliament. And new economic forces—a remarkable spurt of industrialization, conducted with enthusiastic government support—made the new regime anything but a restoration. The revolution had failed to perpetuate the democratic republic; but it had helped decisively to change France.

Prussia and German Unity

If there was anything like a turning-point for the revolution in Germany, it came early in September 1848 over the crisis of the Danish war. The very sovereignty of the Frankfurt Parliament was at stake. Any momentum the revolution still retained was surely lost when the Parliament reluctantly accepted the armistice of Malmö and thus admitted the fragility of its authority. It is tempting to view subsequent efforts at reform in Germany as futile, and indeed the Parliament may well have lost what moral basis and political initiative it once had. And yet, initiative had not yet passed to reaction, though the revolution had clearly lost it. The Frankfurt Parliament continued to sit. None of the rulers of individual states felt strong enough to move against their liberal governments, though events would soon provide Friedrich Wilhelm IV with an opportunity. Until he took it, the confrontation between revolution and counterrevolution remained in a state of suspension.

The March coalition between artisans and middle-class liberals had certainly unravelled by autumn. Not only were the liberals ideologically sympathetic to the idea of economic freedom, as opposed to the principle of guild regulations. They also tended to think largely in political terms. The artisan movement, however, centered almost exclusively on economic and social questions, losing touch even with the left-wing democrats. When a congress of German democrats (representing mostly radical political clubs of the cities) met in Berlin in October, it paid little attention to matters of social reform. The various artisan congresses dealt hardly at all with politics. Moreover, the artisan movement itself was definitively split. Masters and well-established independent craftsmen continued to direct their appeal to the authorities—whether Frankfurt Parliament or the individual states—while journeymen increasingly despaired of a sympathetic hearing from officialdom and began to talk of "self-help." Finally, more impersonal forces were beginning to take the steam out of laboring-class militancy. During the summer of 1848, food prices dropped, production increased, jobs began to open up once more. Conditions did not improve enough to pacify the artisanate completely—the revolution had carried them beyond mere protest. But the economic upswing did take some of the urgency out of the movement.

The Hansemann ministry in Prussia, caught between the large radical contingent in the Prussian Assembly and a growing reactionary movement, was finding it hard to set a middle course. Hansemann attempted a program of reform against rural social grievances, which called for an end to tax-exempt status for many forms of aristocratic property, and proposed the liberalization of local government. In both cases, the radicals insisted on more, and the right stiffened. The left did achieve occasional rapport with the Berlin working classes, but the links were never strong enough to build a truly broad movement. The right had begun to organize quite self-consciously in midsummer, and created a forum in a Berlin daily newspaper, the *Neue Preussische Zeitung* (popularly known as the *Kreuzzeitung*).

It was a delicate situation for Hansemann, and by early autumn he could no longer control it. At the end of July, in the Silesian town of Schweideritz, there had been a small clash between the local (and newly formed) civilian guards and the regular troops garrisoned there. The troops had precipitously fired on the guard, killing fourteen. Radicals in the Prussian Assembly seized on this occasion to attack the military, bastion of reaction. They forced through a resolution denouncing the army for reactionary tendencies, and insisting that it prove its dedication to constitutionalism; officers who could not accept the resolution were invited to resign. Hansemann was understandably anxious to avoid a direct confrontation with the army. He tried at first to ignore the resolution, and then to sidestep it by promising to attend to the incident through the Ministry of War. The left held firm, and demanded execution of its resolution. On September 9, Hansemann's cabinet resigned.

The month of September clearly marked the opening of a reactionary counteroffensive, and Friedrich Wilhelm began to move against the revolution. After defying the Frankfurt Parliament with the Armistice of Malmö, he defied the anti-militarist radicals in the Prussian Assembly by calling General Wrangel to the command of the troops near the capital—the same General Wrangel who had led the troops against the Berlin uprising. The king's choice of a new chief minister was a bit less uncompromising. He named Hermann von Beckerath, then serving as Minister of Finances in Archduke Johann's provisional government of the Reich. It was apparently a gesture of conciliation to Frankfurt. But it never fully materialized, for the reactionaries smelled blood. When Beckerath, while trying to form a cabinet, urged that the king accept a liberal constitution, they persuaded Friedrich to resist. Beckerath withdrew, and the king then called upon General von Pfuel, the man who had helped crush the Polish insurrection. Pfuel compounded this provocation of the radicals in the Assembly by forming a cabinet of non-parliamentarians—mostly royal bureaucrats, of decidedly conservative leanings.

With so much power still in the king's hands, and with liberals and democrats so badly divided, the triumph of Prussian reaction now proved to be relatively easy. Working-class disorders in Berlin provided the occasion for the next move. As employment opportunities reappeared and wages began to rise in the autumn of 1848, the government took the opportunity to cut back its welfare budget accordingly. The laboring poor of the city naturally protested. There were disturbances, erupting into violence on October 16 when the Civil Guard—the middle-class force born of the March Days—killed eleven workers. It was the same old story, in which middle-class liberals refused to countenance popular disorder. In Berlin, however, the democratic left was equally quick to dissociate itself from the workers. After the incident of the 16th, the situation in Berlin remained tense; further troubles were widely expected. They came two weeks later, during another workers' demonstration. This time the demonstrators seem to have been intent upon avoiding violence. But the Civil Guard panicked, and fired into the crowd.

What had been in fact the last gasp of popular agitation in Berlin, the government treated as the prologue to insurrection. On November 2, the king replaced General von Pfuel with yet another army officer, Count Friedrich Wilhelm von Brandenburg, a stern reactionary. On November 10, General von Wrangel returned to Berlin with his troops—and encountered no resistance. He promptly declared a state of siege. The government thereupon disbanded the Civil Guard, suppressed left-wing newspapers, and clamped down on public political meetings. To all this, the protest remained strictly verbal. In a matter of days, virtually all traces of the revolution had been wiped out, leaving only the Prussian Assembly. It was allowed to carry on, but not in Berlin. The government dispatched it to the town of Brandenburg, west of the capital, where it conducted its debates in relative isolation and obscurity.

Few could have doubted that the Assembly's days were numbered. On December 5, the King dissolved it and promulgated a constitution drawn up not by the Assembly, but by the government. The royal constitution nodded to the principles of liberalism: there was a bicameral legislature, with the lower house chosen by universal suffrage. Ministers, however, were responsible not to the legislature but to the crown, which also retained wide executive jurisdiction (including total control of the army and substantial decree powers). Moreover, the franchise was rigged to property qualifications so that, in fact, something less than twenty per cent of the electorate controlled two-thirds of the seats in the lower house.

From one perspective, the Prussian revolution collapsed because the various groups which supported it could not unite to hold it up. Liberals and workers alike welcomed the return of von Wrangel's troops—the liberals because they saw the army as a more efficient force for order in the capital, the workers because they were relieved at the displacement of the Civil Guard. The radicals in the Prussian Assembly had been unwilling to cooperate with the Camphausen and Hansemann ministries, and unable to build any meaningful ties with the Berlin workers. Unlike their counterparts of the French left, the Berlin radicals were more politically-minded than they were concerned with social reform. During the time of the working-class disturbances of October, Prussian democrats were busy voting to strike the phrase "by the grace of God" from Friedrich Wilhelm IV's title and expressing their support of the besieged radicals of Vienna.

From another perspective, however, it is easy to be fatalistic about the triumph of reaction in Prussia. The March revolution had not really gone very far. For that matter, had Wrangel been given free reign, he could probably have mastered the streets in another day or two. In any case, the revolution had left royal power and its most important adjunct, the military, intact. The counterrevolutionaries throughout, however, controlled the most important instrument of coercion—indeed, the only one outside the Civil Guard—and in the absence of a broad revolutionary coalition its ultimate victory ought never to have been in doubt. Friedrich Wilhelm could probably have carried off a successful *coup* when the Camphausen ministry fell. But the King had been intimidated by the March Days and equally by the Prussian election. Besides, he genuinely wished to avoid a bloody civil war. Like the old regime elsewhere, the Prussian regime needed above all a return of self-confidence before it could act. And that return came when the revolution—both in Berlin and in Frankfurt—began to reveal its own weakness.

The Prussian revolution was dead; the dissatisfactions from which it had sprung were not, as the reactionaries well realized. For all the severity of the reaction and the biases of the new electoral law, the right could not turn the election to the new Prussian Landtag into a rout. They did gain a majority, but liberals and radicals together collected about 160 of the nearly 350 seats; all 9 seats in the capital went to the democrats. Anxious to avoid a new uprising, and skeptical of the wisdom of pure repression, the Brandenburg government set out on a policy of calculated social conciliation. Reforms were aimed at the two most volatile groups, the peasantry and the artisanate. Prussian conservatives had not been miraculously converted into liberal reformers; they had developed into more realistic politicians. One of the most reactionary members of the new cabinet, Minister of the Interior Otto von Manteuffel, was also the driving force behind rural social reform. He urged a hesitant king and a reluctant aristocracy to accept the commutation of the remaining manorial obligations to which the peasantry was subject and a variety of other measures designed to alleviate rural unrest. At the same time, Minister of Commerce August von der Heydt inspired the decrees of February 1849 which partially nullified the free-trade *Gewerbeordnung* of 1845 and reestablished certain guild rights and jurisdictions.

The policy was not unique to Prussia. In the smaller German states, the petty rulers too began to gain confidence, and one by one began to displace the liberal ministries of March. In so doing, however, they blended reconsolidation of princely power with paternalistic reform. Everywhere the pattern included concessions to peasant irritation over certain seigneurial rights and reintroduction of some modified guild rights. It is worth noting in passing that the guild reforms were generally keyed to the demands of master craftsmen and represented more a return to the systems that had once prevailed rather than a liberalization of them as journeymen had generally wished. In any event, with their efforts to mollify social discontent, the petty rulers not only helped keep the lid on potentially revolutionary forces. They also made some progress in cementing dynastic loyalty, only further complicating the unifying efforts of the Frankfurt Parliament.

The Parliament's situation was very bad indeed. Reaction was ascendant in Vienna and Berlin, the power loci of central Europe, and liberalism was clearly on the run in the smaller German states. As long as Prussia was busy consolidating its conservative recovery and the Hapsburgs were absorbed by the Hungarian war, the Parliament could expect to complete its constitutional labors unimpeded. But what they would do with the new constitution was not clear. The Schwarzenberg government made clear its intention to maintain the Empire, so that the *grossdeutsch* solution to German unity was no longer possible. At the same time, the liberals had all but lost their leverage in the individual German states. In these circumstances, the constitution voted on March 27 tends to be of only academic interest.

The Frankfurt Constitution envisaged a federal state under an hereditary Emperor, with considerable autonomy for the member states (each of which would have its own legislature). The national parliament featured a lower house to be elected by universal suffrage, and an upper house of appointees chosen by the state governments and legislatures. The federal government—which would control Reich foreign policy, the military, and general economic policy—was responsible to the parliament. It was a characteristically liberal constitution, except perhaps for its concession in the matter of universal suffrage. But by spring 1849 the prospect of acceptance looked more remote than ever.

The weakness of the Assembly is clear enough. What should also be kept in mind is the weak position of the smaller states. In most of them, the dynasties naturally dreaded elimination, or even the inevitable reduction in status that was bound to come with federalism on the Frankfurt plan. But they, too, lacked leverage. Now could they resist unification if some larger power—say, Prussia—desired it? Indeed, one day after accepting the constitution, the Frankfurt Parliament "elected" Friedrich Wilhelm IV Emperor of the new German Reich. It was, to be sure, a decision reached reluctantly on the part of most liberals, who had few illusions about what had been going on in Prussia since November. But it also seemed the only possible choice.

It would have been one thing to serve as Emperor of all Germany in March of 1848; it was quite another in 1849, with conservative forces widely reestablished. The terms were not totally unattractive: they amounted to the opportunity for Prussian ascendancy over Germany (though the Frankfurt liberals would not have thought of it that way). With the exception of the little *Kreuzzeitung* party on the extreme right, spokesmen of all persuasions of Prussian politics urged their King to accept the offer, at least in principle, perhaps subject to some minor modifications. Friedrich Wilhelm, on the other hand, had already announced in private his feelings about accepting a *Schweinkrone,* as he called it, offered to him by "master bakers and butchers." He had vowed that the unification of Germany could only be accomplished by his peers, the princes, and not by the masses. But the mood of the Prussian public gave him pause when the delegation from Frankfurt offered him the crown. Instead of a flat refusal, he virtually left the decision up to his brother princes: if they could accept the constitution, he could accept the crown. Not unnaturally, the parliamentary delegates took this response for a refusal.

Their colleagues in Frankfurt were not so sure. They saw a ray of hope in Friedrich Wilhelm's response, and began to work on the smaller states for acceptance of the constitution. The petty dynasties were similarly puzzled by the Prussian King's declaration. Should they take it for an invitation to reject the Frankfurt constitution? Or should they take it as a veiled willingness to assume leadership of Germany? Most of the small states, to Friedrich Wilhelm's embarrassment, decided upon the second interpretation, although the middling states—Hanover, Saxony, and Bavaria—all resisted acceptance.

Friedrich Wilhelm decided at this juncture that he had left the door ajar when he should have closed it firmly. Actually, the resistance of the middle-sized states provided him with sufficient excuse for clarifying his earlier declaration. But he preferred to offer an ideological excuse, which was probably more candid. He could not, he announced in late April 1849, accept a crown from a popularly elected assembly. At the same time, conservative elements which had urged an affirmative response to the original offer now began to reconsider the implication of accepting the Frankfurt constitution. The Prussian lower house was still favorable, and therefore the government dissolved it. The struggle for unity was over.

Most of the Frankfurt liberals realized it, and gave up the ghost. When their governments did not formally withdraw them from the Parliament, they simply went home on their own. Only the little knot of democrats held on, although they decided to adjourn the rump Parliament to the presumably more sympathetic environment of Stuttgart. From there, they pathetically appealed for a new revolution to rid Germany of the old regime once and for all. It was the occasion for a final spasm on the left. There were risings in eight or ten cities, some of them silly little skirmishes led by radical ideologues, some of them more substantial affairs. In portions of the southwest, a few army divisions even went over to the democrats; in Dresden, democratic rebels momentarily deposed the King of

Saxony. In several cases, Prussian help was necessary to put down insurrections; while they were at it, the Prussians scattered what little remained of the Parliament in Stuttgart.

The important point to be made about the troubles of 1849, however, was that they included so few of the groups which had made the revolutions of 1848. The peasantry stayed aloof, and with but a few exceptions the artisanate was only marginally involved. The insurgents of 1849 were more often lower middle-class types, political democrats and republicans; the revolutionary fervor had long since been drained from the German masses.

There was a coda to the German unification movement, played out in 1849–50, which deserves some mention since it demonstrated that conservatism and particularism were not necessarily synonymous, at least in Prussia. One of Friedrich Wilhelm's closest advisors, Count Josef von Radowitz, convinced his King that a policy of unification under conservative auspices was feasible. His plan was for something more than the old Confederation, something less than the Frankfurt model. First it envisaged Prussia at the head of a medium-sized, unified confederation, and second, a larger confederation still which would include Austria and which existed primarily for the sake of foreign policy. Prussia used its assistance to Saxony and Hanover in the repression of 1849 to extract their agreement. Radowitz drew up a constitution for this new Bund, and invited the other states to send delegates to a new German parliament in Erfurt.

The lesser states doubtless felt pressure from Prussia to accept this odd new scheme, even though some right-wing Prussian particularists and political opponents of the more moderate Radowitz opposed it. But the small and middling states of the south also had support from Austria. Schwarzenberg had always been opposed to German unification, and he sought to restore the weaker Confederation of old on the Empire's northern border. His backing encouraged Bavaria and Württemberg to refuse the invitation to the Erfurt Parliament, and their decision eased the way for the withdrawal of Saxony and Hanover. The Parliament met, in March 1850, with representatives only from Prussia and a handful of the smallest states. Meanwhile, Schwarzenberg engineered a counter-parliament in Frankfurt, meant to prepare the restoration of the old Diet of the Confederation.

In these circumstances, it was pointless for the Erfurt Parliament to continue, and conservatives in Prussia who had originally approved the idea now urged its abandonment. But Radowitz and Friedrich Wilhelm clung to it, and Schwarzenberg was equally stubborn on his side. A showdown seemed inevitable. It nearly came some months later when the ruler of Hesse-Cassel, who had aligned with the Austrians, appealed to the Frankfurt Diet for assistance in a dispute with his parliament. The Erfurt Parliament claimed an equal right to Frankfurt's. There was an impasse, hot words were exchanged between Vienna and Berlin, and troops on both sides mobilized.

The war for German unification could have been fought in November 1850 rather than 1866 had Friedrich Wilhelm not decided to back down. Support within his own ruling elite was hardly unanimous, and Russia, no friend of German unification, was ominously siding with Austria. Friedrich Wilhelm IV finally decided to dismiss Radowitz and accede to the Hapsburg plan for restoration of the old German Confederation.

Like so much else in 1848, this last act of the German revolution clearly anticipated developments of the next generation. German unification, it seemed obvious, would have to be achieved by military means, if dynastic particularism and Hapsburg antagonism were to be overcome. Moreover, since Prussia alone had the military resources with which to stand up to the Hapsburgs, unification would demand Prussian leadership. And that in turn entailed that a unified Germany would have to be created on terms acceptable first of all to the Prussian monarchy and aristocracy. 1848 did not achieve German unification. But by apparently eliminating the option of liberal constitutionalism, it pointed out plainly the path that unification would have to take.

The Roman Republic

The battle of Custozza had exploded the dreams of Italian nationalism in 1848. Custozza's sorry sequel, the battle of Novara, likewise cut short the republican epilogue to the revolutions. This definitive reestablishment of Hapsburg military power in Italy left the republicans in Rome, Florence, and Venice without much hope, though they carried on the fight into the summer of 1849. In general, the story of their defeat, like so much of the story of Italy during the revolutionary year, is a military narrative, and can be quickly told. Even the famous Roman Republic merits attention more for its drama and episodes of heroism than for its intrinsic historical significance.

The principal Austrian effort was directed at Venice. After a lengthy blockade and bombardment of the city, Manin's republicans finally gave in late in August, surrendering the last stronghold of republicanism on the peninsula. The Austrians had also assisted Grand Duke Leopold of Tuscany in his struggle against the republicans who had chased him from Florence. At the end of May, Leopold retook the city, just after Neapolitan armies had conquered the Sicilian separatists in Palermo.

The most spectacular republican experiment had taken place in Rome. The democratic provisional government of Carlo Muzzarelli had staged elections to a Constituent Assembly, but many still loyal to the Pope viewed participation in the election as defiance of the Holy See. Abstentionism among moderates was high, and the Assembly was lopsidedly republican. Even though the Assembly proclaimed the Roman Republic in February 1849, there was some hope that Pius IX could be persuaded to return and make his peace with a constitutional government. His flight and continued absence not only alienated loyalists in Rome; it also troubled the European powers, who viewed the Pope as a legitimate sovereign displaced by revolution. There could be no doubt of Austrian hostility, of course, but in addition French Catholics were beginning to talk about intervention.

When Mazzini arrived in Rome in early March, he shared these concerns, though he did not share the desire for the return of the Pope. At best, he hoped to moderate the disturbances which marred the Republic's early months, especially the anti-clerical demonstrations and depredations upon church property. Made a member of a new ruling triumvirate on March 29, he tried to restore some semblance of order to the turbulent city and at least give the Republic a better reputation abroad.

Mazzini was no red republican. His impulses were basically political: the abolition of monarchy, the establishment of a republic, the achievement of national unity. He rejected socialism, and for that matter the conditions in Italy hardly existed which could give rise to such a persuasion. In a famous exhortation "To the Italian Working Class," written in 1860, Mazzini implored the workers to avoid "Materialism," which leads "through the worship of *self-*

interest, into egoism and anarchy." Mazzini was not ignorant of social unrest and during his brief period of power he inspired a number of social reforms—mostly to the benefit of the peasantry. But disorder offended his strong moral rectitude as well as his political sense. "Here in Rome," he said, "we may not be moral mediocrities."

Mazzini's efforts, to some extent successful, impressed neither the Pope nor the French. On April 20, Pius issued an allocution unequivocally condemning the republic. This document, known as *Quibus Quantisque,* not only dashed hopes of conciliation. It also marked out the main lines of Pius' Papacy for years to come, affirming the sanctity of Papal temporal power and repudiating liberalism and constitutionalism in almost every form. In many respects, it was a clear anticipation of Pius' famous *Syllabus of Errors* of fifteen years hence.

Louis-Napoleon had himself hoped Pius would make some compromise with constitutionalism, but the French President had already been formally committed to intervention by a vote in the National Assembly. On the same day that Pius issued *Quibus Quantisque,* the President issued orders for the French expeditionary force under General Oudinot to set sail for Rome. Had it not been the French, it would have been the Austrians and Neapolitans, and the republicans would have had as little chance against them.

The legendary defense of Rome, conducted by the famous republican and Italian nationalist Giuseppi Garibaldi, has been described at greater length and with greater eloquence than are possible here by the famous English historian G. M. Trevelyan. Garibaldi won some early victories, but was soon outnumbered and worn down by the French. He gave up resistance at the end of June 1849, and, after a series of incredible adventures finally escaped, though his troops were entirely destroyed and dispersed. Mazzini too escaped, though he refused to sign the formal surrender prepared by the Roman Assembly. The French occupied the city —and indeed a French contingent remained there until 1870—while Pius reestablished authoritarian government under a commission of three cardinals. The Pope himself did not return until April 1850.

Chapter 6

1848: Failure and Achievement

No feature of the revolutions of 1848 has attracted more attention than their failure—their failure, that is, to establish durable reforms, their failure to resist the countercharge of reactionary forces after such a short time in power. The apparently robust movements of February and March soon proved surprisingly frail, a development which has since prompted both regret and ridicule from historians and which gave Trevelyan the opportunity for a famous *mot:* "1848 was the turning-point at which modern history failed to turn."

The trouble with Trevelyan's remark is its implication that some odd quirk interrupted the natural development of historical forces. In point of fact, the revolutions represented nothing like a world historical movement that could no longer be denied. Shrewder, more flexible rulers could have denied them, at least temporarily, without much difficulty. Only archaic military planning and royal squeamishness about mass slaughter kept the armies from crushing the rebels at the very outset. Indeed, that there was streetfighting at all was in large part due to the stubbornness of the authorities and their clumsiness in resorting to force.

Inept leadership and mistaken judgment did have a large responsibility in the outbreak of the revolutions; one simply cannot review the record of February and March without admitting the role of these "accidental" elements. But there is danger in going too far in this direction too—in seeing the fact that revolution happened at all as a fluke, an illusion, or, as the Comte de Falloux facetiously put it, as "an effect without a cause." If revolutions of that sort fail, explanation is hardly necessary. 1848 does not fit the category. It was a time of widespread economic discontent, sharpened by the privations of the crisis of 1846–47. There was angry frustration over the governments' repeated refusals to countenance any political reforms. Individual leaders like Guizot and Metternich became the focus for every sort of dissatisfaction, the object of every sort of antagonism. Official intransigence had put the anti-governmental forces in a surly mood, not about to slink away when the authorities threatened to disperse reformist demonstrations. From the fact that the revolutions could have been avoided, in other words, it does not necessarily follow that there was no good reason for them to happen.

There was a sort of broad, collective desire for change which sprang from all manner of dissatisfactions and which varied in intensity from place to place on the continent, but was always strongest among the urban bourgeois and artisans. Yet it rarely reached the extremity where large and strategically located groups of men were prepared to attempt, or at least to accept, that which human societies have always found difficult to do—break with the past. Just what produces the willingness to make that break is a matter of debate. Perhaps it takes a more massive economic dislocation than 1848 experienced, driving men to desperate lengths to improve their lot. Perhaps it demands a more serious frustration of social and political ambitions, ultimately alienating men from the system of social values and rankings in which they have been unable to move upward. Or perhaps it takes a greater ideological exaltation, so that men's commitments to the realization of certain principles drive them to extreme acts. Whatever the ingredients, 1848 lacked them in sufficient measure.

This has always been clearest when it comes to the governments of 1848. All of them, whatever their political composition, were still basically "moderate" in the political contexts of their countries. Whatever their degree of sympathy with the urban poor, they were all anti-radical, and stood in constant fear that the impressionable *demos* would fall under the spell of fire-eating demagogues ready to destroy the whole social order. And so the new governments tended to think of themselves not as the agents of change, but rather as a moderating influence, a brake upon the revolution.

Profound and durable revolutions are not made with such governments at the helm. Truly revolutionary governments must either be composed, or come under the influence, of men who are more ruthless, more fanatical, men who cannot conceive of achieving their ends apart from destroying some existing institutions and, if necessary, the people who support their preservation. What this generally means is that governments must also be willing either to use or to condone the use of violence, of coercion—terror is still perhaps the best word. No continental country produced such a government in 1848, or even very many men who could have manned such a government if one had had the chance to exist.

The absence of a classic revolutionary government in 1848 is easy enough, then, to document. But what is more difficult to say is whether such governments—had they seized power, as for example was so pathetically attempted in Paris on May 15—would have had any support beyond that of a relative handful of urban workers. The majority of Europe's population was of course far removed from the capital cities in which the revolutions had suddenly exploded. Most of provincial Europe gave a sort of tacit consent to the initial stage of revolution—doubtless because there was little that could be done beyond accepting the *faits accomplis*, but probably also because the existing governments were unpopular and some gesture of dramatic change was likely to be welcomed. Yet did these silent sanctions constitute anything like a mandate for sweeping change, for wholesale renovation of the social and political order? There is admittedly no way to be certain, but the French election of April 1848 and the provincial response to the June Days suggests that rural masses are not by definition apathetic and inert. What is certain is that 1848 gives no examples of the peasants pressuring the political leaders for more radical policies, forcing the revolutionaries to be more revolutionary—as happened, for instance, in France during the summer of 1789.

If we conclude that a government of revolutionary terror was unlikely either to have appeared or to have lasted long in 1848, then it would seem that the governments which did exist were dependent upon the consent of the governed to sustain their rule and legitimate their reforms. This proved particularly hard to obtain, for reasons already described in some detail. In brief, the moderates in government found it hard to satisfy both left and right. Unable to sustain the reformist fronts of February and March, they also failed to conciliate the conservatives linked to the old regimes. Had the governmental moderates stuck to the modest reform programs of the pre-revolutionary months, they might not have alienated at least those conservatives not devoted to the blackest reaction. But invariably those programs grew more ambitious in the course of 1848. In the Empire, for example, the liberals of March 1848 complained primarily of censorship; a year later, reformist forces produced the Kremsier Constitution. Finally, the governments proved unable to capture the imagination of the rural masses, to find some way to bind them to the revolutions as, for instance, the sale of church and noble property committed important sections of the French peasantry to the revolution of 1789. If the French peasants of 1848 were grateful for the franchise, the forty-five centime surtax had a contrary effect. Abolition of serfdom does not appear to have made peasants in the Empire devoted followers of the liberal cause; not a hand was raised in defense of the revocation of the Kremsier Constitution. In December 1851, there occurred the single instance of rural resistance to reaction. The French, however, had the benefit of nearly four years of the intense politicizing impact of the republic, something denied the rest of Europe; even so their uprising was highly colored by local grievances and conflicts.

Only in France and, later, in the Papal States, did the revolutions actually bring a change in the regime. Elsewhere, much of the structure of the old regimes remained intact, and much of their personnel within reach of the levers of power. 1848 was not a year for executing retrograde monarchs or exiling reactionary elites. A few displays of the strength that remained in those elites were sufficient to reactivate conservative self-confidence, and the counter-revolution was under way.

Simply because events fail to have the results sought by their authors does not mean that they failed to have any results. Therefore, if we cannot talk about the success of the revolutions, we can at least talk about their impact.

To begin with, there can be little question that the revolutions gave authoritarian government a new lease on life, particularly in central Europe. The rigidity of those regimes would almost certainly have turned to brittleness before too much longer, and a serious challenge from below would have snapped rather than bent them. But 1848 necessitated changes, principally in personnel, which rendered the governments more resilient. The new leaders were able to combine repression with concession in a way that preserved their dynasties, and in large part the structure of authoritarian rule, for the next half century or more.

Moreover, the developments of 1848 seem to have had a way of narrowing the options for the future. In Piedmont, for example, whose government soon came into the hands of Cavour, the military defeats of 1848 and 1849 showed clearly that any further attempts to expel the Hapsburgs from northern Italy without foreign assistance would have been foolhardy. Geography, if nothing else, dictated that such assistance would have to come from France. But this in turn meant that the Piedmontese would more than ever have to confine their ambitions to northern Italy, since French troops continued to guarantee Papal temporal power in Rome. Such were indeed the main lines of Cavour's unificationist policy, suggested but also limited by 1848.

The great revolutionary year also closed off certain paths to nationalists in central Europe, primarily by the fact that the Hapsburg dynasty emerged from the revolutions rejuvenated and in more capable hands than before. 1848–49 was the last time for a half-century that Slavic federalism got a serious hearing in the Empire, whose Slavs were thus left with little choice but to agitate futilely for greater autonomy while gradually coming to the conclusion that their independence and the existence of the Empire were incompatible. By also raising the nationalities question to a top priority in Imperial politics, the revolutions faced the dynasty with the difficult but inevitable choice: continue complete centralization and risk another—and more successful—1848, or bargain with the nationalities and share control of the Empire in order that it might continue to exist in some form. Typically, however, it took the crisis of military defeat in 1866 to prod the Hapsburgs into the conclusion of a bargain with their most troublesome subjects, the Magyars.

Hapsburg revival also spelled the end of *grossdeutsch* unificationism and left liberal-nationalists groping for some way to effect the *kleindeutsch* scheme. After Friedrich Wilhelm's decision to reject the crown offered by Frankfurt, this was not easy. Besides, the fiasco over the Erfurt Parliament demonstrated that Prussian-sponsored unification efforts would lead to conflict with Austria, and Prussian conservatives preferred the traditional policy of cooperation with the Hapsburgs in order to keep the lid on revolutions. The failure of constitutionalist unification left German nationalism in a corner from which it could only be rescued by a turnabout in Prussian policy.

Bismarck engineered that reversal in the 1860s, achieved German unification under conservative Prussian auspices, and forced the liberals to accept it. It has been said that the liberals' inability to unify Germany in 1848 so discouraged many middle-class liberals that they turned eagerly to Bismarck, in spite of their ideological reservations about this former firebrand of the *Kreuzzeitung* circle. In other words, nothing fails like failure, and German liberal nationalists were interested first of all in success. But, in fact, the experience of 1848 does not seem to have demoralized German liberals so completely. In Prussia especially, they took advantage of the new parliamentary structure to remount their campaign for political reform. The rigged franchise which called itself universal suffrage was intended to minimize the radical vote, presumably centered in the poorer classes. But it could not choke off middle-class reformism, which within a few years had built up a remarkably potent delegation in the Prussian Reichstag. Indeed, Prussian liberalism was strong enough by the early 1860s to provoke a major constitutional crisis and bring Friedrich Wilhelm IV's successor to the verge of abdication. It was on this occasion that Bismarck was called to lead the government, and his ultimate victory over the liberals was only realized with great effort. The liberals were anything but meek lambs waiting to be led by the first successful politician who came along.

The experience of 1848, then, tended to intensify reformist convictions of Prussian liberals rather than undermine them. In France, the older generation of liberals was somewhat less firm. A good many Orléanists who had been advocates of limited monarchy and parliamentary government showed up in the ranks of the Bonapartists, driven there no doubt by the great red scare of 1849–51. They accepted authoritarian rule as the price of order and even the prerequisite of prosperity; many of them accepted prestigious government positions as well. But there were a number of liberals who had regretted—even protested—the *coup d'état*, and who thereafter went into political retirement. When Napoleon III began rather gingerly to loosen up restrictions on opposition politics a decade later, a few of the old personalities (like Thiers) re-appeared, but were accompanied by a new generation of liberal spokesmen.

There were rather more familiar figures around when republican-ism reemerged in the late 1850s, and mostly they were moderates like Garnier-Pagès, Marie, and Carnot. It was not so much that moderate republicans had somehow managed to come out the vic-tors on the left as that the multiple repressions of the Second Re-public had badly scattered most prominent radicals. By the end of the empire, a left wing had appeared, composed largely of younger men, who were still a far cry from the revolutionary left of 1848. The real radicals stayed underground, though they surfaced dramatically in 1871. By and large, if the events of 1848–51 helped shake up re-publican personnel, it is hard to see that they had any profound impact on the elite of the movement. More or less the same divisions remained between "political" and "social" republicans; the same gulf separated middle-class democrats from the radical social reformers. It was more the experience of 1852–75 which helped shape the republicanism of the future, particularly by concentrating attention on such questions as the role of the church. Probably 1848's main contribution to subsequent generations of republican politicians was to cure them definitively of any weakness for a strong constitutional executive. It was otherwise with the French masses, for whom the experiences of the Second Republic were something like the begin-nings of a process of political conversion. The first results were evident in the popular response to the *coup d'état*. The Empire was careful to keep expression of mass opinion under control for the next eighteen years, but the decade of the 1870s revealed steadily increasing mass commitment to the republic, a commitment which surely had its roots in 1848.

The political impact of 1848 was thus varied and complicated; but the broader social impact is even harder to determine. In the generation after the revolutions, western and central Europe began in earnest the process of large-scale industrialization. But because great changes followed the revolutions, were they therefore in some sense a consequence of the revolutions? To take a more specific ex-ample, it has sometimes been argued that Germany's great spurt of industrialization in the 1850s and 1860s was in part due to middle-class despair and disgust with politics. Resigned to the perpetuation of authoritarian rule, says this thesis, the bourgeoisie devoted its energies to the new industries and thus helped to make Germany, when unified, the continent's leading industrial state. The trouble with this position is that it would be extremely hard to prove, even if there did not exist the important example of post-revolutionary Prussian liberalism to contradict it. Supposing that one could ever establish an accurate psychology of the German middle classes in this period, is it clear that it would have been a more important factor in industrialization than a host of larger social and economic forces?

In the Italian states, it would be difficult to show that 1848 had any noticeable impact on social structure or economic life. In the Hapsburg Empire, abolition of serfdom cleared the way for the creation of a much larger class of peasant proprietors, but also for a much larger group of agricultural proletarians. Large estates remained the rule in the Empire, and the increasing efficiency of agricultural techniques in the second half of the century cut labor needs. Since the peasant was no longer tied to the soil, free to move only with the permission of the landlord, migration on an unprecedented scale began to swell the cities. The movement was particularly pronounced in Austria, which gradually began its own progress toward the urban-industrial society, while most of the Slavic areas tended to lag. In the German states, 1848 had done little of consequence to retard the decay of the traditional artisanate; the protective statutes granted during the period of reaction were indifferently enforced, and the assault of heavy industry proved irresistible. At best, the revolutions bought the artisans a little time. They did, however, provide a valuable experience in politics. The German working classes learned the value of organization, of uniting against employers in order to achieve their economic demands, and numerous efforts of varying success continued through the 1850s and '60s to form these proto-labor unions.

In all of these areas, the demographic boom of the prerevolutionary years continued in the second half of the century. In France, it stopped cold, and the French population growth stumbled along sluggishly for the rest of the century. With 35.8 million souls in 1851, France accounted for about 14 per cent of the total population of the continent; on the eve of World War I, there were only 39.6

million Frenchmen, just 9 per cent of the continental total. In those sixty-odd years the French population grew at a rate of only 13.6 per cent, as compared to 78 per cent for Great Britain and 57 per cent for Germany, or for that matter as compared to the French growth rate of 26.9 per cent between 1801 and 1851. At the same time, the elaborate structure of rural industry, with its millions of semi-peasant semi-artisan types, began to crumble. Small-scale manufacturing in the countryside and the towns declined sharply, producing (if at all) only for local needs and no longer competing in regional markets. Migration to larger towns and cities picked up markedly (though the population crisis kept French cities from sheer numerical superiority until the twentieth century). Though it can be just as dangerous to attempt to locate some cause and effect relationship with the revolution of 1848 here as elsewhere, it seems at least plausible that these developments were a product of the protracted political and economic crisis of 1846–51. The inflationary crisis which suddenly became a depression converted the position of these social strata from occasionally precarious to virtually untenable. Competition from the cities, pressure—in the form of taxes, for example—from the government, the constant danger of economic catastrophe finally forced large segments of rural and small-town France to the limits of its ability to absorb stress. First there was protest, most spectacularly in December 1851, to be followed by surrender. It is an intriguing hypothesis which, if substantiated by further research, would help explain one of the great social upheavals of nineteenth-century Europe.

The almost incredible series of reversals which shook the European continent between 1848 and 1851 have naturally prompted all manner of attempts to encapsulate the experience of the revolutions into a single, telling insight—most of them elaborations on the thought of contemporaries of the revolutions. One popular view has it that 1848 only announced future upheavals which, taken together, gave the modern world its shape. Marx seems to have thought something like this, though a French radical named Louis Ménard put it best when he entitled a book, published in 1849, *1848: Prologue to a Revolution*. This approach runs the obvious danger of suggesting nothing more than that the past influences the future. Disregarding that, however, and conceding that

1848 anticipated some of the great developments of subsequent years, it is still true that these revolutions were the last with the single exception of the French eruptions of 1870–71—to touch major European countries in the nineteenth century. Before 1905, only France experienced domestic discontent boiling over into violent revolution, and even then the critical stimulus came from foreign invasion. Another school of historians is skeptical of 1848's contribution to future developments, but thinks that its historical role was to undermine old institutions and pave the way for rebuilding. As one of these scholars has put it, 1848 "brought about the end of a world." This suggestion evokes the brilliant Russian radical Alexander Herzen, who viewed the revolutions first-hand and paraphrased its supporters in these words: "We do not build, we destroy; we do not proclaim a new revelation, we eliminate the old lie." Yet clearly there is ample reason to ask just how much destruction the revolutions did, just how many existing institutions they erased, or even challenged seriously.

The experience of 1848 still awaits its encapsulation—not for the lack of effort, but largely because that experience was so complex, even kaleidoscopic, that it has proven unyielding to formulaic expression.

Bibliographical Essay

The following brief bibliography is not designed as a list of sources upon which I drew for this book, but rather as a guide for interested students who may wish to pursue the study of 1848 in greater detail. For that reason, I have in general tried to concentrate on what I consider the most useful of recent scholarship, and the most accessible. More exhaustive bibliographies may be found in some of the works cited below.

Several of the increasingly popular collaborative series on modern history have volumes on the general background to the revolutions of 1848. Of these, perhaps the most useful is the work by Jacques Droz in the "History of Europe" collection, *Europe between Revolutions, 1815–1848*, trans. Robert Baldrick (New York, 1967)*.[1] "The Rise of Modern Europe" series has a sound survey, with a good up-to-date bibliography, by Frederick B. Artz, *Reaction and Revolution, 1814–1832* (New York, 1963)*. The long-awaited subsequent volume by William L. Langer, *Political and Social Upheaval, 1832–1852* (New York, 1969), appeared too late for use here. J. L. Talmon's contribution to the "Library of European Civilization," entitled *Romanticism and Revolt: Europe, 1815–1848* (New York, 1967)*, concentrates heavily on ideology, on the "all-pervasive mood" of romanticism. Somewhat more dour than Talmon, but of manageable length and full of factual details, are the pertinent articles in *The New Cambridge Modern History*, IX: *War and Peace in an Age of Upheaval, 1793–1830*, ed. C. W. Crawley (Cambridge, 1965), and X: *The Zenith of European Power: 1830–1870*, ed. J. P. T. Bury (Cambridge, 1960).

Peter Stearns has given a good overview of social and economic developments in his *European Society in Upheaval: Social History Since 1800* (New York, 1967)*. David S. Landes, *The Unbound Prometheus: Technological Change and Industrial Development in Western Europe from 1750 to the Present* (Cambridge, 1969)*, bristles with provocative suggestions which should keep specialists in lively debate for some time. It is, however, a rather tall order for undergraduates, who may wish to approach the economic history of the period from some of the following

---

[1] Paperback editions are designated with an asterisk (*).

178

national studies: J. H. Clapham, *The Economic Development of France and Germany, 1815–1914*, 4th ed. (Cambridge, 1961)°; Shepard B. Clough, *France: A History of National Economics* (New York, 1939); A. L. Dunham, *The Industrial Revolution in France, 1815–1848* (New York, 1955); the early chapters of Theodore S. Hamerow, *Restoration, Revolution, Reaction: Economics and Politics in Germany, 1815–1871* (Princeton, 1967)°, with a superb bibliography; Arnold H. Price, *The Evolution of the Zollverein* (Ann Arbor, 1949); W. O. Henderson, *The Zollverein* (Cambridge, 1939); Jerome O. Blum, *Noble Landowners and Agriculture in Austria, 1815–1848: A Study in the Origins of the Peasant Emancipation of 1848* (Baltimore, 1948), and by the same author, "Transportation and Industry in Austria, 1815–1848," *The Journal of Modern History*, XV, No. 1 (1943), 24–38; Kent Roberts Greenfield, *Economics and Liberalism in the Risorgimento: A Study of Nationalism in Lombardy, 1814–1848* (Baltimore, 1934), and the same author's "Commerce and New Enterprise at Venice, 1830–1848," *The Journal of Modern History*, XI, No. 2 (1939), 313–333. There is a brief look at "The Transformation of European Agriculture" by Folke Dovring in *The Cambridge Economic History of Europe* (Cambridge, 1965), VI: Pt. 2, 604–672. Studies devoted especially to the peasantry are hard to come by in English, and this badly neglected area of continental history will have to be approached through the general economic histories cited above. The most comprehensive history of the urban workers is in French: Édouard Dolléans, *Histoire du mouvement ouvrier* (Paris, 1948), Volume I: *1830–1871*. In English, Jürgen Kuczynski's *Labor Conditions in Western Europe, 1820 to 1935* (London, 1936) is written from a pronounced Marxist viewpoint. The middle classes have been the subject of a great deal of historical commentary, not all of it terribly edifying. One recent contribution, with helpful bibliographical notes, is worthy of close attention: Leonore O'Boyle, "The Middle Class in Western Europe, 1815–1848," *The American Historical Review*, LXXI, No. 3 (1966), 826–845. See, however, the critique by Alfred Cobban, "The 'Middle Class' in France, 1815–1848," *French Historical Studies*, V, No. 1 (1967), 41–52, and Miss O'Boyle's reply in *ibid.*, pp. 53–56. Of substantially broader scope are Charles Morazé, *The Triumph of the Middle Classes: A Study of European Values in the Nineteenth Century* (London, 1966), and the new work by Félix Ponteil, *Les classes bourgeoises et l'avènement de la démocratie* (Paris, 1968)°.

There is an abundant literature on the dominant political movements and ideologies of post-Napoleonic Europe. David Caute's essay, *The Left in Europe Since 1789* (London, 1966)°, is suggestive, but the numerous categories are often baffling. Guido de Ruggiero's *The History of European Liberalism*, trans. R. G. Collingwood (Boston, 1959)° is full of information, but it was written more than forty years ago and is now rather dated. In many ways, the most helpful introduction to the subject of liberalism is still David Harris' article, "European Liberalism in the Nineteenth Century," *The American Historical Review*, LX, No. 3 (1955), 501–526. One tendency of general studies has been to apply the model of British liberalism a bit too closely to the continent. As a corrective, see Leonard Krieger, *The German Idea of Freedom* (Boston, 1957), and Donald G. Rohr, *The Origins of Social Liberalism in Germany* (Chicago, 1963). Moving further to the left, Frank E. Manuel has written an excellent intellectual biography, *The New World of Henri Saint-Simon* (Notre Dame, 1966)°, of one of the earliest and most seminal socialist thinkers. David O. Evans, *Social Romanticism in France, 1830–1848* (Oxford, 1951), is a gem of concision, with a model critical bibliography. Leo A. Loubère has made some progress in helping to categorize the various left-wing ideologies with his article on "The Intellectual Origins of French Jacobin Socialism," *International Review of Social History*, IV (1959), 415–431. For all his own abundance of categories, J. L. Talmon tends to blur over important distinctions in his *Political Messianism: The Romantic Phase* (London, 1960). In fact, Talmon describes such a tiny fraction of the continental radicals and he so exaggerates the utopian, ideological strain of their thought that his work is of severely limited usefulness. Marxism was still in the process of intellectual formation during the pre-revolutionary generation, but Marx's debt to the earlier socialist thinkers is well established both in Evans' *Social Romanticism in France* and in Isaiah Berlin's *Karl Marx: His Life and Environment* (Oxford, 1959)°. Besides Marx, there were few noteworthy German socialists, though see the book by Carl Wittke, *The Utopian Communist: A Biography of Wilhelm Weitling, Nineteenth-Century Reformer* (Baton Rouge, La., 1950). German intellectual radicalism tended to stay within formal philosophical boundaries, for which the best guide remains Sidney Hook, *From Hegel to Marx: Studies in the Intellectual Development of Karl Marx* (Ann Arbor, 1962)°. The conservatism of the era was more a practice—uphold the status quo—than a clearly-formulated ideology. The exception, of course, would be Hegel, upon whom there is a massive literature; the classic study in English is still Herbert Marcuse, *Reason and Revolution: Hegel and the Rise of Social Theory* (Boston, 1960)°, but see also the newer brief study, with up-to-date bibliography, by J. N. Findlay, *Hegel* (New York, 1963)°.

There is no competent study in English of France between 1815 and 1848; Gillaume de Bertier de Sauvigny's brilliant *The Bourbon Restoration*, trans. Lynn M. Case (Philadelphia, 1967), leaves us stranded in 1830. Even in French, there is no study of equal stature to Bertier de Sauvigny's for the July Monarchy, though Philippe Vigier's bite-size introduction, *La Monarchie de juillet* (Paris, 1965), is a good place to start. The student without French must have resort to Douglas Johnson, *Guizot: Aspects of French History, 1787–1874* (London, 1962), which has some excellent sections on the period from 1840 to 1848, or to T. E. B. Howarth, *Citizen King: The Life of Louis-Philippe, King of the French* (London, 1961). Otherwise, there are the appropriate chapters in the textbooks by Alfred Cobban, *A History of Modern France* (Baltimore, 1965)°, Volume II, and Gordon Wright, *France in Modern Times* (Chicago, 1960). C.-E. Labrousse, *Le Mouvement ouvrier et les idées socialistes en France de 1815 à 1848* (Paris, 1961) cries out for a translator. René Rémond's *The Right Wing in France from 1815 to De Gaulle*, trans. James Laux (Philadelphia, 1966) is essential; John Plamenatz, *The Revolutionary Movement in France, 1815–71* (New York, 1967)° tries to do for the French left what Rémond has done for the right, though in much briefer scope.

Hajo Holborn's *A History of Modern Germany, 1648–1840* (New York, 1964–69), Volumes II–III, is a useful introduction. Otherwise, chapters in Hamerow's *Restoration, Revolution, Reaction* and Golo Mann's *The History of Germany Since 1789*, trans. Marian Jackson (London, 1968), have good introductions to the period. For the reader with German, Franz Schnabel's massive *Deutsche Geschichte im neunzehnten Jahrhundert* (Freiburg, 1947–51), 4 volumes, is still unsurpassed, but see also the collection edited by Werner Conze, *Staat und Gesellschaft im deutschen Vormärz, 1815–1848* (Stuttgart, 1962).

There is no good survey of the Hapsburg Empire in this period in English; in desperation, the reader might fall back on the volumes in *The New Cambridge Modern History*. In German, however, there is Heinrich Ritter von Srbik's masterly *Metternich: der Staatsmann und der Mensch* (Munich, 1954–57), 3 volumes, which is far more than a biography. A. J. P. Taylor, *The Hapsburg Monarchy, 1815–1918* (New York, 1965)°, tends to be flip and chatty and must be approached with some caution.

Since most Italian historiography tends to focus on the successful bid for unification that took place after 1848, the pre-1848 period has gone relatively unstudied. About the best that a reader limited to English can do is consult the responsible survey by A. J. Whyte, *The Evolution of Modern Italy* (Oxford, 1944) or the somewhat more detailed multi-volume study by G. F. H. and J. Berkeley, *Italy in the Making* (Cambridge, 1932–36), Volumes I–II.

Of the several general histories devoted to the revolutions of 1848 themselves, certainly the best-known is Priscilla Robertson, *Revolutions of 1848: A Social History* (New York, 1960)*. Mrs. Robertson's version of 1848 is colorful and entertaining, written in a lively and vigorous style, and succeeds in what is sometimes called "bringing history to life." The book's principal shortcoming, aside from a number of factual slips and a pronounced lack of understanding of the revolutionaries, is that it almost totally ignores precisely what it purports to offer: social history, unless by that term one means a collection of well-chosen biographical anecdotes. For a very brief introduction to the revolutions, one could depend with almost equal profit upon Charles H. Pouthas, "The Revolutions of 1848," in *The New Cambridge Modern History,* X, 389–415. Nearly all the European countries, whether or not they experienced revolution, have a chapter devoted to them in *The Opening of an Era, 1848: An Historical Symposium,* ed. François Fejtö (New York, 1966). There is an absorbing analysis of the outbreak of the revolutions by William L. Langer, "The Pattern of Urban Revolution in 1848," in *French Society and Culture Since the Old Regime,* ed. Evelyn M. Acomb and Marvin L. Brown, Jr. (New York, 1966), pp. 89–118. Langer argues that the absence of adequate municipal law-enforcement agencies in Europe's major capitals meant that, in the early stages of the February and March disturbances, the authorities had to escalate the conflict by throwing in regular troops against the crowds. "As a result," writes Langer, "fairly innocuous aggregations of people quickly turned into bellicose mobs." Students interested in this aspect of the revolutions will find much that is useful in George Rudé, *The Crowd in History, 1730–1848* (New York, 1964)*.

Although the February revolution and the Second Republic have had their share of historians, too few have found their way into English. The only general study of note that has been translated is Georges Duveau, *1848: The Making of a Revolution,* trans. Anne Carter (New York, 1967), with an excellent introduction by George Rudé. For all its merit, however, Duveau's account is highly impressionistic and episodic; there are several French works which do the job better: Paul Bastid, *Doctrines et institutions de la Seconde république* (Paris, 1945), 2 volumes; Louis Girard, *La IIe République (1848–1851)* (Paris, 1968)*; Philippe Vigier's tiny *La Seconde République* (Paris, 1967)*; and best of all, Charles H. Pouthas, "La Révolution de 1848 en France et la seconde République" (Paris, n.d.), which is unfortunately not a published book but a set of mimeographed Sorbonne lectures and rather difficult to obtain. On the February days, the standard monograph is still A. Crémieux, *La Révolution de février* (Paris, 1912), which has not been superseded by Henri Guillemin's newer *Le 24 février 1848* (Paris, 1968). The best work on the economic crisis of the 1840s in France remains C.-E. Labrousse, ed., *Aspects de la crise et de la dépression de l'économie française au milieu du XIXe siècle, 1846–1851* (La Rochesur-Yon, 1956); the relationship between the crisis and the revolution is the subject of an interesting essay by Labrousse, "1848–1830–1789: Comment naissent les révolutions," in *Actes du Congrès historique du centenaire de la révolution de 1848* (Paris, 1948), pp. 1–29. The first volume of Rémi Gossez's work on *Les ouvriers de Paris en 1848* (Paris, 1968) appeared too late for me to use in this book; the long-awaited second volume, which will contain the results of Gossez's quarter-century of research on the June Days, should be out soon.

On the Second Republic in general, it would be useless to try to improve here on the model bibliographical essay by Peter Amann, "Writings on the Second French Republic," *The Journal of Modern History*, XXXIV, No. 4 (1962), 409–429. Only a few additional suggestions will be offered, of which the first is another piece by Amann, "The Changing Outlines of 1848," *The American Historical Review*, LXVIII, No. 4 (1963), 938–953, which makes a case for a revision of traditional opinion on the revolution along a broad front. Another source of what may one day be major revision is the work of the sociologist Charles Tilly. Tilly is directing a massive research project, analyzing the phenomenon of collective violence in France between 1830 and 1960; the project is still some time from completion, the reports thus far are still basically preliminary, and only a few of them have been published. Two of Tilly's forthcoming articles, however, merit special attention: "À Travers le chaos des vivantes cités," which will appear (in English) in the *Proceedings of the Sixth World Congress of Sociology*, and "The Changing Place of Collective Violence," which will be included in *Theory and History: An Approach to General Education*, ed. Melvin Richter, to be published shortly by Harvard University Press. Some of Tilly's central arguments are that serious collective violence often developed directly from more traditional, common violent outbursts, such as the food riot; that collective violence often occurred in relatively stable, secure social groupings and not necessarily in the newer, uprooted groups created by industrialization and peasant migration to the cities; that collective violence was not an exclusively urban phenomenon; and that the form and nature of collective violence seem to have changed distinctly in France around the middle of the nineteenth century. In addition, Tilly does historians a signal service by restoring the resistance to the *coup d'état* of 1851 to its place as a major historical event. Clearly, I have leaned heavily upon his extremely fruitful work in my own essay.

One final suggestion on France: While contemporary observers of historical events are always essential reading, they do not always make the best analysts; particularly in time of revolution, they may be too close to events to organize them coherently and cast them in some meaningful perspective. But the French revolution of 1848 had three contemporaries of authentic genius whose recorded observations, though often widely divergent, are very much worth reading closely. See Alexis de Tocqueville, *Recollections*, trans. Alexander Teixeira de Mattos (New York, 1959)°; Karl Marx, *The Class Struggles in France, 1848 to 1850*, and *The Eighteenth Brumaire of Louis Napoleon*, both available in several editions, but located conveniently together in the Foreign Languages Publishing House *Selected Works of Marx and Engels* (Moscow, 1958), Volume I; and Alexander Herzen, *From the Other Shore* (New York, 1963)°.

Although the language barrier poses serious problems for study of the German revolutions, there is in English one outstanding work. Hamerow's *Restoration, Revolution, Reaction* has made a considerable impact in the decade since its appearance, principally through its emphasis on the importance of the artisanate in the revolutionary movement. But Hamerow's contribution has not stopped there, and he has shed much-needed light on some important corners of 1848's history in three recent articles: "The German Artisan Movement, 1848–49," *The Journal of Central European Affairs*, XXI (1961), 135–152; "The Elections to the Frankfurt Parliament," *The Journal of Modern History*, XXXIII (1961), 15–32; and "1848," in *The Responsibility of Power*, ed. Leonard Krieger and Fritz Stern (New York, 1967), pp. 145–161, a convincing assessment of the causes of the revolution's failure. An even more detailed and extremely useful study of the artisanate has also recently appeared: P. H. Noyes, *Organization and Revolution: Working-Class Associations in the German Revolutions of 1848–49* (Princeton, 1966), who first put forth the thesis about the transition in the working-class movement from statism to organization and self-reliance that I have employed. And, of course, one cannot avoid mention of Sir Lewis Namier's *1848: The Revolution of the Intellectuals* (New York, 1964)°, which, for all its tendentiousness, remains an important work. Marx's studies of France in this period are far more exciting than Engels' essay on Germany in 1848, which is now conveniently included in Friedrich Engels, *The German Revolutions*, ed. Leonard Krieger (Chicago, 1967)°. Leonore O'Boyle has made an argument respecting the German left of 1848 which in some respects anticipated her piece on the middle classes cited earlier; see her "The Democratic Left in Germany, 1848," *The Journal of Modern History*, XXXIII (1961), 374–383, where she tries to relate middle-class radicalism to social structure and social mobility. One of the better general surveys of the German revolutions is not in German, but French: Jacques Droz, *Les révolutions allemandes de 1848* (Paris, 1957), is an extremely useful account, with ample bibliographical indications. Perhaps the finest single study of 1848 was that of Veit Valentin, *Geschichte der deutschen Revolution von 1848–49* (Berlin, 1930–31), 2 volumes, which is available in a not entirely satisfactory

English abridgement, *1848: Chapters of German History*, trans. E. T. Scheffauer (London, 1965). The best reviews of the German-language histories of the revolution are by Hamerow, in his book and also in his article "History and the German Revolution of 1848," *The American Historical Review*, LX (1954), 27–44.

Students can be grateful to R. John Rath for providing the first account in English of *The Viennese Revolution of 1848* (Austin, Texas, 1957). Rath does focus almost exclusively on the capital, however, and for the entire Empire one must turn to Robert A. Kann's *The Multinational Empire* (New York, 1950), 2 volumes, which offers the best statement in English of the nationalities problem at mid-century. There are some helpful observations on the Slavic minorities of the Empire in Hans Kohn's well-known *Pan-Slavism: Its History and Ideology*, 2nd ed. (New York, 1960)°, and Taylor's *The Habsburg Monarchy* has a handy guide to English-language studies of the various minority groups. There is a biography of the new Emperor by Joseph Redlich, *The Emperor Francis Joseph of Austria* (New York, 1929), and a better one of his first minister by Adolph Schwarzenberg, *Prince Felix zu Schwarzenberg, Prime Minister of Austria, 1848–1852* (New York, 1946). The question of Great German nationalism is carefully delineated in Henry Cord Meyer, *Mitteleuropa in German Thought and Action, 1815–1945* (The Hague, 1955). Probably the best German-language study of the revolution is Rudolf Kiszling, *et al.*, *Die Revolution im Kaisertum Österreich 1848–1849* (Vienna, 1948), 2 volumes; for a more complete listing, see the bibliography in Rath.

1848 in Italy has suffered badly from the interest in later Risorgimento history, so that here it is not so much a question of choosing from among a large number of works as it is trying to find even a few things the student may find helpful. Volume III of the Berkeleys' *Italy in the Making* (Cambridge, 1940) is still the most complete narrative in English. Events surrounding Piedmontese policy in 1848 may be glimpsed in A. J. Whyte, *The Political Life and Letters of Cavour* (Oxford, 1930). For Venice, see the colorful account by G. M. Trevelyan, *Manin and the Venetian Republic* (London, 1923); for Rome, E. E. Y. Hales, *Pio Nono: A Study in European Politics and Religion in the Nineteenth Century* (New York, 1954), and G. M. Trevelyan, *Garibaldi's Defence of the Roman Republic* (London, 1907); for southern Italy, Harold Acton, *The Last Bourbons of Naples* (New York, 1961). A. J. P. Taylor puts the problem of Italian unification in a larger context in *The Italian Problem in European Diplomacy, 1847–1849* (Manchester, 1934).

In most cases, the story of the counterrevolutions is contained within the histories of the revolutions themselves; only a few special works deserve mention here. Adrien Dansette, in his *Louis Napoléon à la con-*

quête du pouvoir (Paris, 1961), gives a well-documented account of the Prince-President's early life and political career. There are several biographies of Louis Napoleon in English, none of them quite as satisfactory as Dansette; but see T. A. B. Corley, *Democratic Despot* (London, 1961), and J. M. Thompson, *Louis Napoleon and the Second Empire* (Oxford, 1954). Theodore Zeldin has some helpful insights in *The Political System of Napoleon III* (London, 1958). There are some interesting observations on the role of the army in the Prussian reaction in Gordon A. Craig, *The Politics of the Prussian Army, 1640–1945* (New York, 1964)*. The closest thing to an assessment of the aftermath of the revolutions comes in Stearns' *European Society in Upheaval*.

Chronology of Principal Events

1848

January
12	Insurrection in Palermo
18	Arrest of Manin in Venice
27	Kingdom of the Two Sicilies granted a constitution

February
10	Formation of new ministry, including laymen, in the Papal states
17	Tuscany granted a constitution
22	First disturbances, barricades in Paris
23	Continued street fighting in Paris, fall of Guizot
24	Abdication of Louis Philippe, formation of republican provisional government
27	Reformist demonstrations throughout southern and southwestern German states

March
4	Piedmont-Sardinia granted a constitution
5	Heidelberg conference summons Vorparlament
	First agitation for reform in Berlin
13	Disturbances in Vienna, fall of Metternich
14	Street fighting in Vienna, rioting in suburbs
15	Violence breaks out in Berlin
	Emperor Ferdinand promises a constitution
17	Insurrection in Venice
18	Insurrection in Milan
23	Piedmont declares war on Hapsburgs
31	Vorparlament meets in Frankfurt

April
10	Chartist demonstration fails in London
11	New Hungarian constitution
23	French election for the National Constituent Assembly
25	Hapsburg government announces draft for Imperial constitution

1848 (cont.)

May

2	Viennese demonstration against proposed constitution
15	Pro-Polish demonstration in Paris, abortive left-wing coup
18	Emperor Ferdinand flees Vienna for Innsbruck
	Opening session of the Frankfurt Parliament
26	Formation of the Security Committee in Vienna

June

2	Opening of Pan-Slav Congress in Prague
16	Windischgrätz completes bombardment of Prague, dispersal of the Congress
23–26	Working-class rising, civil war in Paris

July

10	Imperial Reichstag opens in Vienna
23	Radetzky defeats Piedmontese at Custozza

August

9	Piedmont concludes armistice with Hapsburgs
23	Government crushes working-class demonstrations in Vienna
26	Prussia concludes armistice with Denmark, ending brief war over Schleswig-Holstein

September

11	Jellachich invades Hungary

October

6	Left-wing rising in Vienna, followed by investiture of the city by Windischgrätz
31	Fall of Vienna

November

15	Assassination of Rossi in Rome, touching off intense left-wing agitation
21	Schwarzenberg forms new Imperial government
24	Pope flees Rome

December

2	Emperor Ferdinand abdicates in favor of his nephew, Franz Josef
5	Friedrich Wilhelm of Prussia dismisses elected assembly, grants royal constitution
10	Louis Napoleon Bonaparte elected President of the French Republic

1849

February
9   Proclamation of the Roman Republic

March
7   Schwarzenberg dissolves Reichstag, grants a new con-
     stitution
23   Radetzky defeats Piedmont at Novara, followed by
     abdication of Charles Albert

April
28   Friedrich Wilhelm IV declines the crown of a unified
     Germany

June
13   Left-wing demonstration in Paris against French inter-
     vention in Rome leads to arrest of radical leaders

July
1   Fall of the Roman Republic to French troops

August
13   Hungarians capitulate to Russian and Austrian troops
23   Venice capitulates after long siege

1850

March
21   Opening of Erfurt Parliament

May
31   New suffrage law in France, disenfranchising nearly
     one-third of the electorate

November
29   Austria forces Prussia to disband Erfurt Parliament

1851

December
2   Louis Napoleon's *coup d'état*, followed by several days
     of violent resistance in the provinces
31   Suppression of the Imperial constitution of 1848, return
     to complete absolutism

Index

PRINTED IN U.S.A.